SHIFT to Professional Paradise

in Stormy & Uncertain Times

S0-ABC-889

VICKI HESS, RN

SHIFT to Professional Paradise

in Stormy & Uncertain Times

Printed in the United States of America
ISBN: 978-0-9789862-1-6

Credits

Collaborative Editor	Juli Baldwin, The Baldwin Group, Plano, TX Juli@BaldwinGrp.com
Copy Editor	Brenda Quinn, Frisco, TX brendalquinn@gmail.com
Design, art direction, and production	Melissa Farr, Back Porch Creative, Frisco, TX info@BackPorchCreative.com

Contents

INTRODUCTION

Believe It...or Not

Okay, all you doubting Thomases...let me set your mind at ease: **Professional Paradise** *does* **exist** – even in stormy and uncertain times.

How do I know? Because I see evidence of it every day when I talk with healthcare colleagues. I hear stories about folks connecting to their purpose and passion in spite of working in very tough conditions, including a pandemic. I regularly witness people who are behind the scenes bring their "A-Game" to work and genuinely care about patients and their families. It's exciting to see concrete evidence of Professional Paradise in healthcare.

But on the flip side, when I look at data from employee engagement surveys and talk with healthcare leaders and staff, I also hear stories of increasing stress, burnout and disillusionment. The challenges are real and so are the opportunities. Our world is volatile and sometimes tumultuous and it's also immensely gratifying and full of hope and love.

Now seems like the perfect time to adapt to survive and thrive.

I can hear some of you thinking... *as pressures increase and times change, can we realistically be expected to maintain this level of commitment to those we serve?*

The answer is a resounding YES!

Deep down, we all know that we chose healthcare because we actually do care. I define Professional Paradise (you'll hear more about this throughout the book) as when you are satisfied, energized and productive at work. The great news is that whether the skies are sunny or stormy, there are always opportunities for making a difference through our work.

Nationally, according to several surveys, around 40% of healthcare employees are disengaged at work – they have sentenced themselves to Professional Prison. This worries me on many levels. When too many employees are not working to their full potential, everyone suffers. When I say "everyone," I mean our communities, organizations, leaders, colleagues and ourselves. I'm sad to see that there are still folks who are waiting for someone else to make them happy and engaged at work.

Now you may be wondering, "What's in it for me to seek Professional Paradise?" Do you mean other than less stress, more energy and remarkable results? You need more? Well, it's a good thing there are a number of benefits to an extended stay in Professional Paradise:

- ✦ Enhanced health (lower blood pressure, more restful sleep, reduced incidence of common illnesses and serious diseases);
- ✦ Better working relationships and communication;

✦ Additional smiles and laughter;

✦ Increased meaning and joy;

✦ Improved creativity;

✦ More effective problem solving.

In this book, not only will I give you the keys that will free you from Professional Prison, but I will also hand you your Passport to Professional Paradise. I'll show you step by step how you can live the good life at work using a proven, proprietary technique called **SHIFT** that's already being used by many people to connect to what's important – especially when the going gets rough and stormy. The five steps of the *SHIFT* technique are simple but not necessarily easy, common sense but not common practice.

Let's face it. There are a lot of things you have no control over that affect your job satisfaction – things like your responsibilities and duties, your salary, your hours, your boss, etc. These elements are, for the most part, pre-determined. But I'm here to tell you that those things don't entirely determine the quality of your work experience. Professional Paradise doesn't depend on your coworkers, your organization, the commute or the cash. You determine whether you reside in Professional Prison, Professional Paradise or someplace in between.

Some of you are saying "Darn it!" You were thinking you could blame your prison sentence on someone or something else (such as the boss, coworkers, patients or the organization).

Now is a good time to stop and flip this perspective. The great news is that you don't have to wait for someone else to do something to be engaged at work. There's a lot that's within your control. You have the choice and the ability to create a Professional Paradise you've never even imagined until now, no matter what you do or where you work. And you can do it right now, today.

If you doubt the concept of Professional Paradise, that's fine. For now, I'm asking you to simply be open to the possibility that Professional Paradise exists. Surely you have at least one friend who loves his or her job and would describe it as Professional Paradise. Keep this person in mind as you read. Think of how happy he or she sounds when you ask, "How's work?"

Finding Professional Paradise is not only possible, it's a certainty – if you're willing to make a few changes. You may be skeptical that any of this is possible, and that's okay. You don't have to believe yet. You just have to do one thing: **Pack your bags!**

PART I

PARADISE...PRISON... OR SOMEWHERE IN BETWEEN?

Palm Trees and a Warm Breeze

Where is *your* Professional Paradise?

We were on the airplane making our final approach into the island airport. My husband, Alan, and I looked at each other and smiled.

We'd spent months planning this trip…scheduling time off from work, finding someone to care for the children, coordinating household logistical issues and, of course, setting up all the travel arrangements. At last we were on vacation – peering out the window at the postcard-perfect view below: crystal-clear skies, sapphire-blue water, emerald-green vegetation, miles of pristine beaches and the majesty of the mountains rising up from the interior of the island.

"Wow," I thought. "Now this is paradise!"

Paradise. The word has existed in some form or fashion since the 12th century and has evolved through the Iranian, Greek, Latin and French languages. The earliest meaning referred to extraordinary walled gardens or royal hunting grounds. But check any modern English dictionary, and you'll find the contemporary definition of paradise: *a place known for favorable conditions, special opportunities and abundance; a state of supreme happiness, delight or bliss.*

What could be better than that?

When I hear the word "paradise," of course I remember my tropical heaven on earth. And I think many people have that same notion of paradise – an exotic locale where the sun always shines and life comes easily. But others have a completely different idea of paradise. For them, it might be the thrill of rafting down a wild river canyon, spending the day being pampered at a luxurious spa, shooting under par at Pebble Beach or conquering a double-black-diamond slope with fresh powder. Or perhaps the good life is curling up with a great book in front of a roaring fire, driving a precision sports car on the open road, savoring a five-course gourmet meal or catching lightning bugs with the kids at dusk on a summer evening.

What does paradise mean to you?

Sit back, close your eyes (after you read this paragraph, of course) and visualize your version of paradise. Take a few deep breaths and let the feeling of paradise wash over you. Relax and enjoy as you use all of your senses to experience your nirvana....

At this point, you're likely thinking, "Forget about work! I'm going to paradise!"

Before you run out the door, let me ask you a question: **Why can't you have paradise *at work*?** Why can't you live the good life right where you are?

If you're like most people, you want to believe it's possible but you're skeptical. After all, work isn't supposed to be pleasant. They call it work for a reason, right? You wonder, "Is there really such a thing as Professional Paradise? Does it exist?"

Absolutely! Professional Paradise exists when you feel satisfied, energized and productive. It's easy to see how this is possible every day at work – even when things are challenging.

When you're in Professional Paradise you genuinely enjoy (most of) each day. You're satisfied – you have mental momentum to get the job done. You're energized – you show up and physically get the work done, whether that's at a keyboard, on the phone or related to direct patient care. And, you're productive – your work contributes to the organization's mission, vision and values.

When you create your own Professional Paradise, you work to your strengths, routinely perform at your peak and produce results. Your interactions with coworkers and patients and customers are positive and productive. The work may be mentally and physically demanding but you know you're making a difference. If you have to work for a living, what could be better than that?

Perhaps you're thinking that Professional Paradise comes from working for a particular type of organization or having a certain job. This is most definitely not true. **Professional Paradise is a set of beliefs and mindsets backed up with intentional action.** So often it's not what happens at work, but how we perceive it, think about it and act on it that has a lasting impact.

Consider this: Have you – or someone you know – ever had a fantastic job with a great organization making good money and yet you didn't feel like you were in Professional Paradise? It happens all the time. Maybe you weren't reaching your potential or you didn't enjoy the people you worked with or felt like the job wasn't a good fit.

Professional Paradise is not tied to a specific job, organization, position or process. Rather, it is tied directly to your state of mind. When I was in my twenties and worked as a sales trainer for a computer company, I loved traveling for my job. I was on the road two to three times each month for two or three days at a time. I had the opportunity to visit new cities, see the sights and visit out-of-town friends. And, of course, I got my work done. This was Professional Paradise for me.

Fast forward ten years and add a husband, two children and a dog. That same training job with all the traveling would have been the opposite of Professional Paradise – what I call Professional Prison. The job, the work, the company…none of it changed. What changed was my perspective or mindset.

Am I starting to convince you yet?

Rest assured, Professional Paradise is not a mirage or some version of Fantasy Island. In fact, it's grounded in scientific study. Teresa Amabile and Steven Kramer report in *Harvard Business Review* that performance is driven by our state of mind. Their research, based on more than 12,000 diary entries by workers over three years, shows a direct connection between employees' inner lives – including their perceptions and emotions – and performance: "People perform better when their workday experiences include more positive emotions, stronger intrinsic motivation (passion for work), and more favorable perceptions of their work, their team, their leaders, and their organization." In other words, we all do better at work when we have a positive perspective. This seems like common sense, but it's nice to know that scientific research has actually proved the point.

Furthermore, in a *Time* magazine cover story "The Science of Happiness," Richard Davidson (known as "the king of happiness research") says, "Happiness isn't just a vague, ineffable feeling; it's a physical state of the brain – *one that you can induce deliberately.*" Since paradise is defined as supreme happiness, this research is good news! It means **you don't have to depend on others for your happiness or your paradise. You can create it yourself** – on a regular basis – even at work!

You'll soon discover that I'm an insatiably curious person. I love to ask questions, conduct informal surveys and do research with my clients. I've asked more than one thousand people what makes them happy at work – what makes them feel satisfied, energized and productive. The responses vary from "getting the job done effectively" to "laughing with coworkers." I vividly remember one woman who simply answered, "I would like to be able to say 'I like my job' and mean it."

So, what makes people happy at work?

30%	Successfully completing a task or project
15%	Positive connections with coworkers and customers
15%	Receiving appreciation from others
12%	Teamwork
12%	Money
16%	Various other responses

Notice that no one listed "doing as little as possible" or "surfing the web" or "shooting the breeze by the water cooler" as their nirvana. Notice, too, that "money" was mentioned by only a small percentage of people. What do you think about the data?

I'm psyched! I love that people think that getting their work done is important. These results (as well as the research cited earlier) support what I have long believed to be true – that Professional Paradise is determined not just by external factors but also by *internal* factors. The meaning and value of *success, positive connections, appreciation, teamwork* and even *money* are in the eye of the beholder. Do you see how this list is closely connected to your state of mind and not actual events?

Ultimately, your perspective determines your degree of satisfaction. According to a report by global consulting giant Blessing White, employee engagement – which I think of as Professional Paradise – is individualized. Why? Because **work is personal.** Our perspectives, as well as our likes and dislikes, are unique. Let's look at some real-life examples.

Sheila is a relatively new physical therapist who values professional development and growth. For her, Professional Paradise is learning about new treatment options and then using them with her patients to facilitate better outcomes. She actually enjoys the extra time spent digging deep into journals to find best practices.

Steve works in the Facilities Department supporting multiple outpatient cancer centers that are part of his health system. He believes he's living the good life when the employees he supports put their trust in him to fix what's broken and maintain what's working. He sees complex mechanical problems as interesting puzzles to be solved. While other people might resent bearing the brunt of frustrations, Steve loves how he contributes to quality patient care through his work.

How about you? Would you find paradise in Sheila's or Steve's situation? If you let yourself dream about an ideal day in

Professional Paradise, what picture would you paint? What story would you tell?

I'll start with what makes me feel satisfied, energized & productive... My Professional Paradise includes:

Learning new things

Connecting with people

Creating models and frameworks that help simplify ideas

Helping people find joy in work through laughter and learning

Making a difference for patients through my work with healthcare leaders and staff

You can see from this list that most aren't driven by external circumstances. Even when quarantined at home during the COVID-19 pandemic, I was able to learn new things, virtually connect with people, create models, etc. I could still be the Chief Paradise Officer of my job in stormy and uncertain times.

Take a moment now to really think about your Professional Paradise. The first step to achieving anything you desire in life is to paint a clear picture of the end result. It's well worth your time, energy and effort to get perfectly clear about what you are striving for. Once again, sit back, close your eyes, take a few deep breaths and use all of your senses to visualize a day in Professional Paradise. Remember, workplace Utopia is different for everyone. There's no right or wrong answer. Go with what feels "true" to you.

Do you have it? Great! Now write down your thoughts on the followng page. (The act of writing gives value to the ideas and creates momentum.)

Think about internal and external things that make you feel satisfied, energized and productive. **This is your Professional Paradise!**

_____

_____

_____

_____

_____

Perhaps you're thinking, "This sounds great, Vicki. But is it realistic? Can I really get to Professional ParadisParadise – especially knowing that things will never be the same since the pandemic occurred?"

Almost everyone can find Shangri-La at work through a *SHIFT* in viewpoint, thoughts and actions. (Note: Sometimes it takes external help to get unstuck and change unproductive beliefs and mindsets. That's okay! This is the time to reach out to your Employee Assistance Program or someone who is professionally trained to help.)

I'll say it again because it bears repeating – the Professional Paradise you seek is not entirely dependent on your job, your boss, your customers, your coworker or what's happening around you. It is dependent on your inner world (your mindset, thoughts and viewpoint) more than your outer world.

That might lead some people to think that getting to Professional Paradise is about positive thinking. That's a good start, but it's much more than that. You won't achieve less stress, more energy and remarkable results simply by changing the way you think. You have to take action to put your thoughts into practice. Your mindset drives your actions which in turn drive outcomes.

MINDSET ⟶ ACTIONS ⟶ OUTCOMES

You can find Professional Paradise in most any work situation *if* you're willing to open your mind and take some action. Are you ready?

Jailhouse Blues

Doin' time in Professional Prison

Picture a prison. What comes to mind?

Barbed wire…bars…locks…cold, bare cells…orange jumpsuits…guns… threatening people…confinement…hopelessness…despair.

It's not a pretty picture.

It's hard to imagine that these images could be related to work, but unfortunately, too many people feel like they're doing time in Professional Prison (metaphorically speaking, of course). In fact, a recently released report on employee loyalty from Walker Information (published in Harvard Business Online) states that approximately 25 percent of employees "feel trapped in their jobs."

Like Professional Paradise, Professional Prison is not a physical place. Instead, it's a state of being – **a mindset that drives unproductive actions and, ultimately, undesirable outcomes**. And, just like Professional Paradise, it's a function of internal drivers more than external drivers. Those who perceive that they're trapped at work create their own mental barbed wire and lockdowns that keep them imprisoned. They often see others as threatening or ominous (like inmates) instead of helpful and supportive. They view a complaining patient or family member, challenging coworker or difficult boss as someone who is out to get them personally, much like the bully in the prison exercise yard. As a result, they're always waiting for the other shoe to drop, so to speak. In their world, anxiety and uncertainty are the common elements of each day – regardless of what is happening around them..

Sometimes, people in Professional Prison put themselves in solitary confinement. They keep to themselves and want others to leave them alone so they can "do their jobs in peace." These individuals believe that avoiding other people will make their life easier. I'll never forget the time I was training customer registration clerks in a call center, and one of the participants said (*and she meant it*), "This job would be great if it weren't for the patients." Sounds like this job was not a good fit!

Then there are those who join the "Chain Gang" at work. People stuck in Professional Prison want company. After all, it can get lonely in lockup! These Chain Gang members are drawn to each other because they enjoy commiserating with people who are just as unhappy as they are. Sometimes, they even try to "recruit" more coworkers. When Prisoners get around peers who are teetering between Paradise and Prison, they tend to crank up the rumor mill, spread malicious gossip, put a negative spin on good news and criticize everything the organization or senior leadership does. This is often done without conscious thought, but that doesn't make it any less dangerous. Do you have a chain gang in your workplace?

To be sure, there are different "degrees" of Professional Prison. Some people feel as if they've been sentenced to life in a maximum security facility. Maybe they work in an especially high-stress job or their job requires that they work long, arduous hours. Or perhaps they have a boss who is perpetually unfair and unreasonable. These are external factors that can be difficult to improve without changing careers, jobs or organizations. I'm not suggesting that you put up with bullying or incivility at work. That's not acceptable and you should get help.

However, know this: **Sometimes, adjusting your perspective about external factors is what makes them more tolerable.** The strategies you'll discover throughout this book will help you do just that.

Another degree of Professional Prison is similar to "sleeping one off" in the county jail. Although this still involves being "behind bars," the sentence is short, and before long the Professional Prisoner is free. An example of this is the pandemic crisis that affected everyone in different ways. It's one of those times when you think, "This is different than anything I've ever dealt with!" You feel trapped, panic-stricken, but you have no choice except to show up and do the work. The fear and uncertainty can make routine responsibilities seem like hard work.

If you've ever done a stint in Professional Prison (and who hasn't?), you likely felt stuck in your job. You probably experienced pressure, a lack of energy, maybe even sheer misery. Perhaps you were negative, complained about everything, overreacted to situations or became easily overwhelmed. You might have found yourself calling in sick when you weren't ill or dreaming of greener pastures in some other organization.

Do you regularly suffer from the sleepless nights (or days) and that awful feeling you get in the pit of your stomach before you go to work? This is a sure sign of being stuck in Professional Prison.

If you stay in Professional Prison long enough, you soon forget what freedom feels like. Over time, you become hopeless, resigned to your plight as a Prisoner, and you start to think that these feelings are normal. Eventually you accept the four walls of your "cell" as a dead end, and you settle into a self-imposed life sentence. Think about literally being stuck or locked up. After a while, you'd physically experience the effects of being trapped – you'd likely feel anxious, panicky and out of control. That's why many people who stay in a self-imposed Professional Prison long term suffer from chronic stress-related illnesses like headaches, panic attacks, ulcers, high blood pressure and back problems.

Here's what's really interesting: Many people, when challenged to do something about their prisoner status, say things like, "I don't have a choice" or "What am I supposed to do about it?" They see themselves as victims and believe that their prison sentence was imposed by someone or something else. But remember, Professional Prison is not about where you work or what you do; it's a reflection of how you view your work. To prove my point, the following is an example of two different people in the same work situation. One is in Professional Prison while the other is living the good life at work.

Sam works in the revenue operations department of a healthcare organization. Sam's new boss, Marco, is younger than he is and has only been with the organization a few months. Marco has an impressive resume and was the top choice for the manager position. Sam even participated in the interviewing process and recommended Marco.

However, just a few weeks after Marco started, Sam began to feel micro-managed. Marco's attention to detail and constant follow-up were suffocating. Sam was used to operating independently – he and his former boss had an informal agreement that Sam would be left alone as long as he produced results. He'd really liked his job until all this "under the microscope" business began. Each time Marco asked Sam a question about work that was in progress, Sam grew more resentful and angrier. He saw these questions as a direct assault on his character, work ethic and proven performance. Soon, even small questions that Sam wouldn't have noticed in the past became incredibly annoying. Just three months into Marco's leadership, Sam felt "sentenced" to his job. He was locked in Professional Prison.

One of Sam's coworkers, Ravi, was also involved in the interviewing process and thought Marco was a good choice. Ravi was particularly happy that a new manager was coming on board because he felt like his last boss was never around and didn't support the team.

You can probably guess what happened next: Ravi welcomed Marco's management style. Ravi saw it as coaching and mentoring rather than micro-managing. Each time Marco checked in, Ravi took advantage of the opportunity to forge a strong relationship, seek his advice and learn new elements of the job. Ravi appreciated the assistance and was motivated by his boss's attention. He saw opportunity where Sam saw only frustration. For Ravi, this was Professional Paradise.

Neither employee was right or wrong. Sam's and Ravi's perspectives of Marco's leadership style were vastly different. As a result, they had completely opposite mindsets about work. This is a perfect example of how your mindset has such a strong influence on your ability to live the good life at work.

Just as different people have different ideas about Professional Paradise, so it is with Professional Prison. Everyone sees it differently.

Clearly, Prison is not where you want to be! It makes you wonder, "Why do people stay locked up in Professional Prison when they could be enjoying Paradise instead?"

To be sure, some organizations and leaders make it tough to get to Paradise. They may even perpetuate a negative mentality through a variety of less-than-thoughtful employment practices. If this is the case, maybe it's time to go in search of a job that's a better fit for what makes you feel satisfied, energized and productive.

Sometimes, however, you may be powerless to change external things, but you can change your response to them. That's one way to change the outcomes and results you experience every day on the job.

I've found that people often continue to work in Professional Prison because it's the path of least resistance…it's comfortable. I know this sounds crazy – how can "prison" and "comfortable" appear in the same sentence? It's called *institutionalization*: the process by which real inmates becomes so accustomed to the four walls, three meals and structure of prison life that they actually prefer it over freedom.

For the Chain Gang member, sometimes it's simply easier to maintain a self-imposed prison mindset than do what it takes to escape. Mentally staying put and being miserable is the path of least resistance. This may sound counterintuitive, but look around, and you'll notice it happening all over the place. Think about the Dilbert® cartoon – a whole consumer-driven product line created to complain about work.

I'll bet some of you are thinking, "That's not me. Why would I want to stay trapped in Prison?" or "You don't understand – I have my reasons why I can't make any changes at work."

You have every right to stay locked up if that's what you want. You also have the opportunity to get on the path to less stress, more energy and remarkable results at work. Remember, both Prison and Paradise are states of being. You have a choice about your mindset and your actions.

Whether you've been wrongly convicted, you're in a prison of your own making or you're a repeat offender, you can continue in Professional Prison or you can make a daring escape and head to Professional Paradise. Where would you rather be?

Put your objections on the back burner and keep reading with an open mind. You just might discover that you've had the key to your freedom all along.

Out on Parole

Are you a Professional Parolee?

So far, you've created your vision of Professional Paradise and learned about Professional Prison. Now the question is, where do you spend most of your time – in Professional Prison, Professional Paradise or somewhere in between?

Before you answer that question, carefully think about your typical daily work experience – not your best day or your worst day. Try to be objective and avoid any judgment as you formulate your answer – it's important that you answer honestly. Then draw a vertical line on the Prison-Paradise Continuum below that best illustrates where you are:

Professional
Prison   **Professional**
                                                              Paradise

Are you already living the good life at work – having fun and basking in the sun in Paradise? Are you regularly connecting with what makes you feel satisfied, energized and productive? If so, congratulations! But don't stop here…keep reading. Why? Because the strategies you learn in Part II will make it easier for you to stay in Paradise and make your time there even more rewarding.

If this exercise has confirmed what you've been feeling in your gut – that you're stuck in Prison – don't despair. Just keep reading. *Please, please* keep reading. I truly believe the *SHIFT* steps will give you the perspective you need to change and the tools you need to escape. Too often, people think they have to quit their jobs in order to get out of Prison. Before you change jobs, try changing your *mindset* about your job. Sometimes that makes all the difference.

But what if you're neither in Prison nor in Paradise? If you placed yourself somewhere in the middle, you're on what I call Professional Parole. *Merriam-Webster's Dictionary of Law* defines parole as "the state of freedom resulting from a conditional release of a prisoner who has served part of a sentence and who remains under the control of and in the legal custody of a parole authority." Being out on parole is a whole lot better than being in prison, but parolees are not completely free…they can't leave town, and they certainly can't jet off to paradise.

Professional Parole is a similar concept. You're not so miserable that you feel completely trapped in Professional Prison, thank goodness, but you're not "free" and living the good life at work either. Some days you're productive and in the zone; other days are spent moving slowly and watching the clock. There are many great things about your job as well as some big frustrations. Professional Parole is – you guessed it – a state of being, **an apathetic mindset that leads to reaction instead of proactive action.** Things aren't bad enough to make you quit, but they're unpleasant enough for you to feel the suffering in some form or fashion.

You know you're on Parole when you've lost the skip in your step. Maybe you have chronic mild stress and find yourself complaining about little things that never bothered you before, like occasionally having to stay late, a messy common area or a minor change in parking arrangements. Staff meetings and team gatherings aren't as motivating or fun as they used to be, and you go because you have to, not because you want to. You likely spend a lot of time questioning your value to the team or organization, and you may have that nagging feeling that you're wasting your potential, and that there *must* be more to life.

Does any of this feel familiar?

If so, you're not alone. Most people are on Professional Parole. My research indicates that a small percentage of people truly feel trapped in their jobs every day, a slightly larger percentage truly live the good life at work, and the vast majority are stuck in Limbo Land. And it seems my findings are supported by other studies. Based on recurring surveys by the Gallup Organization, over half of today's workers are on Professional Parole. Gallup's results indicate that 16 percent of the U.S. workforce is actively disengaged (Professional Prison), 33 percent is engaged (Professional Paradise) and 51 percent is not engaged (Professional Parole).

Why so many people on Parole? Some have managed to escape from Prison. For them, Parole is simply the next step. Others began their careers or jobs in Paradise, but over time it slipped away from them. They've tasted the good life at work, and they believe they can have it again…they're just not sure how to get it back. Then there are those who've been on Parole their entire careers. Their work experiences have always been just so-so because their negative beliefs about work drive their perceptions and, therefore, their outcomes.

Let's look at some real-life Parolees. Janel works in a small ambulatory care office doing administrative support work for the director. She has a supportive boss and her workload is manageable. The office is close to her house and she gets along with her colleagues. Sounds like Professional Paradise, doesn't it? Well, in recent months, Janel has been discontented and disengaged. She told me, "I miss working in the hospital. I loved being busy and I need some kind of professional development or growth." She doesn't want to change jobs as much as she wants to fix a few aspects of her job that bother her.

Marlene is a Clinical Nurse Educator. She works part time and makes good money. Six months ago her responsibilities were increased to include several remote clinical locations, substantially increasing her drive time. She went from being in the hospital every day to making almost daily trips to other offices, sitting for hours in traffic. She genuinely likes what she does and the people she works with, but she dreads the increased driving. Now she plods through the day, complaining and feeling sorry for herself. She's on Professional Parole.

And then there's Carlos, a respiratory therapist. When I asked him how he feels about his job, he said, "Let me put it this way: Most of my coworkers go to lunch around 11:30. I purposely wait and go later in the day so the afternoons go by faster. I figure if I can just make it to lunch, the rest of the day won't be so bad." Yikes!

How would you describe Professional Parole? Jot down a few words or phrases here.

Professional Parole feels like…

_____

_____

_____

The next logical question is, why do people *stay* on Parole? In some cases, for the same reason people stay in Prison: It's the path of least resistance. But when it comes to Parole, I think there are four other reasons why most of us stay put.

The first is **fear**. Fear is a great immobilizer. Too many people won't even let themselves imagine Professional Paradise because they don't want to be disappointed. Their internal voices knock them down with fear and uncertainty. "What if I take this promotion, and I don't like being a manager?" "What if I look at things differently and it backfires?" Not too long ago, I met an accounts payable clerk who was highly dedicated and possessed great job skills. She'd been in the same position for a number of years, and work felt stale and mundane. I suggested she apply for an open job in her department that involved additional responsibilities. Her response? "I'm afraid. What if I can't do the new job?"

Some people are Parolees for life because they have **low expectations**. They hold deeply entrenched beliefs that work is something you endure. They've watched their parents, loved ones or role models go to work day after day for nothing more than the paycheck. And because they think being unhappy at work is standard operating procedure, they don't even know they have a choice. If you don't know Paradise exists, Parole doesn't look so bad compared to Prison.

The third reason is a **lack of personal accountability**. Ouch! That one hurt! But if we want to get to Paradise, we have to be brutally honest with ourselves. Let's face it, most of us don't want to accept the fact that the quality of our work experience truly is up to us. It's a whole lot easier to blame our boss, our coworkers, our organization or some other factor than to accept responsibility for where we are. It takes courage and strength to admit that it's our fault we've been unhappy or just biding time in a job for months or even years. That's a bitter pill to swallow for anyone. When was the last time you checked in with yourself about your priorities and career goals? Have you lost touch with the "old you" who was energized and engaged at work?

Although your manager and your organization obviously have an impact on your work experience, they are not the reason you're disengaged, nor are they responsible for engaging you. *You* are responsible for engaging you. **You are the Chief Paradise Officer (CPO) of your own life**. It's up to you to create your own Professional Paradise. You have a choice: do nothing and stay on Parole, slide backwards into Prison, or *SHIFT* towards Paradise.

And that brings us to the final reason why so many people never get off Parole – **they simply don't know how**. I believe that many people genuinely want less stress, more energy and remarkable results at work and are ready to take control, but they don't have the tools to make it happen. Fortunately, this book has the solution. The first step is to get off Parole using the *SHIFT* steps I'll share with you. Then you can go one better and head toward your own Shangri-La at work.

POWs and WOWs

The signs of Prison and Paradise

Like many situations in life, where you are in your work experience is not usually the result of a few major events, but rather the accumulation of many minor events over time. Take, for instance, the institution of marriage. A loving, enduring relationship is built over a period of years through many daily choices that reflect how much the spouses respect, support and treat each other. Likewise, a few big fights don't push a couple to divorce. Behind every failed marriage is a mountain of seemingly insignificant arguments, countless misunderstandings, scores of disappointments and years of distrust.

People who find themselves in actual prison and paradise don't suddenly appear there. Although a single illegal act may be the culminating event that finally lands a criminal in prison, it's usually the result of a myriad of bad influences and years of delinquency. Independently wealthy people who live the good life every day likely didn't win the lottery and find themselves in paradise the next day. Most got there through years of hard work, innumerable smart business decisions and prudent financial choices.

And so it is at work.

It is the compounding of your responses to many individual events, situations, interactions and experiences that puts us in Prison, Paradise or somewhere in between. I call these factors POWs and WOWs, depending on whether they are essentially negative or positive. Let's take a closer look at each one.

The Random House Unabridged Dictionary tells us that a pow is "a heavy blow." Have you ever experienced a figurative heavy blow at work – an event, situation or interaction that sucker punches you, distracts you, aggravates you and just plain leaves you feeling bad? That's a POW in a nutshell. It's something bad or negative that happens to you – a metaphorical body blow or right uppercut to the chin.

During the height of the crisis, the Covid-19 Pandemic was a POW of monumental proportions. We all experienced it differently depending on our jobs, financial situation, home life, etc. It is probably the biggest, most impactful POW that any of us have experienced.

Instead of focusing on this BIG POW, let's look at smaller examples that happened as a result of the virus. Stop and think of a POW you've recently experienced. How did it make you feel?

POWs are either *internally* or *externally* generated. Internal POWs are self-inflicted, created by you, such as showing up late for a meeting to find everyone waiting on you, procrastinating on a project or making a careless mistake on a report. Some internal POWs come from your mindset – how you perceive things and react to them. Being so worried about a situation that you can't focus on your work or assuming a colleague is blowing you off because he or she hasn't responded to your email are good examples.

External POWs, on the other hand, are the result of non-controllable situations or other people's actions. They happen *to* you instead of *within* you. Examples might include having to work from home with small children to supervise, a computer issue that occurs minutes before a report is due, or someone who is upset because they can't visit a family member who is ill. Many of the external POWs we experience are related to change, lack of control, uncertainty, or rules and regulations.

POWs caused by other people can originate with patients, family members, other customers, vendors, competitors, coworkers, direct reports or leaders. For instance, an angry patient hits the call bell to complain, one of your team members is out sick during crunch time, or a supplier suddenly announces they can't meet your needs for personal protective equipment. Leaders and staff alike experience POWs. Think of the department head who learns from the vice president that the productivity goals for the quarter have been raised without her input, or the organization that discovers a group of physicians is moving to another health system. See the chart on the next page for more examples of POWs.

Internal POWs
Procrastination; poor time management
Fear; worrying about things before they happen
Not meeting goals, objectives, deadlines
Falling short of your own high expectations
Indecisiveness
Lack of commitment or focus
Being disorganized
Making mistakes; lack of attention to detail

External POWs	
With Coworkers	With Patients/Customers
Poor or no communication	Complaints
Uncertainties of a new boss or team member	Not returning calls or calling too often
Poor performance by others that negatively impacts you	Not doing what is recommended
Differing opinions; conflicting priorities, goals or sense of urgency	Unrealistic/unreasonable expectations
Lack of recognition from leaders or peers	Changing scope or specifications
Interruptions	Project delays
Gossip	Quality concerns
Direct reports who don't share important news	Financial issues

When you get hit with a POW, either you get riled up or you shut down. It's the innate "fight or flight" reaction. You might get angry or annoyed, or become filled with anxiety. POWs sap your energy and enthusiasm, and can leave you feeling disheartened, disappointed, distrustful and disengaged. You often experience physical changes as well. Your heart rate increases, your blood pressure might shoot up and your palms start to sweat.

When POWs pile up day after day, you become imprisoned. Over time, the negative thoughts and reactions to external events lead to a sense of hopelessness and create the feeling of being trapped. A few POWs here and there are no big deal. Everyone – even those in Paradise – experience POWs from time to time. We all do. It's the perpetual presence of POWs – and the lack of ability to manage them – that pushes you into Professional Prison.

POWs, and the way you to respond to them, are like ripples in a pond. Their impact extends beyond you to affect coworkers, customers, teams, even entire organizations. Think of a recent encounter where a teammate perhaps overreacted, jumped all over you and then apologized, saying something like, "Sorry. I'm in a bad mood because (fill in the blank)." That's the ripple effect of POWs.

What POWs do you frequently experience at work? In the space on the following page, write down three common POWs you get hit with and identify each one as internal or external.

POW	Internal?	External?
Example: Forgetting materials for an important meeting	✓	
Example: Your coworker forgets materials for a meeting		✓

Notice that the outcome is the same in the two example POWs, even though one is internal and one is external – there are no materials for that important meeting! If *you* forget the materials, you might beat yourself up over your mistake. The situation plays out differently if it's your coworker who forgets the materials. You'd likely still be angry, but you'd blame your coworker. Either way, you have a meeting to save. And either way, you can control your reaction and find a solution using the *SHIFT* steps.

Look back at your external POWs. Are they within your control? Probably not. But guess what? *It doesn't matter!* What is within your control is how you respond to them – your mindset and your actions. That may sound idealistic, but it doesn't mean it isn't true.

Now let's *SHIFT* gears (pun intended) to something a little more pleasant...

You just got the call. The personal protective equipment order finally arrived! *WOW!*

At last, the project your team has been focusing on for weeks is complete – on time and under budget! *WOW!*

Interesting…you've just learned a new computer program that will save you hours of time! *WOW!*

A *wow* is a joyous exclamation. *Merriam-Webster Dictionary* also defines it as "a sensational hit or a striking success." A WOW as I define it is something that makes you feel satisfied, energized or productive. Sound familiar? That's our definition of Professional Paradise.

WOWs get you jazzed. They create joy, delight and pleasure. When you have a WOW, you feel like you're in the zone, at the top of your game, performing at your peak. You are energized, your stress level is low, and you have a skip in your step.

Think of a WOW you've recently experienced. How did it make you feel?

Have you ever noticed that when you say "WOW!" you automatically smile? Say it aloud right now and see what happens. You just have to smile because of how your mouth forms the letters. Pretty cool, isn't it?

Like POWs, WOWs can be either internal or external. Internal WOWs come from your viewpoint or your response to certain things, such as noticing a stunning sunset while you're sitting in traffic or feeling fulfilled when you serve someone else (even if they don't notice). One of my favorite internal WOWs is solving a problem or coming up with a great idea all on my own. Now that feels good!

External WOWs come from other people or situations. A WOW could be a surprise bonus or raise, a coworker pitching in to help you on a busy day, or a senior executive publicly acknowledging your efforts at a staff meeting.

Internal WOWs
😃 Finishing tasks and projects
😃 Learning a new skill
😃 Feeling like you've made a difference
😃 Finding creative solutions to problems
😃 Laughter and fun
😃 Getting paid what you think you're worth
😃 Using your talents and strengths

External WOWs	
With Coworkers	With Patients/Customers
😃 Teamwork and synergy	😃 Acceptance of help
😃 Helping or mentoring one another	😃 Returned calls
😃 Appreciation from teammates or your boss	😃 Happy, easy-going customers
😃 Personal accountability or initiative by direct reports and coworkers	😃 Solving patient problems and issues
😃 Creative problem solving	😃 Community appreciation
😃 Being given an exciting new responsibility or opportunity	😃 Positive word of mouth about your services
😃 Freedom and autonomy	😃 Appreciation from patients and their families
😃 Positive interactions with others	😃 Positive reactions to ideas

Which WOWs click with you? Take a moment now to jot down three common WOWs that get you jazzed and then indicate whether each is internally or externally driven.

WOW	Internal?	External?
Example: You just finished a project, and you give yourself a big pat on the back!	✓	
Example: You just finished a project, and your boss gives you a big pat on the back!		✓

Did you have more internal or external WOWs? Interestingly, people tend to *notice* internal WOWs more than external ones because we're often not "present" enough in the moment to recognize the external ones. I have a friend who is always so busy thinking about the next project or assignment that she genuinely doesn't hear the accolades she receives from her boss and teammates. As a result, she feels unappreciated when in fact the opposite is true. What WOWs have you missed lately?

As you've probably guessed, an accumulation of WOWs puts you squarely in Professional Paradise. When you consistently experience

WOWs on a daily basis, you'll find that you are absolutely living the good life at work.

You've probably also surmised that you're on Professional Parole when you regularly experience both POWs and WOWs. Remember our description of Parole – some good stuff, some bad stuff; some good days, some bad days. That back and forth is the result of POWs and WOWs.

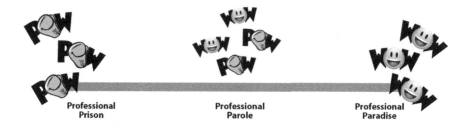

| Professional | Professional | Professional |
| Prison | Parole | Paradise |

Where you are on the Prison-Parole-Paradise continuum is subjective and personal. One POW doesn't land you in Prison; one WOW doesn't put you in Paradise. Just like the marriage example at the beginning of this chapter, **it's the cumulative effect of many individual POWs and WOWs that determines the quality of your work experience**. The amazing thing is that WOWs are experienced even in the most challenging situations. With the pandemic, many team members were asked to work long hours in scary situations, yet they found a sense of family and support all around them. Small WOWs – like a shoulder to cry on or a fresh donut – add up to sustain your Paradise moments.

Right now you might be asking the million-dollar question: "How many WOWs does it take to get to Professional Paradise?" Great news! That is up to you to decide. Just as you created your own vision of Professional Paradise in Chapter 1, *you* determine when you've arrived there. Generally speaking though, it's relative. When you steadily experience significantly more WOWs than POWs you'll be on your way.

Here's an analogy that might help you put POWs and WOWs in perspective: Imagine that you're standing in the middle of a vast field of dead weeds. It's an ugly sight. You bend down and pull a weed. In its place, you plant a flower seed. You continue to work your way through the field, pulling weeds and planting seeds. Now this is one huge field, so you come back day after day, pulling weeds and planting seeds. Before long, you start to notice a difference. The flowers are starting to grow and bloom. At first, there are just a few scattered among the weeds. But as time goes on, the flowers start to overtake the weeds. You keep pulling and planting, pulling and planting. The more flowers you see, the more you pull and plant. Then, one day, you return to the field to a truly magnificent sight…flowers as far as the eye can see. Yes, there are still a few weeds here and there, but you don't notice them. The beauty and fragrance of thousands of flowers is enchanting and consuming.

That's how I see the transition from Professional Prison to Professional Paradise. Every time you *SHIFT* a POW to a WOW, it's like pulling a weed and replacing it with a flower seed. A WOW or two starts to pop up here and there. That's where it starts – one WOW at a time. You discover you like the WOWs, and you work to *SHIFT* even more POWs to WOWs. You're moving quickly towards Professional Parole. There are still some POWs, but you continue to replace them with WOWs. Until the day comes when the WOWs outnumber the POWs, and all you can see is the beauty of Professional Paradise. Get the picture?

POWs and WOWs are the individual pieces – the events, circumstances, situations and your responses – that, taken together, create Prison, Parole or Paradise. POWs and WOWs are the day-to-day evidence of where you are on your journey.

If you're in Prison or even on Parole, it may feel impossible to get to Paradise. But don't worry. In Part II, I'm going to teach you how to *SHIFT* your POWs to WOWs. Try *SHIFT*ing just one POW to a WOW with the simple, proven techniques I'm going to give you. Do you believe that you can transform one confrontation with a patient into a positive connection? Can you turn one personal mistake into a learning experience? Can you find one way to communicate better with your teammates? If you can do it once, then you can do it a hundred times – and then you're on your way to less stress, more energy and remarkable results at work.

PART II

SHIFT:
YOUR PASSPORT TO
PROFESSIONAL PARADISE

People who know me say I am Little Miss Glass-is-Overflowing. What can I tell you? I've been this way my whole life. I'm just a sunny person. I worked with a business consultant a few years back who helped me figure out just what makes me so optimistic. Is it simply in my DNA, or is it something I do?

After lots of great questions from the consultant and some extensive soul searching, I realized that, for me, living the good life both in my job and at home involves effort. Yes, some of it comes naturally, just like some people are naturally athletic. But even people without any natural talent can typically get good enough to play a sport and enjoy it.

Likewise, just about everyone can create their own Professional Paradise. It just takes determination and practice. Yet the effort is not unpleasant. You know how good you feel after a great workout at the gym? Well, you feel the same way when you work out your *SHIFT* muscles and transform your POWs to WOWs. The results are worth the effort.

And that brings us squarely to the "how-tos." So let's get started…

What is *SHIFT*?

SHIFT is an acronym that describes a series of steps you can use to transform a POW to a WOW. It's a proprietary technique I've developed over a number of years that simplifies the process of changing ineffective, detrimental thought patterns and actions into positive, beneficial thought patterns, actions and habits.

SHIFT is much more than just positive thinking. It's a way of looking at situations and events differently and making the necessary adjustments to create better outcomes. The steps are designed to help you discover where there are disconnects and make deliberate changes to get back on track. The benefits of using *SHIFT* are vastly improved productivity, performance and results, less stress, more energy and more positive connections with coworkers and customers. In short, the outcome is Professional Paradise!

The *SHIFT* methodology is proven. I've been sharing this concept for years, and thousands of people have learned and applied the principles. It works for everyone, regardless of age, gender or ethnicity. It works for every position and level in the organization – individual contributor, leader and senior executive. I've taught it in a wide array of healthcare areas, from technology to risk management to financial services to security. It works for any POW you might experience. It just plain works!

In this section, I'm going to teach you the five *SHIFT* steps in detail and then give you several opportunities to practice *SHIFT*ing with actual POWs you've experienced at work. However, the individual steps will make more sense if we first examine the *SHIFT* methodology on a macro level. To *SHIFT* POWs to WOWs and start living the good life at work, conceptually you must:

1. *SHIFT* your work beliefs.

2. *SHIFT* your mindset.

3. *SHIFT* your actions.

4. *SHIFT* your habits.

When you do these four things, your outcomes will *SHIFT* and your work experience will dramatically change for the better. The *SHIFT* process is truly transformational. It is, in fact, your Passport to Professional Paradise.

What You Believe is What You Receive

How your beliefs affect the quality of your work life

I've mentioned several times (repetition reinforces, right?) that Professional Paradise, Prison and Parole are products of your state of mind – outcomes of your internal world rather than your external world. When I first began developing the *SHIFT* technique, I was very curious about that. Why does one person see the sky as partly cloudy and another sees it as partly sunny? How can one team member think a coworker has a strong work ethic, while her teammate perceives the same coworker as lazy? Why do two people see the exact same event, situation or interaction differently?

Now that's a complex question with a complex answer. Personality, individual preferences and mood are certainly key factors. But **the single most important factor in how we view the world is our belief system**. According to researcher Rogene Buchholz, "Beliefs define the world for an individual and constitute an information system to which a person looks for answers."

Beliefs are the foundation not only of our inner world, but also of our actions and reactions in the external world. Think back to the principle I shared in the first chapter about how your mindset drives your actions which drive your outcomes:

MINDSET ➤ ACTIONS ➤ OUTCOMES

Now we're going to expand that principle. When you experience some kind of event or situation (internal or external), that experience either creates a new belief, confirms an existing belief or contradicts an existing belief. The more your experiences confirm your beliefs, the more deeply entrenched your beliefs become. Conversely, the more your experiences contradict existing beliefs, the more likely you are to modify them. For example, if one of your direct reports misses a deadline on something important, it might confirm a belief that he or she – or employees in general – are not responsible. On the other hand, if all your direct reports consistently deliver on their commitments, you would likely start to change your belief about employees being irresponsible.

Your beliefs determine your state of mind (and your state of mind directs your actions which produce certain outcomes). Now here is where it gets interesting! The outcomes are, in effect, events or situations that either create new beliefs, or confirm or contradict existing beliefs. It's an ongoing cycle:

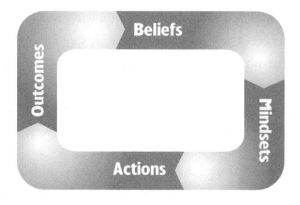

In the example on the previous page, the missed deadline (a POW) confirms your belief and makes you aggravated (your mindset). Your frustration drives you to set rigid due dates for all reports and to make your team work over the weekend (your action), which makes your direct reports resentful (the outcome). Despite the new guidelines – or perhaps because of them – your employees are now disgruntled and disengaged and still don't consistently meet deadlines, further reinforcing your belief that employees aren't responsible. The cycle continues…and so do the POWs!

Our *work* beliefs are the foundation of our mindset, actions and outcomes on the job. We all come to work with beliefs that act as a lens through which we see, experience and interpret every event, situation, interaction and circumstance. They are the "why" behind our thoughts and feelings at work.

Consider a work belief about punctuality and its importance (or lack thereof). Dee's work belief is "Good workers arrive on time," while Zack's work belief is "Good workers get the job done." In each case, the belief determines the mindset (be on time vs. okay to be late), which drives the actions (get to work on time vs. get to work whenever). If the rules or culture of this particular workplace dictate that either action is fine, then both Dee and Zack will likely have positive outcomes, such as being productive and feeling good about their work ethic. These WOWs contribute to a Paradise state of being and reinforce each person's notion that her or his work belief is correct. See how it plays out?

Differing work beliefs are the genesis of many challenges and conflicts in the workplace. Problems arise when our work beliefs are not in sync with the organization's values or when we work with others who don't share the same work beliefs. If Zack's tardiness affects Dee's performance (a big POW), then they need to create a positive solution that will work for both of them. If Dee is annoyed but her productivity isn't affected, then she should let it go. Either way, she can *SHIFT* the POW to a WOW and reduce her stress.

Many factors go into creating our belief system about work. Even the word "work" is full of extremes. Check any dictionary and the definition "employment or a vocation" is typically the first one you'll see. But keep looking and you'll find references to "toil," "effort" and "success." You know you're in trouble when the basic definition can lead to differing beliefs.

The primary inputs that establish our work beliefs are gender, cultural background, age or generation, upbringing, and personal work experiences. I could write an entire book on work beliefs, their origins and how they affect our ability to create Professional Paradise, but for the sake of brevity, let's take just a quick look at each of these factors.

> **Gender.** We already know that gender is a compelling factor in communication style, relationships, our concept of success, our approach to problem solving, how we define our roles in life, and our notion of work/life balance…just to name a few! Is there anyone who *doesn't* think that gender is a compelling factor in the development of our work beliefs? I didn't think so. Enough said.

> **Cultural Background.** As the world continues to shrink, we will undoubtedly find ourselves working more often with coworkers, suppliers and patients from other cultures and regions of the world. Traditions, values and business customs — which vary dramatically from culture to culture — have an enormous impact on work beliefs.

Age or Generation. Grandpa doesn't view the world the same way his digital native granddaughter does. The same is true in the workplace, where never before have so many people from different generations worked together at once. A workplace with Millennial, Gen X and Baby Boomer employees is a perfect breeding ground for diverse work beliefs and therefore conflicting ideas about how and what should be done on any given day. The Baby Boomer's Professional Paradise could well be the Millennial's Prison and vice versa.

Upbringing. Most people begin forming certain beliefs about work at a young age. As toddlers, we read books about firefighters, nurses, teachers, business people and ballerinas. As we grew older, the messages we received about work continued throughout our school and college years. Our parents and teachers unwittingly planted ideas – some negative, some positive – about work and career throughout these formative years. An anonymous respondent to one of my mini-surveys about work beliefs learned from an early age that work stinks. The message in her house was "you work because you have to." On the other hand, a friend of mine learned growing up that work is enjoyable and something to look forward to. His father entertained him and his siblings with stories of the interesting people and exciting places he experienced while on the road as a traveling salesman in the food industry.

Personal Work Experiences. As we enter the workforce and begin to have our own positive and negative work experiences, our work beliefs evolve. In many cases, the beliefs we develop on our own are more powerful than the ones we learned growing up because the experiences they're based on directly impacted our emotions, our status, maybe even our wallets. Just the other day, I heard someone say, "You don't get to pick your job. You just need to get one and stick with it." *POW!* Obviously this person has some negative beliefs about choices and flexibility.

All of these different factors and influences – gender, cultural background, age, upbringing and personal experiences – come together to create a belief system that is the foundation of our work life.

Here's another response I received from my mini-survey: "My mother raised me as a single parent. We didn't have a lot of money, and she needed to work. I remember seeing her become physically ill before going to work. There was no love lost between her and her supervisor. She really dreaded going to work and dealing with him. As a child, seeing this really got to me. I didn't know much about work, other than it obviously wasn't pleasant. When I started working and then became a supervisor, I promised myself that I would create a work environment where everyone showed respect for one another." This is a profound example of how work beliefs affect not only our career choices and work experiences, but also the experiences of those we work with.

I hope you're starting to understand why your work beliefs are so important. Do you see how they can have a huge impact on your definition of Professional Paradise, Prison and Parole?

What are *your* work beliefs?

Identifying and recognizing your (often subconscious) work beliefs, assessing their value and consciously choosing to keep or *SHIFT* them is directly connected to your ability to get to Professional Paradise. Take a few minutes now to thoughtfully answer the following questions:

✦ How do you think your gender affects your beliefs about work? What about your cultural heritage or ethnic background?

✦ Which generation do you belong to? How do you think that impacts your work beliefs?

✦ Which two or three messages or beliefs about work did you learn from parents, teachers or others when you were growing up? For example: "Dad works; Mom stays at home" or "Never trust the boss."

✦ What beliefs have you formed based on your own experiences in the working world?

✦ How do all of these beliefs you've described impact you at work?

✦ Which harmful, detrimental beliefs do you need to *SHIFT* to more helpful, constructive beliefs?

Now that you've gained a better understanding of your own work beliefs, it's equally important to enhance your awareness of your coworkers' beliefs and to acknowledge that their beliefs are more than likely different from yours. Pay attention in conversations and meetings to others' actions and reactions, and consider how the actions might be based on an individualized set of beliefs. You can even ask your coworkers what beliefs they bring to work or start a discussion at a staff meeting. Teams function better and have more synergy when team members acknowledge and respect each other's unique point of view.

Let me now ask you the most important question of all: **Do you *truly believe* it's possible to create Professional Paradise and have less stress, more energy and remarkable results at work?**

The answer to that question is crucial. If you don't believe Professional Paradise is possible for you, the *SHIFT* steps will be far less effective because your belief system will work against them. You must truly believe that you can live the good life at work, or you'll never get to Professional Paradise. Why? Because **what you believe is what you receive!**

If you're already a believer, great! If not, that's okay too. There's nothing wrong with being skeptical. In fact, convinced skeptics often become the biggest believers. I challenge you to finish this book and then come back to this all-important question.

From Alcatraz to Shangri-La

An overview of the *SHIFT* concept

We focused on identifying and *SHIFT*ing your work beliefs in the last chapter. Now let's give our attention to your mindset and your actions.

SHIFT Your Mindset

One of my favorite authors, the late Wayne Dyer, says in *The Power of Intention*, "When you change the way you look at things, the things you look at change." Please re-read that quote now and let its meaning soak in.

In essence, it means that when you change your perspective and your reaction to a situation, it has the *net effect* of changing the situation itself. For example, what would happen if you looked at the massive traffic jam you might find yourself in as a chance to listen to a book or podcast? If you could *SHIFT* your perspective, you would in effect transform the event from a highly annoying pain in the neck to a bit of entertainment or a personal development session. Consider the impact if you *SHIFT* your mindset about a coworker who appears to be distracted and disengaged. When you look closer, you realize that she is sad about something that happened earlier in the day. When you don't take her behavior personally, you open up a chance to connect with her to provide support. *When you change the way you look at things, things change.*

When we get hit with POWs, we often make them worse by obsessing about them. We "awfulize" the circumstances, letting our thoughts rule the day and imagining a disastrous ending to the stories of our life. This is what I call Fly Away Thinking™ – the self-made "tornado" in our brain that takes external circumstances and turns them into whirling dervishes of fear, anxiety and frustration. It's the out-of-control, ever-faster-spinning spiral of negative thoughts that cause volatile emotions and knee-jerk reactions.

Funnel Thinking™, on the other hand, is taking charge of negative, unrestrained thoughts and focusing them into a more productive mindset. You create a mental "funnel" that eliminates pessimistic, unconstructive thoughts and pulls in the ones that are advantageous and constructive. As the name implies, Funnel Thinking forces you to carefully choose and allow into your mind only those specific thoughts that lead to a WOW.

One of the easiest ways to go from Fly Away Thinking to Funnel Thinking is WC^2. WC^2 is an abbreviation for What Can We Control? Asking yourself this question is a good way to stop the mental "tornado." Every day at work, we know there will be POWs – some big and some small. The only thing they all have in common is that we have a choice in how to respond to them.

In our house, we have this sign up in several places. The reason that WC^2 is shown on a ring here is that I liken it to a superhero's secret decoder ring. Keeping this mantra in mind is the antidote to any mental "kryptonite" that comes your way.

You can download this sign at www.ProfessionalParadise.com

I put the signs up during the pandemic to remind my husband and me that there were still things we could do something about. We couldn't change the stormy and uncertain elements of the virus, but we could control a lot of other things. We could control what we decided to consume (from the media, our friends and the refrigerator). We could control the effort behind the work we did. Most importantly, we could control how much we worried or fretted about what was happening.

Let's put Fly Away Thinking and Funnel Thinking into context. Imagine that you arrive at work tomorrow to discover that your boss – whom you really enjoy working for – is leaving the organization for a new job. Your initial response is "Congratulations!" Then reality sets in! You begin to wonder, "Oh no…how will this affect me?" and negative thoughts flood your mind. But the truth is that you don't know how this "story" will end. You have two options for finishing it. One is to let your Fly Away Thinking generate a less-than-pleasant ending to the situation. The other is to use Funnel Thinking to create an entirely different outcome. Let's take a look with WC^2 in mind:

Fly Away Thinking	Funnel Thinking
✓ This will change everything! Why does bad stuff always happen to me?	✓ My boss has resigned and is leaving in three weeks. I'd better learn all I can before she leaves.
✓ This is our second new boss in two years! I knew it wouldn't last.	✓ This is just one more chance to change and grow.
✓ I was so happy with my boss. What if the new boss isn't as good as my boss now?	✓ The new boss could be even better, and I might enjoy working with him even more.
✓ What if they promote one of my coworkers?	✓ Senior management did a great job when they hired my current boss. They'll do a good job again.
✓ I bet this will cause turmoil and chaos!	✓ My boss's boss is supportive of our department. I'm sure the transition will be smooth.
✓ I'd never be considered for the job even if I wanted it.	✓ I enjoy working for this organization, and I'm doing well in my job.
✓ I can't think about work right now.	✓ I have work to do now.

Notice how Funnel Thinking fills your tank and gives you more energy, while Fly Away Thinking is an energy guzzler and drains you. Doesn't it make much more sense to simply keep your thoughts focused on what you know as of today instead of letting your thoughts spiral out of control? Don't jump to conclusions, make assumptions or worry about something that *might* happen in the future. The only part of your manager leaving that you can control is your reaction to it. Which reaction will you choose?

If you just can't help wondering about things to come, then at least be an optimist. I always say, **"If you don't know the ending to a story, then why not create a happy one?"** Before you start worrying about all the bad things that could happen, spend time envisioning the "happily ever after" version of the situation.

Mastering your thoughts is one of the most important principles you can learn. Identify them as harmful or helpful. Pay attention to the assumptions you make – are they mostly negative or positive? Notice how you tend to envision the future – is it with a lot of "what if" scenarios? Much of the time, your mindset is the only thing that remains negative long after a situation is over. Are you ready to let go of your Fly Away Thinking and try a new thought pattern? I promise, you'll be happy you did!

SHIFT Your Actions

Many people believe the secret to creating desired outcomes is simply to think positive thoughts. I believe it takes more than wishful thinking to change your reality – it takes action! The action corollary to Wayne Dyer's thought principle comes from Robert Collier, author of *The Secret of the Ages*: "If you don't make things happen, then things will happen to you." You can't simply sit back and think. You also have to *do* something in order to produce positive results.

Imagine you're going to host a special dinner party for friends. Your first step is to think through the guest list and envision the invitations. You mull over the decorations, picturing the table in your mind. You research recipes and create an impressive menu. Sounds like a great party! But what if you were to stop right there – at the thinking stage? When your guests arrived, you could tell them all about the beautiful decorations and the delicious menu, but you wouldn't have any food to serve them. This wouldn't be a dinner party; it would be a big tease! Your guests would literally be hungry for more. Get the picture?

To get to Professional Paradise, you must *SHIFT* your actions as well as your mindset. Many actions – especially those that occur in response to POWs – are spontaneous, without much thought as to the consequences. Although these automatic reactions can be helpful – like yanking your hand away from a hot stove – much of the time they do more harm than good. They tend to be impulsive, sometimes irrational and typically all too hasty. Add to that the fact that they're often counterproductive and prevent positive connections with others, and you can see why you want to *SHIFT*.

The trick to finding WOWs at work is to **intentionally choose your actions after *objectively* assessing the circumstances**. Thoughts are the first step, but it takes purposeful, constructive and intentional action to get to WOW.

Now let's put it all together to show how *SHIFT*ing your mindset and your actions can move you from Prison to Paradise. I'll use a recent incident to illustrate: I've been having problems with my phone dropping calls. When I'm on the road and need to be in contact with my clients, if my phone isn't working properly, it's a big POW. So I decided to call the technical support line at my wireless company for help. I'm going to share two different versions of how that call might have transpired. You decide which one seems more like a WOW.

Scenario #1:

As I looked for the toll-free number, I remembered the last few times I called the support line – things hadn't gone well. I was already aggravated because I had a lot to do and this call would probably take 20 minutes that I didn't have.

I called the phone number, a little edge in my attitude already. Of course, I got the ever-annoying automated attendant which told me I needed to listen to the choices because they'd recently changed. Yeah, right! Do they really think people have memorized their choices? I selected technical support, and after a few rings I heard, "All of our agents are currently busy assisting other customers…we appreciate your patience." (Obviously they don't know how impatient I am.)

My jaw was clenched; my pulse sped up. The on-hold music was interfering with the tunes playing in my office. If only I could've delegated this to someone else. Why me? Why did my phone have to have problems? This was such a pain! I was ready to give the tech support person a piece of my mind….

I'll stop right there because I'm assuming you've lived through a similar experience and can guess how the rest of the call went. Now, the other version:

Scenario #2:
As I looked for the toll-free number, I remembered the last few times I called the support line – things hadn't gone well. I decided to be prepared for a long wait, so I grabbed a proposal I'd been working on. I couldn't afford to sit idly with all the work I had to do.

I dialed the phone, and of course, I got the ever-annoying automated attendant, which told me I needed to listen to the choices because they'd recently changed. I laughed as I wondered out loud, "Who keeps changing these choices and why?" I selected technical support and heard, "All of our agents are currently busy assisting other customers…we appreciate your patience." I was ready for this. I lowered the volume on my headset and got busy reviewing the proposal. Focusing on my work, I lost track of the time, and before I knew it a tech support person came on the line. I was calm and ready to talk about the issue and get it resolved.

Once again, I'll stop there. You probably have a good idea how that call ended. Here is my question for you: What stayed the same between the two scenarios and what changed?

What stayed the same?	What changed?
✓ I had a lot to do.	✓ I had a proposal ready to work on.
✓ I got the automated attendant.	✓ I laughed at the automated attendant.
✓ I was put on hold.	✓ I made good use of the wait time.
✓ I spoke with a technical support person.	✓ I was calm and level-headed when I spoke with the support person.

Basically, the event itself – the mechanics of the call – stayed the same. What changed was my mindset and therefore my actions. I put on my imaginary WC^2 ring and decided to manage what I could manage. The big difference in the second version was my non-emotional, objective viewpoint about the experience. I bet you're wondering which of the two scenarios actually happened. If you guessed the second, you're correct. I did start with Fly Away Thinking that led down a negative path. I started to feel aggravated but this time I caught myself, *SHIFT*ed and enjoyed the second experience.

Here's another true-life story of someone who *SHIFT*ed her mindset and her actions to transform a POW to a WOW: Roxanne works in the marketing department of a large health system. Recently, one of her coworkers totally re-created a communication strategy that Roxanne had spent hours working on. At one point in her life, Roxanne would have stormed up to the other employee and loudly confronted her about her actions. But after a while she realized that this approach wasn't getting good results (as you might imagine).

Once she learned to SHIFT, she focused on what she could control. Roxanne assumed positive intent on the part of the coworker. She decided to recognize that her coworker wasn't trying to torture her, nor was she out to get her or "one up" her with the changes. Instead, she figured the coworker was simply trying to make a positive contribution to the organization and was unaware how much her "touch-ups" upset Roxanne. Using the *SHIFT* technique, Roxanne talked with her coworker about the incident, but in a way that enhanced their relationship instead of strained it. Note once again that the situation didn't change – but Roxanne's mindset and actions did. That's the power of WC^2 and *SHIFT!*

Einstein's definition of insanity is often quoted: "Doing the same thing over and over again and expecting different results." If you're as smart as Einstein, you'll choose to *SHIFT* your mindset and *SHIFT* your actions the next time you get hit with a POW.

The ultimate goal, of course, is not only to get to Professional Paradise, but to stay there permanently. That's where the final piece comes in – *SHIFT*ing your habits. Whether you realize it or not, you've developed habitual responses to the POWs you commonly experience. To live the good life at work long term, you have to eliminate those harmful habits and replace them with new, helpful habits that lead to WOWs. In other words, **you must create a habit of consistently *SHIFT*ing your POWs to WOWs.** We'll talk about how to do that in Part III. For now, let's keep *SHIFT*ing!

SHIFT to WOW

The 5 Steps to SHIFT

At last, I'm going to give you your Passport to Professional Paradise – the *SHIFT* technique. First, I will walk you through the five steps necessary to *SHIFT* any POW to a WOW. Then, I'll share three *SHIFT* Strategies that will show you exactly how to put the steps into practice. When you're done, you'll be well on your way to less stress, more energy and remarkable results at work.

What does *SHIFT* stand for?

 Stop and breathe.

 Harness harmful knee-jerk reactions.

 Identify and manage emotions.

 Find new options.

 Take one positive action.

Let's dive in and look at each step individually. Imagine that you've just experienced a POW. Take a minute to vividly remember one of the POWs you wrote down earlier. Now…

Stop and breathe.

This first step is pretty straightforward. Notice that you're feeling stress or anger. Then, actually say, "Stop!" If you're alone in your office or car, you can speak the word. But POWs often hit us at inopportune moments in the midst of a crowd. No worries. Simply say, "Stop!" loudly *inside your head.* When you think or say "Stop," the messages that are firing throughout the brain are literally interrupted, allowing you to replace them with calmer, more rational thoughts.

Then take a deep cleansing breath. You don't have to get in a yoga pose or take a giant breath that draws the attention of everyone around you. But you do want to capture the benefits of deep breathing. I know from my nursing training that deep breathing increases the concentration of oxygen in the blood and releases endorphins which promote relaxation. It also causes your brain to begin making alpha waves, the kind of brain waves that gently calm you down. This is exactly what you need when you've been hit with a POW. Your deep breathing helps you achieve a relaxed body state that permits increased brain functioning and decreased knee-jerk responses.

Some POWs take you by surprise while others are more predictable. Making a deep breath a conscious process slows down your reactions and buys you time – time to collect yourself and decide if you want to continue down the path you are on or change directions. Fortunately, you have everything you need to execute this first step wherever you are – in a cubicle, in a conference room, in a patient room, or in the hall.

*H*arness harmful knee-jerk reactions.

When you go to the doctor for your annual physical, he or she checks your reflexes by tapping a little hammer just below your kneecap. Your leg should jerk forward automatically. (If it doesn't, something's up!) You don't decide to kick your leg up, it's an involuntary reaction by your nervous system. That's where the term "knee-jerk reaction" came from, and now, it commonly means something you do automatically without thinking.

Knee-jerk reactions are our automatic, unthinking responses to POWs. The classic knee-jerk reaction that many people think of is the "fight or flight" response. Physiologically, humans are wired to either "put up their dukes" or "run for the hills" when challenged. In the days of the cavemen, this automatic reflex was very helpful when one was confronted by a hungry saber tooth tiger or a charging woolly mammoth. This knee-jerk reaction literally saved lives!

However, in today's healthcare environment, fight or flight can get us into trouble. More objective thinking and different actions are usually far more effective. Fight or flight in response to a POW can range from storming out of the room to becoming a "shrinking violet." Other common knee-jerk reactions include taking things personally, sarcasm, raising your voice, complaining, sulking, talking fast, name calling, blaming others and talking about people behind their back.

If you are not *consciously* evaluating your thoughts in response to a POW, then you are letting knee-jerk reactions take charge. Negative knee-jerk reactions perpetuate, amplify and exaggerate the effects of a POW. Harnessing them keeps you from making a fool of yourself and gives you the chance to make conscious decisions and choices.

Learn to identify your knee-jerk reactions and determine if they are harmful or helpful. One of my big pet peeves is waiting in lines. I know that's a POW for me. When I see a line, I take a deep breath, unclench my hands (my knee-jerk reaction) and then look around to see how I can entertain myself while I wait. Knowing that I'm likely to get impatient in lines helps me keep my knee-jerk reactions in check.

In the heat of a POW, you may not feel like you can harness your knee-jerk reactions. But I'm here to tell you that, with practice, you will be able to. So, how do I do it? It's pretty simple. At the first sign of a negative knee-jerk reaction, take a deep breath in and let it out slowly. Then ask yourself, **"Is (my reaction) going to improve the situation? Who will be most negatively affected by my reaction?"** Usually the answers are "no" and "me." You are the one whose blood pressure is escalating, whose pulse is racing and who's starting to sweat. Your knee-jerk reactions might be bothersome to others, but they are always more detrimental to you, and that's reason enough to stop!

Using the *SHIFT* steps creates *positive* knee-jerk reactions rather than harmful ones. In the long run, negative responses create more stress, anxiety and trouble in your life. Everyone benefits when you harness your negative knee-jerk reactions, but you benefit the most.

*I*dentify and manage emotions.

According to Wikipedia.com, "emotion, in its most general definition, is a complex psychophysical process that arises spontaneously, rather than through conscious effort." The definition goes on to say that emotion "evokes either a positive or negative psychological response and physical expressions, often involuntary, related to feelings, perceptions or beliefs…in reality or in the imagination." Sounds kind of complex and scientific, doesn't it? Put more simply, **our emotional response to a POW causes our knee-jerk reaction.** But in terms of *SHIFT*ing the pattern, we must first stop the knee-jerk reaction. Once we've harnessed that, then we're in a position to identify and manage the emotions behind it.

The first part of "I" is to identify the negative emotions you're experiencing. That means you have to make a conscious effort to notice where in your body you feel these emotions and then name them. I feel anxiety as a queasy stomach; someone else might feel it as a headache. Each of us experiences emotions differently, so the key is to know yourself.

The second part of this step is to manage the negative emotions. Once you know which emotions you're dealing with, you can choose to break the pattern. Have you ever been in an argument with someone where voices were raised and emotions were running high – and then the phone rang? One of you stopped to answer the phone, and greeted the caller with a sunny "hello." It's like a switch was flipped. The person who answered the phone was still angry but was able to temporarily put his or her emotions on hold.

That's what I mean by short-term management of negative emotions. This step is about learning how to flip the switch (in a helpful way) on your emotions to put you on the road from POW to WOW. I'm not recommending that you turn them off or shove them under the rug. I'm suggesting that you *manage* them so that you can proceed – consciously – in a positive direction. Talk to yourself in a calm rational manner such as, "I'm not going to get worked up over this" or "I don't know what's going on, so I'm going to assume it will end positively."

Another great way to flip the switch is to gain some perspective. What difference, *truly*, does it (the POW) make? And more importantly, what good will it do you to continue with the negative emotions? Let's say you receive a report from a colleague that contains a few errors. Instead of taking it personally or feeling frustrated and upset, put the situation in the proper perspective. "Okay, so there are a couple of mistakes. I know this person worked hard on this. It will take me ten minutes max to correct them. This is no big deal."

If you find that your emotions are troubling or running on a loop that is not helpful, now is the time to ask for help. Access the services of your Employee Assistance Program (EAP) or find an outside therapist to help. This is especially true when dealing with past trauma. When the effects of the trauma are getting in the way of you living your life, it's time for professional help.

In the course of a day at work, I'm not suggesting that you do an in-depth analysis of your deep-seated emotions and fears. I'm simply pointing out that it's a good idea to identify and manage your emotions in the heat of the moment because the person they hurt the most is *you*.

Find new options.

This step puts you in a proactive position instead of a reactive one. When you take a few minutes to consider new options, you move closer to WOW and closer to Professional Paradise. The absence of the negative knee-jerk reaction can be filled with the excitement of fresh ideas. This is a great time to stop and answer the question, "What Can We Control?" Having choices provides a feeling of being in control, which most people appreciate. Being creative and thinking of a variety of options opens up possibilities that may have gone unnoticed in the past.

When considering new options (by "new" I mean an approach that's different from the one you might typically use), of course you want to think about specific action steps that will get you to WOW. I invoke the "Rule of Three" to find new options:

1. *What has worked in the past?* Think about another time when you were hit with this particular POW and remember what worked. For example, when a family member complains, think back to someone with a similar problem whom you were able to make happy, and try that option. Remember how your calm response created the space for a helpful resolution and made your day go a lot easier.

2. *What would someone you admire do?* Think of someone you know personally or respect from a distance and figure out what s/he would do in a similar situation. I'm not crazy about getting involved in confrontational situations. Someone I used to work with was assertive in such a positive way. When I'm getting ready to have a tough conversation, I think, "What would Denise do?" This is a tool for moving forward.

3. *What would someone who's objective do?* This third tactic builds on the first two. What if you were observing this situation from an outsider's perspective? All too often we take things personally when they aren't personal at all. Put yourself in the shoes of an onlooker and see what options appear. From a distance, things often seem funny, light hearted or even ridiculous (if you engage your sense of humor).

Remember, there is *always* more than one way to complete a task or solve a problem. Try the Rule of Three to find new options, and you'll be well on your way to Professional Paradise.

*T*ake one positive action.

Once you've discovered new possibilities, the final step is to choose at least one that feels right for the situation and **take action!** This is the action part of *SHIFT*. It takes what was merely positive thinking and moves it toward reality. Remember, thoughts alone rarely achieve anything. You must act if you want a better outcome.

MINDSET ⟹ ACTIONS ⟹ OUTCOMES

You can certainly choose to implement more than one option, but one is the minimum needed to create a true *SHIFT*. Which option will produce the best results? Which one will get you one step closer to less stress, more energy and remarkable results? Which one will create the biggest WOW? Once you decide…take action!

That's it! Those are the five steps to *SHIFT* any POW to a WOW. Using this technique, you can transform virtually any negative or unpleasant situation into one that's not only tolerable, but also productive and beneficial. Here's a real-life example that illustrates all five *SHIFT* steps and will put the puzzle together for you.

It had been a long day. I was on the tarmac in a crowded airplane in Charlotte, NC, and we were next in line for takeoff. Many flights to destinations south of there had been cancelled or delayed due to bad weather, but it seemed like we would be okay. Only one hour until I'd be back in Florida driving home

And then the pilot came on the overhead speaker and said, "I was afraid it was too good to be true. We're being asked to stay here and wait while air traffic in the West Palm Beach area clears out. We're going to park the plane out here and shut off one of the engines to save fuel. I'll update you as soon as I know anything more." *POW!*

I needed to *SHIFT* from POW to WOW. Here's exactly what I did on that plane:

Stop and breathe. I firmly thought, "Stop!" and then reminded myself to breathe. I leaned back in my seat, closed my eyes, unclenched my fists and took several deep breaths. I imagined myself as a wet noodle and reached a state of relaxation in my body.

This slowed down my heart rate and respiration. It eased my muscle tension and helped me think more clearly. It helped me move from my sympathetic nervous system being dominant to the parasympathetic nervous system. This allowed a much calmer response.

Harness harmful knee-jerk reactions. My initial reaction was to start complaining to the people sitting around me. (Funny – that also seemed to be the reaction of just about everyone else on board.) I also had a strong desire to jump up, run screaming toward the nearest exit and get off the plane! However, I recognized that these knee-jerk reactions were neither practical nor helpful. I harnessed them before I caused myself more stress.

Identify and manage emotions. I took note of my sweaty palms and queasy stomach. I acknowledged that I was feeling frustration, aggravation and, yes, some anxiety about the possibility of not getting home. Fortunately, I quickly realized that dwelling on these feelings was not going to clear out the skies above Florida or get our plane off the tarmac any faster. I chose to put things in perspective – in the scheme of my life, or even my week, was this really a big deal, even if I had to spend one night sleeping in a hotel near the airport? No, it wasn't.

Find new options. I tried to think of a few constructive or relaxing things I could do while we sat and waited. But I didn't want to read the magazine in the seat pocket, and I wasn't sleepy. What else was there to do? What part of this could I control (WC^2)? I decided to use the Rule of Three and thought of my friend Ed, a world-class business traveler. I wondered, "What would Ed do?" I figured he might catch up on some work, listen to some music (he has a great iPod collection), make a few phone calls or read.

*T*ake one positive action. In this case, I decided that the music would be a great option – it's a wonderful stress reducer for me. My music selection is upbeat and always puts me in a good mood. So out came the my phone. I also decided to read a book which was a very pleasurable way to pass the time. I had successfully *SHIFT*ed a POW to a WOW.

Luckily, our delay was only about 20 minutes. However, we ended up circling over West Palm Beach for a while and then sitting on the tarmac there for close to an hour before we could get to our gate. But I had my *SHIFT* steps in place by then. What could have felt like Prison instead turned into a little slice of Paradise.

You might be wondering when to use *SHIFT*. I try to use it all the time – whenever something starts to create stress in my life – whether I've caused the problem or someone else has. Unfortunately, when I'm tired and cranky, rushing or upset, I don't always remember. I end up paying for that when I feel angry, anxious or worried. The great news is that you can use *SHIFT* for coping with big, highly stressful events like a pandemic and everything that comes along with it. And you can also use it for everyday nuisances such as a difficult person, having to reschedule a meeting or an offhand comment from a colleague.

After I developed the *SHIFT* technique and began using it, I quickly realized that it's effective in all different types of work (and personal) situations. However, I also observed some common themes. The *SHIFT* technique tends to fall into three main categories of use at work:

✦ **Viewpoint*SHIFT*** – Producing better outcomes in tough situations

✦ **Connection*SHIFT*** – Creating positive relationships with coworkers and others

✦ **Solution*SHIFT*** – Finding the best solutions to your most challenging problems

Let's learn more about each of these and practice using them to *SHIFT* your POWs to WOWs.

Viewpoint*SHIFT*

Producing better outcomes in tough situations

Do you get defensive or take things personally? **POW!**

Ever assume something without having all the facts and then realize you made a mistake? **POW!**

Do you overreact to minor issues that just don't matter in the scheme of things? **POW!**

If you answered "Yes" to any of these questions, then a Viewpoint*SHIFT* is just what you need to turn those POWs into WOWs.

Are you familiar with the hit song "I Can See Clearly Now" that was written and recorded by Johnny Nash in the 1970s? Here are just a few lines of the lyrics:

> *I can see clearly now the rain is gone*
> *I can see all obstacles in my way.*
> *Gone are the dark clouds that had me blind.*
> *It's gonna be a bright (bright), bright (bright) sunshiny day.*

I like that song because it reminds me of a Viewpoint*SHIFT*. You see, a Viewpoint*SHIFT* clears away misconceptions you may have about certain situations and allows you to see events and people more objectively. It shines light on the situation, so to speak. As a result, you become more adaptable and open minded – you see things more clearly. A Viewpoint*SHIFT* will help you systematically change your mindset and your actions in order to reduce your stress and create more energy in any difficult situation.

According to *The American Heritage Dictionary*, viewpoint means "a [mental] position from which something is observed or considered." Your viewpoint is the lens through which you see the world. It influences every experience you have and every action you take. One person sees the glass as half empty; another sees it as half full.

Have you noticed that when you complain or are unhappy at work, it often has to do with your internal thoughts (specifically your viewpoint or mindset) about the situation and not necessarily the event itself? Suppose your manager sends you an email asking you to contact her later in the day. All of a sudden, you assume the worst and become consumed with worry. Instead of focusing on other work, you create all sorts of negative scenarios in your mind, none of which have a happy ending. It's not the email that creates the drama; it's your viewpoint about the email that causes all the trouble. Your manager might want to give you good news – perhaps she received a compliment about you. Sometimes a pessimistic viewpoint keeps us trapped in Professional Prison or on Parole because we create obstacles in our minds that don't exist in reality.

How often do people in the workplace have different viewpoints? *All* the time. Usually that's a good thing. Different viewpoints unleash fresh, creative solutions and can produce impressive results. But differing viewpoints can also become roadblocks to remarkable results and create great strife and stress in the work environment. Think about a typical office or patient care unit on a typical day with a typical team. With 10 or 15 people on the team, there are countless opportunities for differing viewpoints about many situations. Add in other departments, leaders, patients and suppliers, and you have literally hundreds of chances for conflict and clashes to erupt. I believe that people often become defensive when someone disagrees with their viewpoint because they assume they are being personally attacked. So, they tend to fight back instead of listening to the other person's concerns and considering that another perspective might be valid.

A Viewpoint*SHIFT* is crucial whenever you need **perspective**... when you:

+ Feel defensive or take things personally;

+ Make a mountain out of a molehill and get worked up over a situation that doesn't matter when you look at the big picture;

+ Don't like how someone is doing something and you can't seem to let it go;

+ Worry about things that haven't even happened yet;

+ Overstep your bounds and get involved in someone else's business;

+ Make assumptions without having all the information.

Each of these signs is a clue that your mindset is more than likely contributing to your POWs. Has your outlook ever gotten in the way of creating positive connections with coworkers or producing remarkable results? Take a few minutes right now to think about a time when your viewpoint alone was the cause of your problem.

The great news is that with a Viewpoint*SHIFT*, you can change your perspective and create more WOWs. According to Zen Buddhists, when you have a Beginner's Mind you see many possibilities, you lack preconceptions and your outlook is broad and deep. On the other hand, those with an Expert's Mind often have limiting views which shrink their viewpoint. Isn't that interesting? You would think you'd want an Expert's Mind, when in reality the Beginner's Mind is more beneficial. A Viewpoint*SHIFT* helps you foster a Beginner's Mind.

Now let's take a look at a Viewpoint*SHIFT* in a real work-related situation. Rosalie is a manager in the Human Resources (HR) department of a mid-sized hospital. She oversees benefits administration and her "customers" are the employees of the organization. Rosalie and her staff recently orchestrated a conversion to a new software system that automated many of the functions they used to do by hand. As a result, employees can now go online 24-7 for benefits information instead of calling the HR department during business hours.

Rosalie was sitting at her desk working when an employee just walked into her office. She'd seen him around, but didn't know his name. He walked right up to her desk and, before she could get a word out, said "I'm Maurice from the Environmental Services. I'm here to tell you that I don't appreciate what you've done. It's ridiculous that we have to go online to check benefits. Not everyone sits in front of a computer all day, you know. If you don't do something to fix this right now, I'm going to go to my boss and complain." *POW!*

Rosalie immediately became defensive. She stood up behind her desk. "I beg your pardon?" she retorted. "You can't just barge in here and tell me how to do my job!" She was seething inside. "Who does he think he is?" she thought. Who was this guy to question her judgment? He had no idea how carefully she and her staff had worked to make sure the new system was easy to use. What nerve!

Now, I'll walk you through the five steps of a Viewpoint*SHIFT* that Rosalie used to change her POW to a WOW.

 ## *S*top and breathe.

Rosalie was definitely worked up. But she prides herself on maintaining her professionalism. She feels that as an HR leader it's her job to model positive behavior. She decided she'd better get back in control. "I've got to stop and calm down," she thought. She invited Maurice to sit down and then took a deep breath as she sat back down.

 ## *H*arness harmful knee-jerk reactions.

Typical knee-jerk reactions when you need a Viewpoint*SHIFT* include lashing out at others, automatically assuming you know what's going on, raising your voice, presuming the worst-case scenario, not giving others a chance to express their opinions, and thinking others are out to get you.

Rosalie's knee-jerk reaction was to defend herself from the perceived attack. Her automatic fight response kicked in, and she stood up and lashed out at Maurice. Fortunately, she caught herself and thought, "This isn't appropriate. Plus, getting mad isn't going to help anything." She quickly apologized to Maurice and suggested they start over.

Identify and manage emotions.

Common emotions when your viewpoint is out of whack include defensiveness, resentment, exasperation, resistance to change, concern and cynicism. Rosalie initially felt attacked. She resented Maurice for questioning her decision-making process, and she was offended by his remarks and his threat to go to his boss. This whole transition hadn't even been her idea – it was forced on her to begin with! She recognized all the unproductive feelings that were welling up. She stopped the Fly Away Thinking and made a conscious effort to engage in Funnel Thinking.

 ### Find new options.

Rosalie reminded herself that her goal was to serve the employees and to adequately address their concerns. She quickly ran through some options in her mind that would move both her and Maurice to WOW. The ideas Rosalie considered are the same options you can use for a Viewpoint*SHIFT*:

✦ Give yourself time and space to think things through before taking any action.

✦ Consciously choose to write a happy ending to the "story."

✦ Collect more data and get all the information before making assumptions, judgments or decisions.

✦ Quit taking it personally (QTIP).

✦ Let go of old grudges and hurt feelings.

✦ Assume others are acting with positive intent.

✦ Decide to be more open minded and genuinely listen to others' ideas and perspectives.

✦ Use the Rule of Three (what worked in the past, what would someone you admire do, what would someone who's objective do).

*T*ake one positive action.

Rosalie realized she was taking Maurice's comments personally when they weren't personal at all. She decided it would be more productive to look at things from his viewpoint, so she began asking him questions in an effort to learn more. She wanted to be sure she clearly understood his concerns. As they talked, she began to appreciate that he was frustrated despite all of her hard work. After all, it wasn't that surprising that someone with limited computer access would be upset that he could no longer get his information personally. This new program wasn't going to please everyone – her team had discussed that very issue at the beginning of the project.

Do you agree with the options Rosalie chose? What would you have done? After talking with Maurice – and later, with other members of his department – Rosalie and her team encouraged employees who didn't have computer access at work to contact the HR department for their benefits information and questions. Since the vast majority of employees had computers, the new system greatly reduced her team's workload. They were more than happy to continue to personally serve those employees who called in. Now that's a **WOW** – for everyone!

Some of you may be thinking, "Why did Rosalie have to change her viewpoint? Why didn't Maurice change his?" Ideally, everyone involved in a situation should engage in a Viewpoint*SHIFT* in order to create the best outcome. But in reality, the only viewpoint you can change is your own. You can be stubborn and say, "If others won't change their viewpoint, then I'm not going to change mine," or you can step up and own your half of the interaction and get much better results.

That is exactly what is so fantastic about a Viewpoint*SHIFT* – **you**

can change the whole tenor of a situation by simply changing your viewpoint. Your ability to be flexible and open-minded provides endless possibilities for resolving conflicts to your satisfaction and living the good life at work.

What will it be: a victim viewpoint or a Viewpoint *SHIFT*? The choice is yours!

Letting go of your own biases and judgments… **WOW!**

Walking in someone else's shoes… **WOW!**

Seeing things for what they are – no big deal… **WOW!**

ViewpointSHIFT Exercise

This is your chance to apply what you've learned and a valuable step in creating a *SHIFT* habit. You may be thinking, "I don't want to do this exercise," but I assure you that practicing and personalizing the steps are crucial to making them work for you! (To download a free 8.5" x 11" version of this exercise, go to www.ProfessionalParadise.com.)

1. Under "POW," give a brief description of a recent situation where you felt defensive or believed you were the victim, blamed, wronged, etc., including your viewpoint of the situation.

2. Under "S," write the word STOP. (This will help you remember to say "Stop!" and breathe the next time you're hit with a POW.)

3. Under "H," list the harmful knee-jerk reactions you had in response to the POW you described in Step 1.

4. Under "I," list the emotions you experienced.

5. Under "F," list as many ideas as you can think of that are new options for the scenario you described.

6. Under "T," write down at least one action you will take if you are faced with this POW again.

7. Under "WOW," list the positive outcomes that would result from this Viewpoint*SHIFT*.

POW	Stop and breathe	Harness knee-jerk reactions	Identify & manage emotions	Find new options	Take one positive action	WOW

Connection*SHIFT*

~~~~~~~~~~~~~~~~~~~~~~~~

Creating positive relationships with coworkers and patients/customers

Coworkers getting on your nerves? **POW!**

Got cranky family members you'd like to avoid? **POW!**

Don't see eye to eye with your boss or direct report? **POW!**

In my own research with more than one thousand people, when asked what makes them happy at work, a full 42 percent cited positive interactions with other people as the most important factor in workplace satisfaction. These interactions included creating connections with coworkers and customers, receiving appreciation from others, working effectively on teams and demonstrating care and concern for others. In addition, numerous studies have shown that the quality of an individual's relationship with his or her immediate leader is the most significant factor in turnover and retention. In other words, your connection (or lack thereof) with your boss is a significant factor in the quality of your work experience.

A Connection*SHIFT* is a tool for turning relationship POWs into WOWs. It creates a positive association between people. The intentional act of establishing a connection with someone in order to better understand their position is a living example of the words of St. Francis of Assisi (made popular in modern times by Stephen Covey): "Grant that I may not so much seek to be understood as to understand."

At the most basic level, a connection occurs when two or more things are joined together. Connections are at the heart of healthcare because little gets done without some degree of interaction or joining together with others. Think about it: Organizations must connect with their patients, the community , their suppliers, the board and their shareholders. Departments must connect with one another in order to deliver outstanding patient care. **Without connections, there is no healthcare**. Read that again and let the full impact of its truth sink in.

Ultimately, all of these interactions come down to individuals – people like you and me – connecting with each other on a personal basis. Who do you have to connect with in order to get your job done – coworkers, teammates, leaders, colleagues in other departments, patients, vendors? Which connections are positive and which ones *aren't but should be*? Remember, you don't have to be fast friends with everyone. You just need to work with them when the need arises.

Unfortunately, workplace connections are a primary source of POWs for most people. Because there are so many factors that affect relationships, there are lots of things that can go wrong. Let's look at some common causes of relationship POWs.

Interpersonal disconnects are often the result of conflicting work beliefs. Think back to the belief chapter and all the things that go into the belief system that drives our thoughts and actions on the job. It's easy to see how connections can be hindered or damaged when our work beliefs conflict with others' beliefs.

Bad first impressions make for a lot of relationship POWs. Consciously or unconsciously, we all form first impressions that directly influence our desire and willingness to connect with others. Customer service experts tell us that you have only six seconds to make a great first impression. That's fast! So in the first few seconds you meet someone, talk to them on the phone or read an email from them, you are deciding how you will connect with them – and they with you! Allowing a negative first impression to hinder a connection is definitely a knee-jerk reaction – one that can be hard to overcome.

A final reason for weak connections is the way we communicate these days. In an electronic world, it's far too easy for people to avoid face-to-face interactions. As a result, connections between people become muddled (if they exist at all). Even though they work in the same building or on the same floor, people use texting or email to address tough issues, avoid confrontation and cover their backside. This use of technology almost always backfires because there's simply too much room for misinterpretation.

Whew! It's no wonder people aren't connecting!

Thank goodness you have the Connection*SHIFT* strategy in your toolbox. Use it anytime you want to create a strong link with others:

♦ Meeting with a new patient and his or her family;

♦ Completing inter-departmental projects;

♦ Dealing with unhappy customers;

♦ Working with your boss or direct reports;

♦ Networking with colleagues outside the organization;

♦ Collaborating on a team project.

A Connection*SHIFT* will help you get along better with others. But I'm not suggesting that you roll over and take it when conflicts arise or people upset you. In fact, I'm suggesting the opposite. A Connection*SHIFT* allows you to "speak your truth" in a way that others are able to hear. It's one thing to tell a coworker in a respectful manner that you're disappointed about something he did; it's quite another to blame, complain and accuse him. See the difference? You speak your truth in both instances, but using *SHIFT* creates a relationship WOW instead of a relationship POW. A Connection*SHIFT* also helps you remain calm and objective so you can hear other people's "truths" behind the noise of their defensiveness, knee-jerk reactions and negative emotions.

There are many reasons to make the effort to create positive connections with everyone you interact with at work. Connection WOWs lead to a less stressful, more peaceful workplace. Sounds good, doesn't it? But I want to make certain you understand that this is much more than "feel good" stuff (although I'm not sure why feeling good isn't a big enough benefit for us all!).

There are many tangible benefits to *SHIFT*ing relationship POWs to WOWs. As an individual, you're *guaranteed* to get your work done more easily, more quickly and with better results. Let me say that again. You are guaranteed to get your work done more easily, more quickly and with better results. Compare a day spent butting heads to one with positive connections, and you'll know exactly what I mean. For the organization, connection WOWs translate to less overtime, increased safety, quality, efficiency and productivity. Oh yeah, and one more: happier patients (which leads to positive word of mouth in the community)!

Let's see how a Connection*SHIFT* works in the real world. The story takes place in a small community hospital. Our cast of characters includes Kimi, a 28-year-old registered nurse in charge of her unit, and Michelle, a 48-year-old veteran pharmacist. Kimi is exasperated by pharmacy orders that are consistently late. She's had several phone conversations with Michelle and feels that Michelle isn't on board with the new technology the hospital purchased. Now another medication order is missing, and Kimi is certain Michelle has purposely delayed it just to spite her.

Kimi needs a Connection*SHIFT* in the worst way!

 Stop and breathe.

When Kimi got the news about the missing medication from a fellow nurse, she started to lose her temper. "Stop!" she said to herself and took a deep breath to calm her nerves.

 Harness harmful knee-jerk reactions.

Typical knee-jerk reactions for connection snafus include being critical or defensive, gossiping, making inappropriate comments, exhibiting negative body language or voice tone, blaming, being confrontational, walking away, mentally shutting down or not accepting responsibility. Poor patient/family member connections can cause employees to complain, pass the person off to others, have a negative attitude, or do sloppy work.

Kimi's immediate reaction was to call the nursing manager to complain about the pharmacy problems. She also would've loved to have stormed down to the pharmacy and had a blunt conversation with Michelle. Instead, she harnessed her reactions and went to the break room to cool off.

Identify and manage emotions.

Connection POWs might cause you to feel isolated, irritated, annoyed, disliked, unkind, threatened, picked on or singled out. Since connections always involve two or more people, remember to also consider the possible negative emotions of the others involved.

Kimi acknowledged her frustration. This was stressful. Late medications created lots of problems with physicians, for her unit and for her patients. She knew she had to connect with Michelle to resolve this issue once and for all.

 ## Find new options.

Here are several options Kimi – and you – can use to make a Connection*SHIFT*:

- ✦ Practice *Swan Seeking*™ – find at least one good thing about the other person.

- ✦ Ask others questions to learn more about what's happening with them (seek first to understand) and carefully listen to what they say.

- ✦ Rehearse your lines before any kind of conversation to make sure they are positive.

- ✦ Envision a strong connection in advance of a meeting or interaction.

- ✦ State that you want to create a positive connection with the other people involved.

- ✦ Apologize for any hard feelings that arose as a result of a misunderstanding.

- ✦ Use the Rule of Three (what worked in the past, what would someone you admire do, what would someone who's objective do).

Do you remember the story "The Ugly Duckling" by Hans Christian Andersen? The ugly duckling hatched among a group of ducks who did not take kindly to his odd looks. So he left and went looking for a place where he fit in. Eventually, he found other animals who accepted him for what he was – a swan. He'd been a swan all along, but none of the other animals had seen his potential. All too often we only see the ugly ducklings in others, when in fact they are beautiful swans. And the way we see others has a direct impact on our relationships. Which do you look for in others – the ugly duckling or the swan? They are one and the same. The only thing that changes is your mindset.

Make a choice to look for the good in people – to do some "Swan Seeking." When a negative trait pops into your mind, work to create a positive connection instead. There is good in everyone; you just have to find it. If you did nothing other than Swan Seeking, you'd turn many of your relationship POWs into WOWs, and you'd be much closer to living the good life at work.

Kimi realized it wasn't reasonable for her to assume Michelle had done this on purpose. Although Michelle was aloof and seemed a bit smug, Kimi had to admit she was the consummate professional (Swan Seeking). Michelle would never intentionally hold up a medication. Perhaps she needed to visit the pharmacy and talk with Michelle to find out more information.

 Take one positive action.

Kimi calmly headed to the pharmacy. When she arrived she said to Michelle, "Do you have a minute to talk about the pharmacy orders on my unit? I know we've had some problems, and this will give us a chance to iron out some things that might be getting in the way." Kimi asked some questions and learned about some challenges the pharmacy had been having with the new software. In the end, they both realized they experienced similar challenges at work, and they felt better about their relationship.

I bet I know what you're thinking: "But you haven't met my boss or my coworkers. They are impossible to get along with!" The Connection*SHIFT* strategy works with all kinds of people, even the most challenging ones. You might just have to be a little more patient and a little more assertive with a really tough connection. What will it be – a connection shambles or a Connection*SHIFT*? The choice is yours...starting today.

*Listening without interrupting...**WOW!***

*Connecting with your boss more effectively
so that she accepts and values your input...**WOW!***

*Taking the time to learn more about a difficult person's interests
and hobbies, and really enjoying yourself...**WOW!***

Connection*SHIFT* Exercise

This is your chance to apply what you've learned and a valuable step in creating a *SHIFT* habit. You may be thinking, "I don't want to do this exercise," but I assure you that practicing and personalizing the steps are crucial to making them work for you! (To download a free 8.5" x 11" version of this exercise, go to www.ProfessionalParadise.com.)

1. Under "POW" give a brief description of a recent meeting or conversation you had with a coworker or patient that created a negative connection, including why you were having a tough time connecting positively.
2. Under "S" write the word STOP. (This will help you remember to say "Stop!" and breathe the next time you're hit with a POW.)
3. Under "H" list the harmful knee-jerk reactions you had in response to the POW you described in Step 1.
4. Under "I" list the emotions you experienced.
5. Under "F" list as many ideas as you can think of that are new options for the scenario you described.
6. Under "T" write down at least one action you will take if you are faced with this POW again.
7. Under "WOW" list the positive outcomes that would result from this Connection*SHIFT*.

POW	*S*top and breathe	*H*arness knee-jerk reactions	*I*dentify & manage emotions	*F*ind new options	*T*ake one positive action	WOW

Solution*SHIFT*

~~~~~~~~~~~~~~~~~

Finding the best solutions to your most challenging problems

Ever disagree with someone about the best way to complete a task or project? **POW!**

Do you get frustrated or stuck when you can't solve a problem on the first try? **POW!**

Tired of being right but not happy? **POW!**

Most people spend a great deal of their time at work solving problems. Stop and think for a minute about your typical day. Isn't problem solving in some form or fashion much of what you do? You might be solving problems for a patient, your boss, direct report, another department or another team member. Or perhaps you deal with technology snafus, time-management challenges or leadership problems.

In my experience, problem solving is also one of the most difficult (yet ultimately satisfying) tasks we face at work. Why? Because very few problems involve black-and-white issues, and there isn't one proven method for solving every challenge or dilemma that arises. Problem solving is also challenging, I believe, because humans have a powerful need to be right. I've studied people in solution-seeking mode for years, and I've observed this time and time again. Do *you* have a strong need to be right? (Be honest!) If so, why?

A Solution*SHIFT* is a potent problem-solving strategy. I'm sure you've heard the saying, "There are three sides to every story: your version, the other person's version and the truth." Likewise, there are three solutions to every problem: your solution, the other person's solution and the *best* solution. A Solution*SHIFT* guides you in objectively evaluating many possible answers – from both parties' perspectives. It allows you to let someone else be right without losing face and offers an opportunity to achieve the **best solution for the situation**. (By the way, "best for the situation" doesn't necessarily equate to a win/win solution.) Isn't that what you really want, after all?

A Solution*SHIFT* does not provide a win-at-all-costs or a give-in solution. Instead, it works within the framework of your objectives and helps you develop several solutions to find the most appropriate one for the given circumstances. It is especially powerful because it enables you to give up your emotional attachment to *your* solution so you can choose a more productive one. Who knows…you might learn to comfortably say, "I didn't think of that" or "I can learn something in this situation" or even the dreaded "I was wrong."

Please note that in situations which involve safety or quality, the solution may be dictated by policies, procedures or laws. In these circumstances, educating the other person about the evidence to support this decision can be very helpful. Knowing the "why" behind a rule often satisfies the upset party.

A Solution*SHIFT* comes in handy with all kinds of problems, conflicts and disagreements. Here are just a few examples of POWs that can be resolved with a Solution*SHIFT*:

✦ You and a coworker must resolve a quality issue.

✦ A family member wants you to alter visiting rules.

✦ Your supervisor gives you a new assignment that you think is unfair.

✦ You and a fellow team member "butt heads" about the best way to complete a task.

✦ Your patient is frustrated with a service issue that you have no control over.

Using a Solution*SHIFT* to transform problem POWs into solution WOWs will give you an ideal resolution plus contentment. And do you want to be right or be happy? Happy is so much more satisfying in the long run.

Let's see how a Solution*SHIFT* can take two professionals from POW to WOW. Anthony works in the IT department at a large academic medical center. He goes onsite to various departments resolving technology-related issues. Estelle is the key contact at one of the largest departments he supports. She can be difficult at times, expecting Anthony to drop everything to come to her office whenever she calls. The support team always works to fix problems right away, but Estelle wants to be bumped to the front of the queue. One day while working with another internal client, Anthony received a frantic voicemail from Estelle: "One of our busiest printers is down, and you need to get over here ASAP! If you can't get it fixed within the next few hours, I'm going to escalate this request to the director!" **POW!**

Anthony was sick and tired of Estelle throwing her weight around, and he wasn't in the mood to deal with her. He was fairly certain based on her description of the problem that fixing the printer would require getting a new part, which would take at least a day or two. His patience was hanging by a thread.

I'm going to use Anthony and Estelle's story to illustrate the steps of a Solution *SHIFT*:

 ## Stop and breathe.

Anthony realized that he was gunning for a fight and that he and Estelle were potentially headed for trouble. "Stop," he said. "I've got to take a minute and think this through." He stepped outside and took a deep breath. He took a few more breaths until he felt his muscles relax. He wanted to make sure his body was not in "fight or flight" mode.

 ## Harness harmful knee-jerk reactions.

Typical knee-jerk reactions to problems and challenges include fighting for your solution, summarily rejecting others' solutions, trying to convince the other person that you're right and he/she is wrong, talking faster, giving up, giving in, and using negative body language such as folded or flailing arms. Watch people the next time you see a disagreement at work and notice the knee-jerk reactions that play out.

Knee-jerk reactions to internal or external customer-related problems tend to be more subtle and passive-aggressive since most people know better than to overtly aggravate their customers. In the case of a stalemate with a coworker, you might talk to yourself, use sarcasm, say something acceptable but with closed body language, or deliberately not return phone calls or emails.

Anthony's natural response was to dig in to his position. He was, after all, "right" based on the "first come, first served" model they used. He hadn't even picked up the phone to call Estelle yet, but he could feel his blood pressure rising again. "I'd better get a handle on myself or I could get myself in trouble," he thought.

*I*dentify and manage emotions.

Without a doubt, unresolved problems will stress you out and sap your energy. You could also feel disappointed, aggravated or intimidated. Or you might feel the need to "win" at all costs, be worried about what the other person thinks of you, or get agitated because you're not getting your way. You can better manage your emotions by making a concerted effort to focus on the *facts* of the problem at hand, not your *feelings* about the problem at hand.

Another critical element in a Solution*SHIFT* is to think about *the other person's* negative emotions because they also play a key role in the problem-solving process. Notice what is going on with the other person. What do you think he or she might be feeling? Focusing on the other party is a great catalyst for being more objective.

When Anthony finally stopped thinking about how he was going to convince Estelle he was right and she was wrong, he was able to acknowledge his frustration. And once he got that out of the way, he could see the problem more clearly. He also knew from past experiences that Estelle could be hot-tempered and stubborn. Thinking through how she might be feeling and how she might react allowed him to better plan his approach with her.

 *F*ind new options.

A multitude of alternative options exist for a Solution*SHIFT*. Some possibilities include:

+ Objectively describe the facts of the situation.
+ Acknowledge that there are many ways to "skin a cat" and accept that your solution might not be the best.
+ Identify at least one solution that hasn't been considered and request that the other person do the same.

✦ Empathize with the other person and share the options that you know of.

✦ Let go of your ego and decide to be happy, not necessarily right.

✦ Once you've chosen the best solution for the situation, release your emotional attachment to your original ideas and say "thank you" to the other person.

✦ Actively listen with an open mind to the other person and his/her solution. Ask questions if necessary to clarify and improve your understanding of the idea.

✦ Agree to reach a consensus solution and commit to supporting it.

✦ Ask others to share their objections to your solution and respectfully consider ways to resolve their concerns.

✦ Agree to compromise.

✦ Use the Rule of Three (what worked in the past, what would someone you admire do, what would someone who's objective do).

Sometimes in a Solution*SHIFT* you simply have to liberate yourself from your ego, let go and move forward with someone else's solution. Ahhhh – that feels good. Then there are circumstances in which everyone agrees to listen objectively and come to a consensus. Sometimes you compromise – each person gives a little in the hope of finding some common ground. And there are those times when you passionately believe in the merits of your solution. That's when you respectfully listen to others' concerns about your idea and develop creative ways to resolve them.

When seeking a Solution*SHIFT*, steer away from absolutes such as, "We go with all of my plan or nothing" or "There's nothing in your suggestion that is workable." Often when we're in the midst of a disagreement, it's helpful to simply state the facts: "It's reasonable that we would have different priorities on this."

In our example, Anthony's goal was to resolve Estelle's immediate problem and still get the rest of his work done for his other departments. After all, Estelle's department's work was important and his job was to be helpful, so he definitely wanted to avoid an argument. He decided to brainstorm possible ideas for an interim solution until the printer part could arrive.

 *T*ake one positive action.

Anthony called Estelle and said, "Estelle, I'm sorry that your printer isn't working. I know it's frustrating for you when it goes down and you hear all the complaints (empathy is a very helpful tool to use). I assure you that I'm working to get it fixed as soon as possible. Please tell me what happened." And then he calmly listened as Estelle vented (loudly). He remained emotionally detached and objectively summarized the facts of the situation for her. They worked together to figure out where in the organization they could pull a "loaner" printer from, and he agreed to get to her office as soon as possible to switch out the printers and diagnose the problem with the broken printer.

Because Estelle is Anthony's internal customer, the Solution*SHIFT* is slanted in her direction. He should be flexible and accommodating, even though he has a policy that supports next-day repairs. If this had been an issue with a coworker in his department, Anthony might have had a more open discussion. Perhaps he would have asked a teammate to be more flexible since they work together toward the same goals in the same area. See the difference?

Anthony recognized that it was in his best interest to let go of being right about the details of the service agreement. He knew that when looking for solutions, **sometimes the strongest thing to do is to bend a little**. As long as he stayed true to himself and his objective, he was in a good position to find the best solution for the situation. Anthony's boss complimented him on keeping his cool and resolving the problem for an important area, and Estelle was a happy customer despite all her huffing and puffing. WOW!

The next time you're hit with a problem POW, which will you choose – a solution stall or a Solution*SHIFT*?

*Being open minded and embracing a coworker's suggestion...**WOW!***

*Giving up the emotional fight for your solution...**WOW!***

*Finding a way to solve a patient problem that works well for both of you...**WOW!***

SolutionSHIFT Exercise

This is your chance to apply what you've learned and a valuable step in creating a *SHIFT* habit. You may be thinking, "I don't want to do this exercise," but I assure you that practicing and personalizing the steps are crucial to making them work for you! (To download a free 8.5" x 11" version of this exercise, go to www.ProfessionalParadise.com.)

1. Under "POW," give a brief description of a recent problem, disagreement or conflict you had with a coworker or patient where there was a difference of opinion about next steps or possible solutions. Be sure to include your idea/solution and the other person's idea/solution.

2. Under "S" write the word STOP. (This will help you remember to say "Stop!" and breathe the next time you're hit with a POW.)

3. Under "H" list the harmful knee-jerk reactions you had in response to the POW you described in Step 1.

4. Under "I" list the emotions you experienced.

5. Under "F" list as many ideas as you can think of that are new options for the scenario you described.

6. Under "T" write down at least one action you will take if you are faced with this POW again.

7. Under "WOW" list the positive outcomes that would result from this SolutionSHIFT.

POW	Stop and breathe	Harness knee-jerk reactions	Identify & manage emotions	Find new options	Take one positive action	WOW

PART III

GRAB YOUR PASSPORT
AND GO!

Destination: Paradise

~~~~~~~~~~~~~~~~

Lead your organization to Professional Paradise

When traveling abroad, a passport is the legal document which allows you to enter other countries. Your Passport to Professional Paradise represents the knowledge and skills you need to travel to your own version of Paradise, and it is now stamped with specific, proven strategies and techniques to *SHIFT* your POWs to WOWs. You can immediately put your Passport to use and be on your way...*if* that is your wish.

Some people are content in Prison or on Parole. They'd simply rather stay stuck in their comfort zone. Could that be you? If you want to get to Professional Paradise, you must first decide that you want to be there. There's a Volkswagen ad that says, "Misery has enough company...dare to be happy!" I wholeheartedly agree.

Most of you, however, are probably quite unhappy in Prison or on Parole and are ready to get out of Dodge. You know you want less stress, more energy and remarkable results at work. Good for you!

Making a conscious decision to *SHIFT* to Professional Paradise is critical to your success. Stephen Covey says, "Start with the end in mind." In Part I, you took the time to develop your vision of Professional Paradise. Now, create a Paradise Vision Card by taking that description and rewriting it on a piece of paper or typing it on the computer. (Or you can download a free Paradise Vision Card from www.ProfessionalParadise.com.) My vision card looks like this:

My Professional Paradise

I see people laughing and people who "get it."

I hear interesting dialogue and discussion about the topic at hand.

I think, "I'm so grateful to get to do this every day."

I say, "How can I be of service?"

I feel positive emotions — hope, joy, contentment, enthusiasm.

I am learning, creating new ideas, connecting people and serving others.

I am paid fairly for my services.

I connect with like-minded people who sparkle and shine with enthusiasm, *and* with people who need a "shot in the arm" to get themselves back on track.

My Professional Paradise is helping people become the Chief Paradise Officer of their job, even in stormy and uncertain times.

Once complete, take your vision card and post it in your office or work area. Attach it to the steering wheel or dashboard of your car. Put it someplace where you're sure to see it several times a day. Every time you look at it, take a minute or two to read it and envision it as if it is already happening.

With your Paradise destination constantly at the forefront of your mind, you will be more likely to remember to *SHIFT* your POWs to WOWs and to direct positive energy toward your goal. You'll begin to recognize the events, situations, interactions and circumstances that match your vision of Professional Paradise.

So how will you know when you've arrived in Paradise? Oh, you'll know, trust me.

More than likely, you'll notice the physical signs first. You'll find that you sleep better, have more energy, are far less stressed and experience better health. You might have fewer headaches and backaches. A healthy mindset supports a healthy body.

As your physical condition improves, so will your mental condition. Your concentration and ability to focus will get better. You'll find that you're more creative in general and more innovative in your problem solving. You'll spend more time "in the zone," so your assignments, projects and tasks will be easier to complete, and the workday will go by faster. And because you'll be creating positive connectionswith coworkers, patients and their families, your communication and working relationships will improve.

All of these things bring about increased productivity which ultimately leads to remarkable results. And at the end of the day, isn't that what you really want – remarkable results, for you and for your organization? Remarkable results mean better performance reviews, which often translate into raises, bonuses and promotions. People who work in Professional Paradise often report that they have more financial success.

There are other, more subtle but just as important signs that you've arrived in Paradise. You'll be internally motivated to succeed. You'll be satisfied, fulfilled and have a sense of purpose. You might even catch yourself smiling more and even having fun! And of course, you'll discover the sense of happiness and bliss you've been looking for all along – even when things are challenging.

Oh yeah…and you'll actually enjoy going to work every day. What a concept!

I'll bet your family, loved ones and friends will notice when you arrive in Professional Paradise. They'll see the changes in you, possibly before you see them yourself.

Your customers (external and internal) will also notice. Paradise is contagious! When you are living the good life at work, your patients will be positively impacted by your work experience. Do you know who else will sit up and take notice when you reach your Paradise destination? Your colleagues, coworkers, boss and direct reports if you're a leader. The quality of *your* work life affects those you work with. You don't just create Professional Paradise for yourself, but also model it for your team, your department, even your entire organization. The number one reason to *SHIFT* to Professional Paradise is to benefit *you*. That's right – it's okay to put yourself first in this case. Why? Because you can't help others get to Paradise if you're not there yourself.

Every time I give a presentation at least one person asks, "Why do *I* always have to be the one to change?" or "Why do *I* have to change first?" I know some of you are thinking that same thing right now. And you may already know the answer deep down: because you're the only person you have control over and because you're the one who wants to work in Paradise.

Mahatma Gandhi said it best: "Be the change you want to see in the world." I think this is especially valuable wisdom in the workplace because we spend so much of our time working – more time, in fact, than just about anything else we do. So step up and become the model for others to follow. When you become the change you want to see and create your own Professional Paradise, you give others permission to do the same.

When you start to *SHIFT*, you'll notice a ripple effect that will be felt across your workplace. In his bestselling book *The Power of Intention*, Wayne Dyer shares research that just one person operating at a higher level of consciousness affects as many as *90,000 other people* who are stuck at a lower level. Talk about a ripple effect of the greatest magnitude!

Of course, you can't create Professional Paradise for someone else – that's an individual responsibility. But you can stay in Paradise yourself and be a delight to work with. Through your mindset and your actions, you can enhance the quality of work life others experience when they interact with you. Your ability to change your viewpoint, foster positive connections and find productive solutions contributes to your Professional Paradise as well as theirs. When *you* SHIFT, you literally start an upward spiral of positive energy.

Imagine you and everyone around you working in Professional Paradise each day. Just think about the amazing environment and the spectacular results that would ensue. It would indeed be Shangri-La.

One person has the power to start the groundswell for *SHIFT*ing to Professional Paradise. Why not be that person? You can be the rock that causes the ripple in your work pond and beyond. This is your chance to be a leader – regardless of your position in the organization.

Go ahead…lead your organization to Paradise and beyond!

Work, Sweet Work!

Set up permanent residence in Paradise

Just for a moment, think about how you feel on the last day – or maybe even the second-to-last day – of vacation. If you're like me, you get a knot in your stomach or maybe a lump in your throat. You enjoy the day, but you also start to dwell on the inevitable return to reality.

Wouldn't it be great if you didn't have to go back? Wouldn't you love to stay forever?

Unfortunately, an everlasting vacation isn't very likely. But you can set up permanent residence in Professional Paradise – your very own "Work, Sweet Work!" **You can make Professional Paradise your reality every day, day in and day out.** How?

First, **become the Chief Paradise Officer of your life.** In a nutshell, that means accepting total responsibility for the quality of your work experience and your professional life. No blaming the patients or the boss or the teammate in the next department. Never forget that it is you who is in control. You have the power to imprison yourself or to set yourself free. Being the chief officer of anything involves responsibility, but it also offers great rewards. So hire yourself and get busy!

Before we finish up, let's revisit WC^2. You've been focusing on the question "What Can We Control?". Now let's *SHIFT* the message to remember "What We Can Control."

Thankfully, there are many, many things that we can control in our day-to-day work. It's just a matter of being intentional and keeping the idea front of mind.

Second, **periodically re-evaluate your vision of Professional Paradise.** Do you remember the story I told at the beginning of the book about my job as a sales trainer and how it was Professional Paradise because I enjoyed the travel? Do you also remember how much that same job would have been Prison to me just a few years later when I was married with two children?

Our needs, wants, desires, likes, dislikes, goals and priorities change over time. As a result, how we define and describe Professional Paradise will change over time as well. If you don't stop every so often and reassess your vision of Paradise, you may find yourself locked up in Professional Prison. It's also a good idea to consider from time to time where you are on the Prison-Paradise Continuum. In our chaotic, busy, post-pandemic world, it's easy to fall into the trap of living and working in survival mode – doing just enough to get by and get through each day. Before you know it, a year or two passes, and you look up one day to discover that you've been stuck on extended Parole.

The great news about Professional Paradise is that it's adaptable, flexible, changeable. It can be anything you want it to be – whatever suits you at any point in time. It won't look and feel the same throughout your entire career. As much as I enjoyed my work at the hospital, when I started my own business I found a different version of Professional Paradise – the next evolution of Paradise, if you will.

Right now, go put a reminder in your calendar to re-evaluate your situation at least once a year. Then go to www.ProfessionalParadise.com and download a free Paradise Vision Card and Prison-Paradise Continuum and also put them in your calendar. When the time comes, re-do both exercises and see where you are. Remember, as long as you continue to re-evaluate, redefine and re-envision – and as long as you keep *SHIFT*ing – you will always have a place in Professional Paradise.

The third step to ensuring a permanent spot in Paradise is to **create a habit of *SHIFT*ing POWs to a WOWs**. Without question, you will benefit from the first moment you try the *SHIFT* techniques and strategies. But to create lasting change you must develop a habit. If you want to stay in Paradise indefinitely, you can't just *SHIFT* the occasional POW to a WOW. Nor can you *SHIFT* for several months and then revert back to your old ways. You must create a habit and *SHIFT* to WOW every day.

Your brain works in amazing ways to form a habit. Think back to the time when you didn't know how to use a new phone – before it became a habit. As you learned the steps and functions and apps, you metaphorically cleared a path in your brain for how to navigate the phone and its software. Over time, as you repeated the steps, you created a "rut" in your brain which holds the habit. Now, that rut is so deep and so worn, you can talk to your kids, check your email and talk on the phone while drinking a cup of coffee. Sound familiar?

This hardwiring of the brain is the reason habits are so hard to change. The habit ruts tend to persist, and the deeper they are (metaphorically speaking), the more difficult it is to eliminate them. The longer you've had a habit and the more often you use it, the harder it is to change. This is why stopping a habit is usually always harder than starting one. Think about it: Stop eating desserts or start making healthy dessert choices – which is easier? Stop getting annoyed or start being more patient? The "starting" seems more appealing – not to mention more doable – than the "stopping."

And so it is with POWs and WOWs. Which is easier: to stop your habitual responses to POWs or to start transforming your POWs into WOWs? *SHIFT* is not about stopping old habits as much as creating new, more positive habits. With practice – and distance from old habits – you will see great results and start to live the good life at work.

Stephen Covey, in *The 7 Habits of Highly Effective People*, shares that there are three elements to every habit: knowledge, skills and desire. When these three pieces converge and you do the necessary work, you are on your way toward developing a new habit. Forming a habit of *SHIFT*ing all your POWs to WOWs involves the same three elements:

1. **Knowledge – understanding how your work beliefs and your mindset affect your actions and outcomes.** The knowledge you've gained in this book about getting to Professional Paradise is deeply rooted in changing your beliefs and your thoughts to create new actions and outcomes. Clarify your descriptions of Prison, Parole and Paradise so you can recognize them. Acknowledge and decide to change any limiting work beliefs that are holding you back. Use your new knowledge to get out of Prison and get on with the journey.

2. **Skills – learning and executing the five *SHIFT* steps and applying the three *SHIFT* strategies in the workplace.** *SHIFT*ing a POW to a WOW is a skill which can only be honed through practice – lots of practice. Learning new skills isn't always easy and may "go against your grain" in the heat of the moment. Give yourself a pat on the back or a small "Way to go!" inside your head each time you *SHIFT* a POW to a WOW. No more waiting for the boss or your coworkers to tell you how great you're doing – recognize yourself!

3. **Desire – consistently choosing to *SHIFT* because you want to live the good life at work.** If you consciously notice when you *SHIFT* a POW to a WOW, then you will enjoy the results and want to do it again. Make a concerted effort to monitor your thoughts and actions as they occur and decide if you like the outcomes. If you will just start using the *SHIFT* steps, I guarantee you'll see positive changes.

A Habit*SHIFT* (as I like to call it) typically takes 21 to 28 days according to the latest research. The best way to create a Habit*SHIFT* is to use your thoughts and actions to transform one POW at a time. Every day, for 28 days, use at least one *SHIFT* Strategy, and you'll form a new habit. It doesn't matter which strategy you use – you can use the same one each time or a different one. The steps, of course, are the same for all the strategies. Once you develop the habit of using the *SHIFT* steps, you'll do them automatically without thinking about which strategy you're using.

How can you keep the *SHIFT* steps and strategies on your radar while you form this new habit? One idea is to keep this book handy. When you feel a POW coming on, pull it out and review the *SHIFT* steps. Another option is to get a Passport to Professional Paradise memory card – a quick-reference card that lists the five *SHIFT* steps .(Visit www.ProfessionalParadise.com for more details.)

Finally, if you want to stay in Professional Paradise long term, **pay attention to the care and feeding of your mind.** Your brain really does listen to all the messages you give it. Are you feeding it "food" that is nutritious or toxic? You need some Paradise Brain Food – and I don't mean fresh fish. What can you do for your mindset that will help you on your journey?

For starters, listen to the people around you. Listen to yourself for that matter. What do you say out loud and to yourself about work? You are in charge of your mindset. The images and ideas you put into your mind create the realities and experiences you live. "Garbage in, garbage out" works for your head just like it works in a computer processing system. When your friends ask you about work, do you say things like "I'm getting crushed" or "This job is killing me"? Pay attention to the messages you are sending yourself.

Who do you spend time with at work? Are you hanging out with the Chain Gang in your organization? Do you have lunch with people who are looking for WOWs or with the Dilbert® crowd?

Choose your friends at work wisely. The more positive your peers are, the fewer POWs you will encounter.

Trust me when I tell you that once you get to Professional Paradise, you won't want to leave. In Paradise, you feel more empowered and connected to what makes you feel satisfied, energized and productive. Make a commitment to do what it takes to create your own Work, Sweet Work so you can live the good life indefinitely.

Paradise Found

Postcards from Paradise

All that you seek can be found right where you are.
– Abraham-Hicks Publications

You didn't seriously think I'd end this book without saying it one last time, did you? Professional Paradise – or Prison or Parole, for that matter – is not dependent on your job, your organization, your boss, your coworkers or your patients. Do you see that now? Do you understand that the Professional Paradise you seek is right under your nose, just waiting for you to claim it – even when things are stormy or uncertain?

When you picked up this book, you were likely either a doubter, a curious skeptic or a hopeful believer.

Which one are you now?

I hope you're a believer. I hope you know in your gut, your heart and your head that **Professional Paradise exists, you deserve it and you can get there.**

I'm fond of saying, "If you don't know the ending to a story, then why not write a happy one?" Write a happy ending to your work story. Decide to live happily ever after in Professional Paradise. You can do it – Professional Paradise is within your reach!

You have the key to release yourself from Prison. *Make a break…run for it!*

You have the knowledge and skills to get away from the limiting confines of Professional Parole. *SHIFT!*

You have the Passport that will get you all the way to your very own Professional Paradise. *Leave right now…today!*

And when you get there, kick off your shoes…put up the umbrella… lean back in that lounge chair…feel the breeze on your face…and dig your toes into the warm sand.

I ask only one thing as you live the good life at work – as you experience less stress, more energy and remarkable results…

Send me a "postcard."

Call me, email me (Vicki@VickiHess.com) or visit me on the web and say just two words:

PARADISE FOUND!

Acknowledgments

I now realize that "it takes a village" to write a book. Thank you to all the folks in my village who made the process so exciting and fulfilling.

My personal village is full of great men! To my husband, Alan, I love you just the way you are. Thanks for saying, "Go for it!" so often and then always being my biggest cheerleader. Josh...you are the calm in all storms. You inspire me to push a little harder and give a little more. Thanks for your thoughts and ideas along the way. Last but definitely not least, Brian...you work harder than anyone I know. Thanks for making sure my feet are always firmly planted on the ground.

A note of gratitude goes to Juanell Teague and James Huggins who really got this ball rolling many years ago. Those two days I spent working with you were truly transformational in my journey to serve.

Thank you to Melissa Farr of Back Porch Creative who brought vision and creativity to the cover and inside layout of the book.

Thanks especially to Juli Baldwin, CEO of The Baldwin Group and chief book coach and editor, who helped me take this book to new levels that I never dreamed possible. You pushed and pulled in the gentlest of ways to extract the best I had to give. I've come to appreciate your wisdom, expertise, laughter, positive spirit and loving nature – thanks!

About the Author

Vicki Hess, RN, MS, Certified Speaking Professional

Vicki is your go-to resource for transforming employee engagement at the individual, departmental or organizational level. As the author of 5 books, Vicki inspires clients to act. Organizations that implement Vicki's ideas experience increased productivity, safety, quality, retention, client satisfaction, creativity and more. To read what her clients say about working with her, please visit www.VickiHess.com.

A highly-regarded speaker, author, facilitator and virtual coach, Vicki shares her expertise in employee engagement with healthcare organizations across the country. She has more than 30 years of hands-on business and healthcare experience that she draws upon to provide inspirational and evidence-based strategies for workplace engagement. Using time-tested methods including virtual and in-person workshops, retreats and keynote presentations, Vicki is a much sought-after speaker whose knowledge of the industry makes her uniquely qualified to address the ever-changing priorities of today's healthcare organizations.

Ms. Hess holds a Bachelors of Science in Nursing from the University of Florida and a master's degree in Human Resource Development from Towson University. She was an adjunct professor at Johns Hopkins University Graduate School of Business for five years.

Vicki is one of 300 women in the world to have earned the Certified Speaking Professional (CSP) designation, the speaking profession's international standard for platform skill. She has been voted a TOP 5 Healthcare Speaker for four years.

Vicki has written for AONE Nurse Leader, American Nurse Today, Hospital & Health Network, Becker's Hospital Review, NurseTogether.com and other industry publications and blogs. To learn more about Vicki and to see some of her presentation videos, visit http://www.HealthcareEmployeeEngagement.com

More Ways to *SHIFT* to Professional Paradise

1. **Virtual or In-Person Keynote Presentations**
   Let author Vicki Hess help your employees and leaders develop personal accountability for creating their own Professional Paradise and delivering remarkable business results. Vicki's high-energy, one-of-a-kind presentations are specifically designed to achieve long-term habit change for healthcare leaders and staff.

2. **Employee Engagement Virtual and In-person Workshops**
   Get everyone in your organization in Professional Paradise. Customized sessions focus on specific employee engagement challenges facing your employees and leaders. Virtual workshops offer the benefits of in-person training without the inconvenience and expense of travel.

3. **Resources**
   Powerful tools to help you practice and personalize the *SHIFT* steps and strategies.
   + *SHIFT* Exercise – *SHIFT* any POW to a WOW with this step-by-step guide
   + Prison-Paradise Continuum – where are you...Prison, Paradise or somewhere in between?
   + Paradise Vision Card – clarify and reinforce your personal vision of Professional Paradise
   + Passport to Professional Paradise Reminder Cards – quick-reference cards provide the *SHIFT* steps right at your fingertips

4. ***Engagement Excelerator Virtual Coaching Program***
   Provide your leaders with the tools and resources to sustain engagement over time. Help them lead their teams to Professional Paradise through their leadership actions. Visit www.EngagementExcelerator.com for details.

To book Vicki for your next meeting or conference, please call 410.205.5081. For more information about Vicki's other customized, engaging and inspiring virtual and in-person keynotes and presentations, visit **www.VickiHess.com**.

Find FREE Downloadable Tools at
www.ProfessionalParadise.com

To bring Vicki to your organization, visit
www.VickiHess.com

Other Books by Vicki Hess:

SHIFT to Professional Paradise:
5 Steps to Less Stress, More Energy & Remarkable Results at Work

The Nurse Manager's Guide to Hiring, Firing & Inspiring

6 Shortcuts to Employee Engagement:
Lead & Succeed in a Do-More-With-Less World (Healthcare Edition)

Made in the USA
Columbia, SC
05 June 2020

Addressing ADD Naturally

Addressing ADD Naturally

Improving Attention, Focus, and Self-Discipline with Healthy Habits in a Healthy Habitat

Kathi J. Kemper, MD, MPH

Author of *The Holistic Pediatrician* and *Mental Health, Naturally*

To order additional copies of this book, contact:
Xlibris Corporation
1-888-795-4274
www.Xlibris.com
Orders@Xlibris.com
83548

CONTENTS

To the children, families, and colleagues who have taught me so much and helped me live a more focused, intentional, and fulfilling life. And to Daniel, who makes it all worthwhile.

FOREWORD

WHEN THE MIND spins in twenty directions at once, it is impossible to think clearly, study effectively, work productively, or engage in balanced relationships. Being unable to focus makes even everyday tasks seem unattainable, and trying to do anything that requires concentration often brings intense frustration, anxiety, and demoralization. This is especially true for young children because they cannot describe what they are experiencing and don't know how to ask for help.

The syndrome that goes under the current label of attention deficit hyperactivity disorder (ADHD) crosses all geographic, age, and cultural boundaries. The rate at which ADHD is diagnosed and treated has increased dramatically since the syndrome was first recognized as a specific disorder in the Diagnostic and Statistical Manual (DSM) in the late 1970s. In the US, as many as 10% of males and 4% of females have been diagnosed with ADHD.[1] Many children diagnosed with ADHD also have oppositional defiant disorder and learning disorders; they have an increased risk of developing depression, anxiety disorders, and substance-abuse problems as adults.[2] Almost half of children diagnosed with ADHD never graduate from high school, and fewer than 5% complete a four-year university degree program. These statistics underscore the need for more effective, safer treatments of ADHD.

ADHD is caused by diverse genetic, social, medical, and environmental factors. Studies on twins show that ADHD is highly heritable.[3] The risk of developing it is probably influenced by genes that affect brain levels of dopamine and serotonin.[4] A greater risk of developing ADHD is also associated with fetal exposure to alcohol, tobacco smoke, and lead in addition to a history of premature birth, birth trauma, and serious childhood illnesses. [5-6] As many as one in five cases of ADHD may result from brain injury around the time of birth.[6] Some cases of ADHD may be associated with delayed development of the frontal and temporal lobes of the brain and more rapid maturation of motor areas than in non-ADHD children.[7] Certain food preservatives are known to worsen symptoms of ADHD, and exposure to certain pesticides is also associated with an increased risk.[5]

Professor Kemper's book is a timely response to urgent, unaddressed concerns over the limited efficacy and unresolved safety problems of conventional pharmacological treatments of ADHD. Stimulant medications including methylphenidate (Ritalin) and mixed amphetamine salts (Adderall) are common pharmacologic treatments of ADHD. However, one in three children and adolescents who take stimulants experience significant adverse effects, including abdominal pain, decreased appetite, and insomnia, and 10% have more serious adverse effects including stimulant-induced psychosis.[8] The nonstimulant medication atomoxetine (Strattera) may not be as effective as stimulants.[10] There are also concerns about its adverse effects, including hypertension, increased heart rate, nausea and vomiting, liver toxicity, and possibly increased suicide risk.[11-12]

Professor Kemper's book addresses each of these concerns head-on with practical, well-referenced solutions. Her summary of the scientific evidence for natural therapies is a long-needed and refreshing reply to legitimate concerns about the inappropriate use and overprescribing of stimulant medications in the context of unanswered questions about their efficacy and safety.

Many people diagnosed with ADHD already use natural therapies. Over half of the parents of children diagnosed with ADHD treat their children's symptoms using one or more natural therapies, including vitamins and dietary changes, but most do not disclose this to their child's pediatrician.[13] Avoiding medical jargon, Dr. Kemper reviews the evidence for natural therapies that are reasonable to use alone or in combination with stimulants or other conventional pharmacologic treatments. Throughout the book, Dr. Kemper emphasizes that the strategy should be tailored to the unique symptoms, circumstances, and needs of each child. The ideal treatment depends on the particular symptoms that are causing distress or impairment in social or academic functioning, your child's response to previous treatments (if any), the risk of adverse effects, the presence of coexisting medical or mental health problems, and cultural preferences and financial constraints that limit realistic treatment choices.

Starting with commonsense holistic approaches that benefit the body and mind, Dr. Kemper reminds us of the therapeutic value of regular exercise, adequate sleep, and rational food choices. As Dr. Kemper clearly explains, specialized dietary modifications, including reduced intake of refined sugar and elimination of food colorings and additives, are reasonable first-line strategies in children whose predominant symptoms are hyperactivity and impulsivity. Emerging research suggests that purified omega-3 essential fatty acids can help improve symptoms of both hyperactivity and inattention. Although omega-3s are now widely used for ADHD, more research is needed to determine the most effective kind and amount of omega-3 to use. The critical role of good communication in shaping a cooperative relationship between parent and child is the foundation on which effective practical strategies for achieving behavior changes can take place.

Practical reviews of other natural treatments of ADHD included in the book include a preparation made from the bark of the French maritime pine tree, zinc supplementation, and the amino acid acetyl-L-carnitine.

There is a growing research literature on EEG biofeedback training in ADHD, showing it can result in sustained clinical improvement in both hyperactivity and inattention. Furthermore, when EEG biofeedback training is pursued on a regular basis, the doses of stimulants can sometimes be reduced, resulting in fewer adverse effects, improved treatment adherence, and improved overall functioning. Toward the end of her book, Dr. Kemper summarizes emerging evidence for massage, acupuncture, and chiropractic in the treatment of ADHD.

In writing a practical guide for parents of children and adolescents diagnosed with ADHD, Dr. Kemper has successfully translated cutting-edge ideas and research about emerging treatments from obscure medical references into a book that is both accessible and scholarly. This book will have a lasting impact not only on how ADHD is treated but also how parents, teachers, clinicians, and researchers *think about* ADHD.

Dr. James Lake
Author of the *Textbook of Integrative Mental Health Care*

INTRODUCTION

CHANCES ARE THAT you or someone you love wants to be more focused, deliberate, thoughtful, and attentive while having fun and enjoying life. The loved one could be your child, teenager, spouse, student, neighbor, or even your boss. Maybe it's your family doctor or your favorite salesman, athlete, actor, musician, or comedian. Perhaps your child's teacher has suggested getting an evaluation. Perhaps there's been an official diagnosis of ADD (attention deficit disorder) or ADHD (attention deficit/ hyperactivity disorder). Or perhaps you're wondering if natural therapies might be safer and work as well as medications. This is the book for you!

Abbreviations

If you were born after 1970, you probably use the term *ADHD* (attention deficit hyperactivity disorder) or maybe even AD/HD (attention deficit/ hyperactivity disorder). The term *ADD* (attention deficit disorder) was officially retired in 1987 when the DSM*-III-R was published. Before it was known as ADD, these symptoms had other names: hyperkinetic disorder of childhood or minimal brain dysfunction (MBD). Some people say it's illogical to call a syndrome ADHD or AD/HD when hyperactivity is not essential to the diagnosis. I prefer the esthetics of *ADDressing ADD*! I hope my colleagues who correctly refer to it as ADHD or AD/HD will forgive my preference. Who knows? The next version of the DSM may be back to plain old ADD.

ADD and ADHD are Common

Regardless of what you call it, ADD and ADHD are two of the most commonly diagnosed and costly mental health diagnoses in the US. In addition, many people without a formal diagnosis want to have better focus; make deliberate, well-thought-out decisions; and discover more order in their lives. Millions of children, adolescents, and adults struggle with impulsivity, distractibility, hyperactivity, and their consequences. A growing number of college students and adults turn to medications for an extra mental edge.

---

*   Diagnostic and Statistical Manual

Parents eager to see their children succeed spend billions of dollars on prescription drugs to improve focus and reduce impulsivity.

Keys to Success

Since you have picked up this book and are reading the Introduction, you have already demonstrated the three keys to helping yourself and your loved one address ADD successfully:

1. You care, and you want to help. You are compassionate.
2. You are hopeful that things can be better and humble enough to seek and use help from reliable resources.
3. You focus on fundamentals (otherwise you would have skipped the Introduction).

Your compassion, hope, humility, curiosity, and commitment are the keys to success. You're already halfway there. You can succeed.

How This Book Can Help

This book will help you focus on strengths and innate abilities to accomplish your goals (chapters 1 and 2). It will help you understand and use five fundamental strategies for success (chapters 3-8). It will help you make a plan that works (chapters 9-10), and it will help you choose how and when to use additional help (chapters 11-14). If you're in a hurry, feel free to skip to the bottom line in chapter 15. If you want to dive into more depth and get creative, check out the optional activities at the end of each chapter.

Remember, you don't have to be sick to feel better, and you don't need an official diagnosis to enhance attention, patience, and self-discipline; modulate activity levels; and achieve the true freedom of being able to think, speak, and act deliberately. Let's get started by focusing on *your* goals for your child and existing strengths to help achieve those goals.

CHAPTER 1

What is ADD?

History, Diagnoses, Labels, and Frames

Jack be nimble.
Jack be quick.
Jack jump over the candlestick.

WHAT WAS JACK thinking? He could have burned himself, knocked over the candle, started a fire, or simply singed his clothes. Did Jack (or the person encouraging him to jump) have ADD? For that matter, did Peter Rabbit, who—after being warned not to—ran straight into Mr. Macgregor's garden as soon as his mother was out of sight?

History

Impulsivity and distractibility are nothing new in literature or in life. A nineteenth-century pediatrician wrote about a character named Straw Peter who was fidgety, had trouble paying attention, was impulsive and aggressive, and had trouble learning. Sound familiar? If Tom Sawyer and Huck Finn were alive today, would they be diagnosed with ADD?

Historically, impulsivity and distractibility were considered bad character traits that deserved harsh punishments. To counter our human tendencies to be impulsive, careless, distracted, or disorganized, religions have promoted practices to encourage self-discipline, restraint, and spiritual devotion. Those whose problems persisted were sometimes stigmatized as being influenced by immoral or evil forces (devils) and subjected to ostracism, shunning, penances, or worse.

Impulsive, distractible, disorganized, injury-prone children who are constantly criticized, reprimanded, and harshly punished for their behavior can develop low self-esteem leading to worse behavior problems. The sense of not fitting in, not meeting expectations, and failing to please peers, parents, and teachers can contribute to sadness, worry, irritability, and moodiness, leading to outbursts and oppositional and antisocial behaviors.

Negative Labels Have Negative Effects

A downward spiral of inattention, impulsivity, and negative behaviors is partly due to the discouraging effects of the stigma of negative labels. Labeling someone with ADD or ADHD as lazy or stupid is just plain wrong; the vast majority of people with ADD and ADHD are trying as hard as they can. The problem is not lack of intelligence; it's the need to master specific skills.

Labeling someone with ADD or ADHD as bad or evil is also wrong. Just like everyone else, the vast majority of people with ADD and ADHD want to do well, want to please their parents and teachers, and want to contribute their best to help others. The problem is not lack of willpower; it's the need to build on their strengths to succeed.

Modern Medical Views of ADHD and ADD

Modern medicine views most problems as combination of genetic and environmental factors correctable through medication. Biologists see a perfect storm of nature and nurture to be treated with biochemical remedies. Often, earlier unscientific stigmas persist, handicapping those with ADD in their pursuit of happy, productive lives.

Whether viewed from the perspective of history or biology, one thing is certain: people with ADD and ADHD do not consciously or deliberately choose to be difficult.

Good News

The good news is that despite the challenges, a number of natural strategies grounded in a commonsense focus on the fundamentals can foster the kind of focus and forethought your child needs to succeed.

As the youngest of three children, Michael's family loved him. His mother was an award-winning teacher. But by the time he was nine years old, he was a pest, he was disruptive, and he had trouble in school. Michael was diagnosed with ADHD and put on Ritalin. His mom also met regularly with teachers, worked with him closely herself, and found tutors to help him. Once he found an activity he loved (swimming), a worthwhile goal (winning), and coaches who supported him, Michael developed focus, drive, discipline, persistence, and tenacity in the pool. By the time he was 15, Michael Phelps was off medications, and he became an Olympic swimmer, breaking numerous swimming records and winning more gold medals than any swimmer in history. There's more to Michael's story. Keep reading.

How do you know if you or someone you love has ADD or ADHD?

Diagnosing ADD

There are no lab tests or x-rays that confirm or refute the diagnosis of ADD. The diagnosis is based on whether (a) certain behaviors are more common than in most people and (b) whether those behaviors cause significant problems in different parts of their lives.

Technically, attention deficit/hyperactivity disorder is defined as an early (appearing by age seven years), persistent (at least six months), and pervasive (present in at least two settings) pattern (at least six symptoms) of *shorter*-than-normal *attention span* (distractibility) and *more*-than-normal *impulsivity* and/or *hyperactivity* that disrupts age-appropriate functioning in two or more arenas: academic, social, athletic, artistic, or occupational. Whew! That is a mouthful. Let's just say that the problems of short attention span and impulsivity are more than just a passing phase characteristic of the average toddler or puppy.

Behavioral Checklists

Clinicians use standardized behavioral checklists such as the Vanderbilt or Connor questionnaires to assess impulsivity, distractibility, and hyperactivity. The diagnosis is based on perceptions of behaviors and difficulties. Because perceptions are subjective, most clinicians ask for input from two or more people who see the child in different settings (e.g., a parent, teacher, or coach) to help make the diagnosis and monitor progress. Researchers may use computerized testing protocols to assess response to experimental treatments, but these protocols are seldom used in clinical practice.

Imaging Techniques and qEEG: Future Trends for Diagnosis

Within the next ten years, new brain imaging techniques and laboratory tests may pinpoint brain areas and neurotransmitters that need training or support to improve life for people with ADD. Two promising tools include single photon emission computerized tomography (SPECT) scan, which can analyze activity levels in different parts of the brain, and the quantitative electroencephalogram (qEEG). Noted psychiatrist Daniel Amen uses the SPECT scan to help guide and monitor response to therapy, but this tool is not widely used by other clinicians, and scanning is not usually covered by your insurance. The qEEG often shows a pattern of slower (theta) activity in the parts of the brain involved in organizing and planning. The qEEG can also be used for neurofeedback training to improve the pattern and symptoms (see chapter 13).

What's Wrong with His Brain?

Researchers are trying to understand which parts of the brain and which of its chemical messengers contribute to ADD. Some studies suggest that the brain is just fine, but it develops more slowly in those with ADD than in other people. Other research suggests that the frontal cortex (the parts of the brain concerned with attention, planning, and self-control), the cerebellum (which affects movement, timing, and balance), or areas relating to moodiness and emotions are slightly different in those with ADD. A great deal of research implicates the brain's messenger systems (neurotransmitters such as dopamine and norepinephrine) associated with alertness and internal rewards. This is why most of the medications used to treat ADD and ADHD affect the release, reuptake, or receptors for dopamine or norepinephrine.[*] Although ADD sounds like one diagnosis, there may be different subtypes in which different brain areas and neurotransmitters are affected.

No matter what areas of the brain are affected, it is capable of changing and improving. Though most of us will never become Olympic athletes, we can get stronger with weight training. Similarly, though most of us will never be Mensa candidates, we can enhance our focus, forethought, and organization with good coaching and practice. Regardless of which parts of the brain or body need improvement, healthy habits and a healthy habitat are fundamental for optimal performance.

---

[*] Regardless of how a medication works, the diet must supply the amino acids (such as tyrosine and phenylalanine from healthy proteins) and cofactors (such as vitamins and minerals) that are needed to make dopamine and norepinephrine.[1] Medications cannot replace good nutrition.

What's *Right* with His Brain?

Human beings have many different kinds of intelligence and skills. People who have problems with one or two skills such as focusing or self-discipline often have valuable hidden talents. Many children (and adults) who have ADD are very creative—musically, artistically, or dramatically. They can be terrific innovators and out-of-the-box thinkers. Others are amazing athletes excelling in swimming, running, dancing, martial arts, tennis, or biking. Some are mechanically inclined and can not only take things apart, but put them back together or fix them when they are broken. Others have excellent insight into computers and all kinds of technology. Many children with ADD are attuned to nature; sensitive to changes in weather, animal behavior, or plants; and become wonderful biologists or environmentalists. And some have enormous emotional sensitivity and intuition. People with ADD may have tremendous social skills: forming friendships, collaborating, fostering teamwork, comforting those who are sad, creating comedy, entertaining, or making sales. We can't all be great at everything all at once. But each person with ADD and ADHD has unique and admirable gifts and talents that emerge over time. Let's be patient and curious to watch their beauty unfold and play to those strengths!

Building Skills

The two essentials for an ADD diagnosis are problematic distractibility (poor attention skills) and impulsivity (poorly developed skills related to organization, planning, patience and follow through).

Managing Attention

ADD means poorly developed attention skills. Just as learning to walk requires desire, balance, strength, and coordination, *learning to manage attention requires the following*:

a. Motivation (it's easier to pay attention to things that interest us),
b. The ability to accurately perceive sensory data such as sounds (as words) and symbols (written words or gestures) and process them into meaningful information,
c. Tuning out irrelevant sensory information (e.g., ignoring music or conversation in the background while reading a book), while being flexibly responsive to changing priorities (e.g., responsive to a smoke detector, a cry for help, or ringing telephone),

d. Being able to monitor one's own attention ("Oh, was I listening to the music instead of focusing on the words? Was I imagining my next meal or preoccupied with an overwhelming emotion? How many times have I read this sentence?"), and

e. Skill to redirect attention ("Let's get back to the book.").

Following Directions

Following directions well requires not only attention, but also

a. understanding the meaning of the request,
b. recognizing the tools and skills needed to complete it,
c. assessing their availability,
d. using available resources and asking for help when needed, and
e. monitoring performance.

Other Skills: Organization, Planning, Patience, Following Through

Many people with ADD also have trouble organizing things in space and time. They can be messy, disorganized procrastinators who have a hard time finishing projects or considering long-term consequences. Did I mention impulsive? The skills of delaying gratification, anticipating consequences, following through, planning, organizing, and being patient are challenging for folks with ADD to master. But they are skills. They can be learned and improved with good coaching and practice.

Medical Problems, Medication Side Effects, and Other Problems

Most children with ADD and ADHD are physically healthy. However, it's important to make sure another health problem isn't affecting their behavior. Good clinicians conduct a thorough evaluation to make sure there are no medical problems (such as anemia, insomnia, or an under-functioning thyroid gland), sensory issues (hearing and vision problems), or psychological factors (recent moves, deaths, or other stressors) contributing to distractibility or impulsivity.

Aaron was a quiet slightly overweight teenager whose father was concerned about his daydreaming. His mother was frustrated that he seemed to spend all his time playing computer games when he was supposed to be working on school projects. Aaron had

KATHI J. KEMPER, MD, MPH

suffered from eczema as an infant and developed asthma during preschool. His only medication was an inhaler for his asthma; Aaron wheezed in gym, especially when ragweed was in bloom, and a physical exam showed some eczema patches that he was too embarrassed to show to anyone. After he started new treatment strategy, Aaron still preferred computer games to football; but addressing his asthma, allergies, and eczema helped him participate more fully in gym, concentrate better on his homework, and come out of his room to attend car shows with his dad.

Medical problems such as itchy rashes or stuffy noses can be distracting and can make it hard to focus. Hunger and nausea impair concentration on other things. Pain can lead to desperation and impulsivity. Someone who can't see the screen or hear his seminar leader may find it easier to talk with his colleague or daydream than listen. Poor sleep can result in daytime fidgeting. Thyroid problems can masquerade as spaciness, and treating hypothyroidism or resistance to thyroid hormone can improve ADD symptoms.[2] Iron deficiency can cause fatigue, inattentiveness, restless legs, and other problems.

Betsy was a charming, bright five-year-old whose teacher suggested she come for an evaluation for ADHD because she was always out of her seat. When I asked Betsy why she thought she had come to the clinic, she said it was because she "had to go potty" a lot. Her mom, Denise, thought that Betsy made frequent restroom trips because she had potty-trained late and was afraid of having accidents in her big-girl panties. A careful evaluation showed that Betsy had a chronic, low-grade bladder infection. Once she was treated, Betsy felt more comfortable and more secure. Her frequent trips to the bathroom tapered off, and she was better able to focus on her schoolwork.

Medication Side Effects

Well-intentioned medical treatments can also cause problems. For example, some stimulant medications curb appetites and may lead to mild deficiencies of nutrients that are essential for optimal brain function. Chemotherapy, radiation, head injuries, and other medications (including antihistamines and seizure medicines) can also adversely affect brain function. Looking different because of a medical condition (anything from glasses to hearing aids to casts or braces) can lead to embarrassment, withdrawal, acting out, and trouble in focusing. Please get a thorough medical evaluation to address all your health concerns.

Other Problems that Can Look Like ADD

Many other psychological problems can look superficially like ADD. Being anxious or depressed can make it difficult to concentrate. Stressful situations like a death in the family, a recent move, a change in schools, the birth of a sibling, or living through natural disasters or war can impair attention too.

Learning disabilities make it hard to learn, so children tend to talk or daydream instead. Some of the most common learning disabilities include dyslexia (difficulty reading due to problems processing letters and words), dyscalculia (mathematical disability), dysgraphia (difficulties forming letters or writing clearly), auditory-processing disorders (difficulty decoding and making sense out of sounds and speech even with normal hearing on a hearing test), visual-processing disorders (difficulty understanding visual inputs including symbols and letters even with normal vision), and disorders with understanding spatial relationships, social signals, and using short—or long-term memory. A qualified clinical psychologist best assesses these disabilities with full neuropsycho-educational evaluation. The psychologist can also help you talk with the school about getting appropriate accommodations and assistance to address them.

Types of ADD

Although a healthy lifestyle benefits just about everyone, ADD is not a one-size-fits-all diagnosis. It comes with (ADHD) and without (ADD) hyperactivity. It can coexist with other conditions, such as anxiety, depression, or bipolar disorder. Some people with ADD have learning problems (reading, math, memory, logic, or auditory or visual processing). Some seem angry, moody, irritable, or temperamental, and some are defiant and oppositional. Regardless of the type or subtype of ADD, common characteristics are above-average distractibility and impulsivity that interfere with successfully navigating the modern world.

Classic ADHD (with Hyperactivity)

The classic image is a boy like Dennis the Menace. He is energetic; he talks a lot, interrupts others, acts as if driven by a motor, fidgets and squirms, has a messy room, acts impulsively, and has trouble following rules. He is often admonished to sit still, pay attention, and clean up his room. He drives his parents and their neighbor, Mr. Wilson, a little crazy. As an infant and small child, Dennis may have needed fewer naps or less sleep than other children; and from the time he could crawl, he was always on the go. He frequently gets into trouble in school and is the child other people call hyper or the Energizer Bunny. Dennis may be a handful, but he's often entertaining.

The quiet girl like Luna Lovegood (from the Harry Potter books), who daydreams and is inattentive in class, is a second classic type of ADD. She may be inattentive to parents or teachers, and she may be impulsive; but because she is not hyper, she is not considered a troublemaker, though some of her teachers may consider her slow or spacey. Luna may have suffered from the quiet type of ADD; nevertheless, she was a loyal, selfless, and generous friend.

Atypical ADD

Other kinds of ADD include those who are over-focused perfectionists so intent on their own worries and rigid ways of doing things that they have trouble paying attention to others or adapting to change. They differ from people who suffer from anxiety alone because they are inattentive (rather than hypervigilant) and impulsive (rather than very cautious).

Similarly, some ADD sufferers also experience mood swings, at times being stubborn, unyielding, inflexible, mean, or thoughtless; while at other times being talkative, impulsive, or grandiose; and still other times being very sweet, contrite, and loving.

Outgrowing ADD and ADHD

Previously, ADD and ADHD were thought to be childhood conditions. However, recent studies show that for more than 50% of people, problems with impulsivity, distractibility, and organizational skills persist into adolescence and adulthood. This means that developing healthy habits and learning skills to address innate challenges can have lifelong benefits.

Labels and Frames

Is impulsivity a problem or the beginning of greatness? Consider this quote by Edgar Allan Poe:

The impulse increases to a wish, the wish to a desire,
the desire to an uncontrollable longing.

Longing, of course, can lead to passion, dedication, and great literature.

While one can dwell on diagnostic categories and the negative behaviors associated with ADD (the glass is half-empty), it may be more helpful to focus on its strengths (the glass is also half-full). Focusing on the label or diagnosis can limit a person's self-concept (focusing on the problem rather than their strengths, skills, and potential contributions) and decrease motivation ("Why bother? I've got ADHD, so I'll never get it right anyway.").

In her book *The Gift of ADHD*, Dr. Lara Honos-Webb describes many ways of transforming problems into strengths.[*] For example, high activity may be seen as being full of energy, enthusiasm, exuberance, or vitality. Being off in one's own world may be the sign of a creative or innovative imagination at work. Children and adults with ADD can have lots of good ideas and ask lots of great questions. Impulsivity might be beneficial if being spontaneous, flexible, or adaptable is needed in improvisational theater. Exuberant, creative, flexible people can make great salespeople, performers, and scientists. There's never a dull moment when someone with ADD is around.

> Howard was expelled from high school after he pulled a prank impersonating a member of the school board to convince a construction company to come make a bid for an addition to the school. He has gone through a number of jobs but he has had a stable marriage and three kids despite his diagnosis of ADHD. You may know him better as the host of Deal or No Deal and his stage name, Howie Mandel. Howie has become a champion of understanding and coping with adult ADD.

---

[*] See the Resources section at the end of this book for more terrific books, organizations, and Internet sites for parents, teens, children, and professionals.

KATHI J. KEMPER, MD, MPH

Whether one sees characteristics and behaviors as a handicap or strength depends on the situation and one's mental framework. Being energetic, innovative, and aware of subtle changes in the environment may be useful for an artist, entrepreneur, or someone hunting wild game, but it can be challenging in a crowded classroom. The qualities that wreak havoc in chemistry can make for a successful stand-up comedian.

Table 1.1 Reframing Negative Labels

Negative Label	Reframed as a Positive
Hyper	Exuberant, vigorous
Distractible	Aware of details that others miss
Spacey	Rich inner life
Driven by a motor	Energetic
Emotional	Sensitive
Explosive or Intense	Passionate
Off-task	Creative
Impulsive	Eager, enthusiastic, willing
Inattentive	Listening to a different drummer
Poor concentration	Flexibly aware of changes in the environment
Accident-prone	Fearless
Demanding	Entertaining
Problematic	Filled with endless challenges and opportunities

ADD and Other Challenges

About half of children diagnosed with ADD face additional challenges. They include problems with learning, visual or auditory processing, memory, sleep, moodiness, irritability, anger, resentment, tics (like Tourette's syndrome), or anxiety. Being labeled as bad, difficult, slow, or stupid can lead to low self-esteem and further problems with mood, attention, or behavior.

ADHD also increases the risk of injuries, addictions, unintentional pregnancy, gambling, and impulsive decisions leading to criminal activity. Just because someone has mastered focus, diligence, and discipline in one area of life (such as competitive sports or school), it does not mean that he has mastered those skills across all the domains of living (recreation, interpersonal relationships, work, etc.).

Remember Michael Phelps? After record-breaking victories in the pool, at age nineteen, Michael was arrested for driving drunk and running a stop sign.* A few years later, he was photographed smoking marijuana. Youth with ADD have higher risks of developing substance abuse and gambling, particularly if their ADD symptoms are not well managed.

Genes or Environment?

Part of the tendency for ADD is *genetic*, that is, the tendencies to have problems with attention, impulsivity, disorganization, and impatience often run in families.[3] This means that children with ADD often grow up in families in which one or both parents have problems with distractibility and impulsivity. The household may be disorganized, parenting may be less than consistent, and the adults may not always provide optimal role models for patience, diligence, detailed deliberation, or self-discipline. This is certainly not always the case, and some children with ADD have been raised in homes that are models of quiet, calm, consistent order. While insight and clarity may be helpful, guilt about having or transmitting ADD is not.

The increases in rates of ADD diagnosis have also been attributed to changes in our *environment*. The main suspects have been toxic chemicals, poor diets, and television (electronic media). Thousands of new chemicals have flooded the environment in the last sixty years. Of the 358 industrial chemicals, pesticides, and pollutants found in studies of the umbilical cord blood of American infants, over 200 are known to be toxic to the brain.** Convenient quick-processed foods are often deficient in the nutrients needed by the brain while being loaded with problematic artificial ingredients. Excessive use of electronic entertainment is also linked to problems with attention and impulsivity. All of these changes are common elements of modern American families' lifestyle.

---

* The US and International Olympic Committees and the National Collegiate Athletic Association have banned the use of stimulant medications such as Ritalin. Competitive athletes with ADHD can't use stimulant medications.

** For more information on these studies, see the Environmental Working Group Internet site: http://www.ewg.org/childrenshealth.

Guilt

If you're a parent or grandparent of a child with ADD, you may feel very guilty. You may feel bad for *causing* the ADD or *failing* to manage it without help. You may be overwhelmed with the demands of parenting an exuberant, impulsive, distractible child. Your spouse, parents, in-laws, friends, and neighbors may be pressuring you or in conflict with you about parenting or relationship issues. The school may be telling you that your child is bad, failing, difficult, or may need medication or that you need to feed or discipline him differently. You may be beset by uncertainty about what is best, what the long-term consequences of medications, counseling, etc., may be. It can be overwhelming.

Please stop for just a minute. Take a deep breath. Even if you carry a genetic tendency for ADD, you did not choose it. You did not create it. You did not want it for yourself, and you did not want it for your child. Neither your ancestors nor your child are trying to hurt you, disappoint you, or make your life more difficult.

You cannot undo anything that happened prior to this moment. Neither you nor your loved one can choose another brain or another set of ancestors! Guilt does not solve problems. Guilt is stressful. It does not help you think clearly, plan, or make good decisions. If guilt is not helpful, what is?

Alternatives to Guilt—Three Working Assumptions

Let's make three simple working assumptions:

1. You would like things to be better.
2. You and your loved one are doing the best you can.
3. You cannot try any harder, so you'll need to try *smarter* with new strategies.

If you can accept those three assumptions, I have good news for you: Regardless of what has happened in the past or where things stand right now, there are natural strategies that can help. Natural therapies based on a firm foundation of a healthy lifestyle and a healthy environment can improve attention, focus, relationships, behavior, and the long-term outlook for happiness and success.

Balance

Balance is the key to achieving our goals. We don't want to go from scattered to hyperfocused. We want to be able to focus on what we want for as long as we want and remain responsive to important changes in our environment (such as a smoke detector, a baby crying, or the telephone ringing). We don't want to go from impulsivity to paralysis, unable to decide what to do. We want to be deliberate, cautious, and careful while remaining flexible and fun.

Figure 1

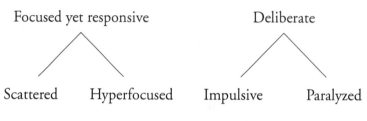

Focused yet responsive   Deliberate

Scattered   Hyperfocused   Impulsive   Paralyzed

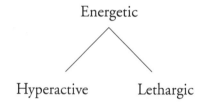

Energetic

Hyperactive   Lethargic

Similarly, most of us would rather be moderately energetic than lethargic or fidgety.

Medications

Before we dive into the details of natural approaches to promoting optimal health and function for those with ADD, let's spend 30 seconds on medications (we'll talk more about medications in chapter 12). They can be helpful for many people. For more details on ADHD medication for children, please see the American Academy of Pediatrics' book *ADHD: A Complete and Authoritative Guide*.

ADD and ADHD are chronic conditions. ADD medications are *not* like taking penicillin for a strep throat; you do not take them for ten days and expect a cure. ADD is a *chronic* condition, so if you use medications, they must be taken every day for as long as you want their benefits. They do not teach new skills.

Because medications can have side effects, don't work for everyone, and are not cures, even eminent organizations such as the British National Institute for Health and Clinical Excellence (NICE) do not recommend medications as the first-line treatment for people with mild to moderate symptoms of ADD. Instead, behavioral strategies and a focus on the fundamentals of a healthy lifestyle are the best place to start.

First-Line Fundamentals

The first-line therapy for any chronic condition is to optimize a healthy lifestyle. This does not mean you should avoid medications, but it does mean that drugs are not a substitute for nutritious food, restorative exercise and sleep, effective stress management practices, promoting positive communication in healthy relationships, and creating a favorable environment for success.

What are the specific elements of a healthy lifestyle that help promote focus and forethought? This book gives you a quick and easy overview. First we'll review the fundamentals and practical ways to take steps to improve; then we'll go over other natural helpful strategies.

Optional Activities

Consider trying one or more of the following:

- Find examples of other famous figures from the past or present, real or imaginary who might suffer from impulsivity, wandering attention, and increased activity levels. What other characteristics do they possess? What do you admire about them? What helped them succeed? Is Tigger's exuberance pathological? Does Dennis the Menace need medication? Are some of their problematic qualities part of what makes them lovable and entertaining?
- See a medical doctor for thorough evaluation to rule out any other health problems that adversely affect attention.
- List your loved one's good qualities. What are her strengths that could lead to success? What are her interests? What gives her the most joy? What do you enjoy most about her?

CHAPTER 2

Goals

Give me a stock clerk with a goal,
and I'll give you a man who will make history.
Give me a man with no goals, and I'll give you a stock clerk.
—J. C. Penney

WHAT ARE *YOUR* goals? What do you want most for the person you love who is struggling with ADD? In my clinic, I routinely ask parents what their goals are for their children. No matter how different the families appear to be on the surface, parents want their children to be happy and successful. Describing long-term general goals like *happiness* is relatively easy compared with describing short-term goals, but they're vital for crafting a plan to help us get there.

Strategic planning is worthless—
unless there is first a strategic vision.
—John Naisbitt

Goals Open Possibilities

Focusing on our goals helps us see many possibilities and makes us better problem solvers. This is one reason why successful companies spend so much time crafting their mission, vision, and value statements before they undertake the details of strategic planning. Both in personal life and in business, if you focus on just the problems of the moment, it's easy to get lost in the details, missing the big picture and big opportunities.

Challenge of Switching from Seeing Problems to Goals

It can be hard to change our perspective when we've looked at something the same way for a long time. As a doctor trained to focus on diagnosing disease, I know how difficult it is to switch from picturing problems to describing a destination. Medicine is full of tools—blood tests, imaging studies, surveys, and questionnaires—to determine a diagnosis. We have very few tools to measure well-being and even fewer words to describe health than to describe disease. Sometimes it helps to work with opposites. For example, the opposite of hypertension is having a normal blood pressure.

Try it yourself. For example, if you're worried because your child has been accident-prone, reframe this into a goal of wanting your child to be safe. Table 2.1 has a list to help you get started.

Table 2.1 Turning Problems into Goals

Problem	Goal
Accident-prone	Safe
Destructive	Productive
Disorganized	Organized
Distractible	Focused
Hasty	Deliberate
Failing school	Successful in school
Inattentive	Follows oral and written directions well
Impulsive	Intentional, deliberate
Heedless	Thoughtful
Hyperactive	Calm, serene
Insomniac	Sound sleeper, rested, vigorous
Learning disabled	Mastering math, reading, or other subjects
Messy	Neat
Procrastinator	Timely, on time, early bird
Spacey	Present, engaged, attentive

Did you notice that the list of problems could also imply immutable character traits? Character is something that is shaped by our choices, not our starting point. If we call a child accident-prone or disorganized, it's easy to give up and just say that's the way he is. When we focus instead on a goal of helping keep our child safe, calm, and neat, or helping him master a subject, we can think of many possibilities for helping him achieve those goals.

Focusing on our goals instead of problems helps us see the world a little differently. We see many more prospects and strategies to get there. We're more creative, and we embrace the bigger picture. Focusing on our goals is empowering!

Before we start looking at strategies for success in chapter 3, I invite you to take a few minutes and reflect on *your* unique long—and short-term goals for your child:

1. **Long-term goal** (for example, be happy or successful):
   Long-term goal   _____

2. **Short-term goals** (for example, be more focused, organized or calm, thoughtful, deliberate, self-disciplined, well-rested, etc.)

   Short term goal 1   _____
   Short-term goal 2   _____
   Short-term goal 3   _____

Optional Activities

What else you can do to identify worthy goals? Here are a few possibilities. Consider picking one or more to do with your loved one to help you establish meaningful goals.

1. Ask your loved one who he admires most in the world. What is it he admires about that person? What are they like? Discuss what it might have taken for them to achieve their success.
2. Read a biography or see a film or play about a person who achieved something significant despite a handicap. Discuss how they did it.
3. Reflect together about your loved one's favorite fictional character. What is it about that character that makes her special? What did she need to succeed?
4. Ask your loved one what he would like to be doing ten or twenty years from now. What does he think it will take to help him succeed? Help him generate as many ideas as possible.
5. Ask your loved one to pretend to be a wise old man (or woman); ask, "Now that you are old and wise, please give me some advice about how you succeeded."

KATHI J. KEMPER, MD, MPH

6. Consider writing a story, doing a play, drawing a picture, or making up a song about your idea of success.

> *First say to yourself what you would be;*
> *and then do what you have to do.*
>
> —Epictetus

CHAPTER 3

Five Fundamentals for Success: Healthy Habits in a Healthy Habitat

Dictionary is the only place that success comes before work.
Hard work is the price we must pay for success.
I think you can accomplish anything if you're willing to pay the price.
—Vince Lombardi

All good coaches know that the key to athletic success is practicing the fundamentals. Success on the field or court and in life takes practice. It takes consistent effort in the desired direction.

Tourist to cab driver: "How do you get to Carnegie Hall?"
Cab driver: "Practice, practice, practice!"
(Old joke)

NO MATTER HOW talented they are, practicing is the key to success for musicians too. For sports, the fundamentals may be running, throwing, catching, and teamwork. For music, they include scales, chords, melody, and harmony.

What are the fundamental strategies that promote focus, attention, organization, self-discipline, and forethought? Most doctors are trained to think about diagnosing diseases and dispensing drugs, so their answers might be commonly used pharmaceutical products. Many people who embrace alternative medicine might mention herbs, acupuncture, or some other natural remedy.

Fundamentals

However, the fundamentals for addressing ADD and optimal mental performance are also fundamental to optimal athletic performance: optimal nutrition (food); a balance of exercise and rest (fitness and sleep); friendships and family relationships built on clear communication; practicing successful emotional self-management strategies; and being good stewards of a healthy and safe environment (see figure 3.1).

Figure 3.1

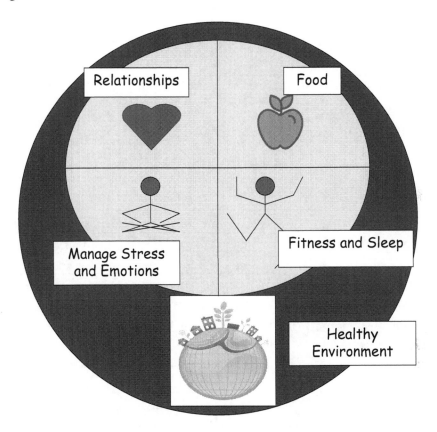

Practice

Particularly for learning new skills, we need to practice, practice, practice. A good coach continues to emphasize the fundamentals (keep your eye on the ball, keep your knees flexed, breathe from your belly) over and over without getting angry with the player who is trying to master it. Similarly, you may need to repeat "inside voice," "hands in your lap," "double-check your homework" thousands of times before the message is heard, understood, internalized, practiced, and finally mastered. Demonstrate calm, loving persistence.

Focus on what you want more than what you don't want. Practice saying what you do rather than what you don't want. Pay attention to the positive goals, and you will get there faster and more comfortably than spending your energy on the things you dislike.

Go with what you want. Stop saying what you don't want. Can you do it? Yes, you can!

Table 3.1 Say What You Want—Stop Saying What You Don't Want

What You Want (Go)	What You Don't Want (Stop)
Keep hands in lap.	Grabbing sister's toys.
Use your inside voice.	Yelling.
Go to bed.	Running around the house.
Eat vegetables.	Filling up on junk food.
Feel grateful.	Whining.
Wait your turn.	Interrupting, blurting out answers.
Be on time for the bus.	Miss the bus and need a ride to school.
Plan ahead and consider consequences.	Following the herd, doing the first thing that comes to mind.
Double-check homework.	Messy, incomplete homework shoved in a book bag or left on the table while rushing off to watch TV or play an electronic game.
Do your best.	Half-hearted attempts.
Ask for help when you need it.	Whining or failing to ask for help when needed.
Do it the first time I ask you. Repeat what I say so I know you heard me.	Task not completed despite multiple requests with a later excuse of "I didn't hear you."
Make your bed and put your clothes away.	Having a messy room.
Take care of your toys, clothes, pets, etc.	Breaking, misplacing, or losing things.

Find a peaceful solution to conflicts with your siblings/friends. Work it out.	Fighting, hitting, screaming.
Remember to bring your homework home and the supplies needed to complete it. Return it to school in the designated folder or notebook.	Forgetting assignments, pencils, notebooks, books, etc.
Tel me what homework you have in language, arts, social studies, math, and science.	Forgetting homework in some subjects.
Start to prepare for the test the week before. Spend 20 minutes per night. Review the outline, the highlighted words, the sample problems, and questions. Ask for extra help to master challenging material three days before the test.	Forgetting about the test until the night before or the morning of, failing to prepare or get help in mastering material, getting bad grades.

Each of the next five chapters gives you easy-to-follow, detailed, specific information on fundamentals. Remember, smart athletes and musicians seek help from good coaches. Be smart. Seek help from a health professional (such as a pediatrician, family doctor, psychologist, counselor, or nutritionist) or support group.

CHAPTER 4

First Fundamental: Food

Eat food. Not too much. Mostly plants.

—Michael Pollan

Janey was a 15-year-old cheerleader who was always smiling and always on the go. Her morning routine included a shower, makeup and hairstyling and a quick manicure before selecting the outfit of the day and rushing out to school. She got to sit next to her best friend in her first period class and her boyfriend during second period, so those classes were fun; but she thought third period was boring, and she could feel her stomach growling. Ravenous, she gulped down pizza, fries, and a diet soda at lunch while chatting with her friends. After lunch, she felt sleepy and bored. By the last period, she was perky again but a little distracted, anticipating cheerleading practice. She loved practices and drills with her friends, and it didn't hurt that they got to practice right next to some of the cutest football players in school. Someone usually brought cookies or granola bars and energy drinks to help them keep their energy up. But after all the working out, by the time she got home after everyone else had eaten dinner, she was starved and still had to do homework, so she grabbed a bag of chips or microwaved an instant dinner while texting and watching TV. Janey's mom was concerned that her grades had fallen from As and Bs as a fifth and sixth grader to Cs in high school. She knew Janey enjoyed cheerleading, but her mom felt frustrated that Janey didn't eat dinner with the family. Janey's mom wondered whether eating better might help her grades.

Paying Attention Demands Optimal Fuel

AS ANYONE WHO has focused on a difficult task for a long period knows, paying attention is demanding. The brain uses about 20% of the body's energy supply even though it takes up less than 5% of our total weight. To function well, it needs a steady supply of high-quality fuel, and it needs the right building blocks to make its messengers (neurotransmitters). Making those building blocks also requires vitamins, minerals, and amino acids.

Good nutrition makes it easier to focus. Research has shown that good nutrition leads to better learning, better problem solving, and fewer behavior problems.[1] What does good nutrition mean? It means:

- Good Timing—a steady supply
- High quality

Good Timing

If you plan to use your brain in the morning, afternoon, and evening, *eat breakfast, lunch,* and *dinner* to make sure your brain has the fuel it needs to succeed. You can't drive your car on an empty tank of gas. Your brain doesn't work well on empty either. Skipping meals impairs mental performance. Eating a healthy breakfast helps us perform better.[2] What you put *in* your body is just as important as what you put *on* your body. You wouldn't leave the house naked. Don't leave the house without eating breakfast.

Avoid topping off the tank. Big meals can make you sleepy and make you lose focus. Eating more than 1,000 calories at a single sitting, like Janey's lunch or a large Thanksgiving dinner, tends to make us sleepy. If you want to stay alert in the afternoon, don't overeat at lunch.

Snacks may be helpful for children, teens, and adults who have a fast metabolism to stay alert and focused throughout the day. Studies support common sense: healthy snacks can improve memory and performance.[3] Be thoughtful about what and how much you snack—chomping down chips or cookies is not a great choice. Healthy snacks include whole grains, fruits, veggies, and protein-rich foods (like peanut butter, organic milk, or cheese).

Janey agreed that she would sit down and eat breakfast at least four days a week. On Sundays, she'd prepare some small containers with dried nuts and raisins to eat on the way to school for the other days. Her mom agreed to shop for those items so they'd be available when Janey wanted them. Janey and her mom started to negotiate lunches; if she made and brought a healthy lunch to school, Janey could bank her lunch money, and her mom would match the money she saved for a special shopping expedition. If Mom made the lunch, she wouldn't match funds. Whatever Janey spent on school lunch or vending machines would be deducted from her shopping fund. They agreed to try it for one month.

High Quality

If it came from a plant, eat it. If it was made in a plant, don't.
—Michael Pollan, *Food Rules*

Get essential nutrients (amino acids, fatty acids, vitamins, and minerals) from food. Avoid junk food that has the same name in every language (e.g., Coke and Big Mac or is served through the window of your car). Our bodies have evolved over thousands of years to get essential nutrients from food (primarily plants and fish), not pills. Dietary supplements and ingredients added to processed foods or energy drinks are no substitute for whole grains, fruits, vegetables, seeds, nuts, and beans.

Table 4.1 Dietary Essentials for Optimal Attention

Dietary Essentials	Foods Sources
Amino acids	Soy, tofu, beans, lentils Seeds and nuts Milk, cheese, eggs Fish, fowl, meat
Essential fatty acids (EPA, DHA, and linolenic acid)	Fish (e.g., tuna, salmon, sardines, and mackerel) Flaxseeds, walnuts Dark green leafy vegetables Animals that have eaten omega-3 rich diets, such as eggs from chickens fed flaxseed, pasture-raised and grass-finished beef, lamb, bison, wild game, etc.
B vitamins, including folate and B12	Beans, lentils, nuts, and seeds Green leafy vegetables, asparagus Oranges and other citrus fruits and juices Whole grains Yeast (e.g., brewer's), dairy, eggs, meat, poultry, fish, and shellfish
Minerals (iron, magnesium, zinc)	Peas, beans, lentils, peanuts, peanut butter Green leafy vegetables (spinach, avocado) Raisins Whole grains, brown rice, wheat bran, and germ Nuts (e.g., almonds, cashews) Dairy, eggs Meat, fish, poultry, oysters

Did you notice that chips, sodas, candy, cookies, fried foods, and processed foods are not featured as good sources of *any* of these essential brain nutrients? Fortified foods are not the same as fresh locally raised, homemade foods. Eat foods our great-grandparents might have grown or caught—sustainably raised fresh fruits, vegetables, legumes, whole grains, nuts, and fish. They are the mainstays of optimal nutrition. Given the conditions under which most modern livestock are raised and the link between animal products and many chronic illnesses (including cancer, obesity, diabetes, and heart disease), I favor a plant-based diet.[4] I'm also a fan of sustaining a healthy fish population because healthy, uncontaminated fish are excellent sources of essential amino acids and fatty acids.

Check out the Web sites for the Natural Resources Defense Council (NRDC.org) and the Environmental Defense Fund (EDF.org) for more information about healthy, sustainable fish, and see the US Environmental Protection Agency (EPA.gov) for information about fish advisories due to mercury and other pollutants.

Amino Acids

Amino acids are the building blocks of many of the brain's messengers. Some small studies suggest that *carnitine* (an amino acid found in meat) can help improve attention and behavior in children and adults with ADD, particularly the inattentive type.[5-6] Where do you find amino acids if you're cutting down on meat? Soy, tofu, peanuts, tree nuts, nut butters, seeds, lentils, and beans are excellent sources of amino acids.

Essential Fatty Acids

Americans are finally getting over the mistaken notion from the 1990s that all fats were bad. In fact, certain fatty acids such as omega-3 fatty acids are actually essential because our bodies cannot make them from other things in our diet. They are also vital for healthy brains because they are an active part of the brain's cell membranes.

Low levels of omega-3 fatty acids are linked to ADD and behavioral problems in both adults and children.[7-8] Supplementing with fish oils (which are rich sources of omega-3 fatty acids) can alleviate ADD symptoms; decrease depression, anger, anxiety, impulsivity, and aggression; and improve academic achievement.[9-15]

Although flaxseed, walnuts, and green leafy vegetables contain the omega-3 fatty acid (linolenic acid), our bodies have to do some major metabolic work to transform it into the *eicosapentaenoic acid (EPA)* and *docosahexaenoic acid (DHA)* that our brains need. On average, we convert only about 5% of linolenic acid to DHA. My advice is to either eat sardines, salmon, or mackerel twice weekly*, one to two tablespoons of flaxseeds daily,

---

* For information about which fish are lowest in mercury and other toxins, see the US EPA Internet site on fish advisories: http://www.epa.gov/fishadvisories/

or consider a supplement containing between 500 and 2000 milligrams of the omega-3 fatty acids, EPA, and DHA.

Matthew was an eight-year-old boy who had seasonal wheezing and year-round problems with attention. His grandfather was taking omega-3 fatty acids for his heart, and he'd read that they could help attention too. Could they? Yes! I recommend an omega-3 fatty acid supplement to most of my patients. Some studies suggest that omega-3 fatty acid supplements during pregnancy and childhood can reduce the risk and severity of asthma too.

Vitamins

The brain relies on B vitamins, including folate, to make the messengers that promote optimal focus and attention. The best food sources of B vitamins are whole grains, beans, citrus fruits, green vegetables (such as spinach and broccoli), low-fat dairy, eggs, fish, poultry, and meat.

Minerals

Deficiencies of essential minerals such as iron, magnesium, and zinc can contribute to difficulties with attention, impulsivity, learning, and behavior. *Iron deficiency* interferes with memory, concentration, behavior, and both physical and mental performance.[17-21] Supplements can improve attention and restlessness in those who are deficient. *Magnesium* supplements have helped children with ADD, especially those who tend to be very excitable, easily stressed, or worriers, and those who also suffer from constipation.[22] *Zinc* supplements can improve behavior for those whose diets are deficient in zinc.[23-24]

The best dietary sources of essential minerals are plants and animals raised on mineral-rich soils. For picky eaters or those who eat poor-quality diets, I usually suggest taking a multivitamin/mineral supplement. If you're not deficient, megadoses probably won't help and may cause side effects.

advice/ or the Natural Resources Defense Council Internet site: http://www.nrdc.org/health/effects/mercury/protect.asp.

Emily was a 13-year-old girl who was a daydreamer; when she came out of her daydreams, she often acted without thinking. Her mother was at her wit's end with Emily's impulsive decisions. For example, Emily had recently decided to save the planet by eating only plain pasta with margarine, fruit bars, and peanut butter. While we tackled her diet, I advised her mom to give Emily a multivitamin with iron, flaxseed oil, and a calcium/magnesium/zinc supplement to ensure she got at least the minimum of her daily needs. I also suggested that they head to the library to find books by Judy Krizmanic, Dorothy Bates, or Stephanie Pierson on healthier ways to be a teenage vegetarian.

Water

Avoid dehydration. Dehydration can impair attention and mood, even in trained athletes.[25] In a small study of first graders, having some water before taking a test led to better attention and greater happiness.[26] If you are concerned about your tap water, have it tested or consider using a reverse osmosis filtration system to reduce or eliminate exposure to heavy metals. You don't need to spend money on bottled energy drinks or vitamin-fortified water. Advocate for environmental policies that keep our drinking and fishing water pure.

Avoid Toxins

Avoid mercury-containing fish and any foods or traditional home remedies from developing countries that may be contaminated with lead or other heavy metals; they are toxic to the brain. Also avoid processed foods that contain artificial colors, flavors, and sweeteners. Schools in the US, England, and Wales that have done so have shown remarkable improvements in students' attention, behavior, and grades. You may think that avoiding chemical toxins is a 21st-century idea, but it was actually anticipated decades earlier by Dr. Ben Feingold.

Was Feingold Right?

In the 1970s, the Feingold diet was very popular but mostly misunderstood. The Feingold diet does not ban sugar, but it does eliminate salicylates (a family of chemicals found in aspirin and a few foods, which are avoided at first but usually reintroduced as tolerated), several synthetic food additives, and certain synthetic sweeteners:

- Artificial colors (petroleum-based certified FD&C and D&C colors).
- Artificial flavors
- BHA, BHT, TBHQ (preservatives)
- The artificial sweeteners Aspartame (now called Truvia), Neotame, and Alitame

Artificial food colors significantly worsen hyperactivity for many people.[27] The Center for Science in the Public Interest (CSPInet.org) has called on the US Food and Drug Administration (FDA) to ban dyes linked to hyperactivity and behavior problems. The colorings the CSPI would like to see banned are listed here.

Artificial Colors to Avoid

o Blues 1 and 2
o Green 3
o Orange 8
o Reds 3 and 40
o Yellows 5 and 6

In studies of Australian and American children with ADHD who received the Feingold diet, 73% had improved behavior within six weeks.[28-29] A rigorous British study of over 1,800 three-year-old children showed consistent significant improvements in the children's hyperactive behavior on a diet free of benzoate preservatives and artificial flavors.[30] Artificial colors and sodium benzoate preservatives increased hyperactivity in healthy three-year-olds as well as school-age children.[31] For more details on the original Feingold diet, see the Internet site (www.feingold.org).

Despite the scientific evidence that avoiding artificial ingredients can improve attention and behavior, many Americans find these diets difficult to follow, and most American physicians do not recommend them. However, I have found that when families are willing to make the effort to focus on healthy foods, use supplements wisely, and avoid exposure to artificial ingredients and environmental toxins, they see remarkable improvements in mood, attention, and behavior. Some have been able to reduce their reliance on stimulant medications. Consider working with your local school and workplace to improve the quality of celebrations by serving party food that is actually nutritious. Like many others, you may discover that if you make it yourself, it's both less expensive and healthier than if you buy it ready made in a bag or a box.

Jacob was a ten-year-boy whose mother, Elizabeth, was a chemist. After reading about the adverse effects of artificial colors in Nutrition Action Newsletter, Elizabeth decided to read some labels on common items in her grocery. She was astonished and dismayed at how many popular kids' foods contained artificial colors and how easy it was to choose healthier items with just a little common sense. Before making a huge decision about what to buy for her family on a long-term basis, she decided to observe Jacob's behavior on days she intentionally served two kinds of food: on Tuesday, she gave him gelatin, candy, and cereal containing artificial red and yellow colors; on Thursday, she gave him similar food without the artificial colors. The difference was dramatic. Being a serious scientist, the next week she switched the menus—Tuesday was dye free and Thursday was loaded. Both Jacob and his teacher noticed the difference too. That was enough for Elizabeth to change her shopping habits. She told me she felt like the food industry had been experimenting on our children, and she decided to join thousands of others in urging Congress to ban the use of artificial colors, flavors, and sweeteners in children's food.

Foods We Love: Sugar, Chocolate, Coffee, Tea, and Salt

There is substantial individual, cultural, and social variability in response to foods. Expectations and beliefs powerfully affect our responses. What do scientific studies show about the effects of some of our favorites?

Sugar

Simple sugars can add enjoyment to our lives, but they can also add unneeded calories and cavities. At least a dozen double-blind scientific studies have shown that sugar does not directly cause hyperactivity. However, eating simple sugars can cause energy swings that impact our ability to pay attention and impair mental and emotional stability. It's better for your brain, your teeth, and your waistline to take in more calories from complex carbohydrates such as whole grains than to consume a lot of high-fructose corn syrup (HFCS) and other cheap sweets.[32]

The modern American palate has become conditioned to seek sweets, and popular advertising links sweets with celebration and reward. Humans need celebration, so these advertising campaigns have been very successful for the corporations who manufacture and sell processed food using HFCS and other cheap sweeteners. Many sweetened, processed food products also contain artificial colors and preservatives. Keep celebrations focused on people and homemade treats to save money and minimize your exposure to unwanted chemicals and empty calories.

Chocolate (Cacao Beans)

Most of us do not munch on pure cacao beans. The chocolate we eat also contains sugar, vanilla, and fat. The cacao itself contains caffeine, phenylethylamine, theobromine, and cannabinoid-like fatty acids. Each of these compounds can influence brain activity. Chocolate is rich in antioxidants, and eating a little bit leads to the release of the body's feel-good chemicals, endorphins.

Different people respond differently to chocolate. Some feel guilty; others are ecstatic. Be a careful observer of your own reactions to chocolate and other foods.

I admit it. After reading some scientific studies linking dark chocolate to lower blood pressure,[33] I started eating about half an ounce daily of dark chocolate purely for medicinal reasons, of course (even though my blood pressure is normal). I am not suggesting, however, that you should give hyperactive, inattentive, oppositional, or impulsive children a daily diet of candy bars!

Coffee

Americans are the #1 consumers of our favorite mind-altering herbal product: coffee. Coffee's caffeine keeps us awake, alert, and attentive. It helps us get going in the morning and stay awake during long, boring car trips. Coffee can also improve short-term memory. Benefits start within 30 minutes and typically last about three to four hours, though they can last much longer during pregnancy and in infants and the elderly who metabolize it more slowly. When the caffeine wears off, fatigue and irritability can set in. Like sugar, coffee can cause swings in energy and attention.

Some psychiatrists and other mental health experts recommend that ADD sufferers avoid coffee to minimize those swings. I hold a somewhat different view. Most of the prescription medications for ADD such as Ritalin and others are stimulant medications that are similar to caffeine. As you might expect, research suggests that caffeine improves attention better than placebos, but it is not as potent as prescription medications.[34-37] Based on this, I sometimes suggest that patients give coffee or tea a trial on weekends to see if they can reduce their medication dose. However, I do not recommend caffeinated sodas or energy drinks because they usually contain artificial flavors, colors, and preservatives that can interfere with overall health and optimal brain function (see section above). Nor is coffee a good substitute for regularly getting a good night's sleep (see chapter 5).

There is a lot of variability in the amount of caffeine in coffee and tea depending on how it's grown and prepared. Beverages usually have fewer side effects than medications. On the other hand, coffee can cause insomnia, jitteriness, anxiety, a racing heart, or even panic attacks, and require frequent trips to the restroom, leading to dehydration. Coffee can be addictive; those who are deprived of their morning cup can become irritable, sleepy, depressed, anxious, fatigued, and have a headache. Withdrawal symptoms can occur in people who drink as little as 1-2 cups daily. Do not drink coffee late in the day. Use common sense.

Tea

Tea contains less caffeine than regular coffee, so it causes fewer side effects, but it can still enhance alertness. Green tea contains less caffeine than black tea or oolong tea. Tea also contains the recently recognized amino acid theanine, which leads to a feeling of calm that can counteract the jitteriness some people experience with coffee.[38] I often recommend iced tea as a summertime remedy to enhance attention, and I enjoy making my own combination of regular and green tea. Avoid premade bottled or canned tea loaded with sweeteners.

Salt

In people who are salt sensitive, salt plus stress can cause higher levels of irritability and anger, just as it can lead to higher blood pressure. This is probably because salt sensitivity is associated with differences in how the nervous system and hormones regulate heart rate, blood pressure, and breathing rate.[39] Americans tend to eat way too much salt because we eat way too much processed food. If you eliminate processed foods (including canned soups, pasta, processed meats, and instant noodles as well as the more obvious chips and pretzels), you will have a lot more control over the amount of salt your child eats, and you may find him feeling more calm and focused.

Food Sensitivities

Avoid foods that cause allergies or sensitivities. Approximately 6-10% of children have allergies or sensitivities to foods. In addition to classic allergies, many people are lactose intolerant and about 1% are sensitive to gluten. Food sensitivity is even more common among those with ADD. The most common food sensitivities are to wheat, corn, soy, milk products, eggs, tree nuts, shellfish, and peanuts.

How do you know if you're sensitive to a food? Start by keeping a careful *food diary*. In some cases, blood testing, skin testing, biopsies (for gluten sensitivity), and elimination diets may be useful (check with your doctor). However, because many reactions are not true allergies in the medical sense, allergy testing could be negative even if a food really does cause a problem. For example, I'm lactose intolerant (so drinking milk makes me bloated), but I'm not actually allergic to milk (I don't get hives or a rash). I rarely recommend conventional allergy testing for foods unless a child has classical allergic symptoms, such as eczema, runny nose, watery eyes, or asthma. However, I often recommend that families keep a food diary to observe the relationship between eating different foods and changes in behavior. Eliminating triggering food(s) can improve mood, behavior, attention, headaches, rashes, constipation, bloating, and nausea.

Studies support the use of few foods or elimination diets (sometimes called oligoantigenic diets) in improving symptoms in over half of children with ADD.[40] An elimination diet typically eliminates all the foods that commonly cause problems: citrus, corn, eggs, dairy, nuts, soy, and wheat, as well as artificial colors, flavors, and sweeteners. All of these foods are avoided for at least two weeks and then slowly reintroduced one at a time every three to four days. If you're not used to it, this is a very restrictive diet that omits most of what Americans consider normal food. (It does allow meat, most fruits, vegetables, beans, seeds, rice, and millet.) Doing an oligoantigenic diet on your own runs the risk of developing a deficiency of one or more essential nutrients. If you decide to try it, please seek professional nutritional help to ensure adequate intakes of essential nutrients while avoiding triggering foods.

Kayla was a healthy teenager who started drinking more milk to make sure she got enough calcium after her grandmother had a hip fracture. Within a week or two, Kayla noticed that she felt bloated and had an embarrassing amount of gas. She was so distracted by her stomach and afraid she was going to explode in class, her grades started to slip. Her parents thought she was just distracted by the stress of her grandmother's hospitalization. But her grandmother quickly figured out the problem. "I found out when I was about your age that milk did that to me too," she told Kayla. Once Kayla figured out that she was lactose intolerant, she switched to a lactose-free brand of milk. As soon as she had the lactose under control, her attention problems evaporated.

Organic or Not?

Although the word *natural* is next to meaningless as a food label, *organic* has a very specific legal definition according to the US Department of Agriculture. Organically raised livestock may not be given hormones or growth-promoting antibiotics. Organic fruits and vegetables are raised without conventional pesticides and without fertilizers made with synthetic ingredients or sewage sludge (yes, that stuff *is* in your conventionally raised produce). A government inspector must certify a farm before its products can be labeled as organic. Companies that produce processed organic foods are also required to undergo federal inspections to be certified. As you might expect, organic crops contain lower levels of pesticides and other agrochemical residues than nonorganic crops.[41] Produce that has the highest levels of pesticide contamination when raised conventionally includes apples, bell peppers, celery, cherries, imported grapes, nectarines and peaches, pears, potatoes, raspberries, spinach, and strawberries (see the Environmental Working Group Internet site for a printable list you can take with you to the grocery store of the produce most/least likely to be contaminated: www.ewg. org). Children who eat organic produce have fewer of these toxic pesticide chemicals in their system than children who eat conventional produce.[42] Children of farmworkers are at particularly high risk of exposure to toxic pesticides. Help reduce their exposure by supporting organic farming.

As modern conventional farming replaced historical practices in the late 20th century, mineral levels in fruits, vegetables, meat, and milk fell. How much? A lot. Up to 76% between 1940 and 1991 according to US government statistics.[43] Organic crops contain significantly more minerals and antioxidants than crops raised with petroleum-derived (so-called conventional) fertilizers.[44-45] Milk from cows that graze on grass (botanically diverse pasture) has higher levels of the essential omega-3 fatty acids than milk from cows that eat grain[46-47]. *Eat organic foods that are low in toxic pesticides and high in essential nutrients.*

More Dietary Tips

Locally grown foods support your local economy, reduce dependence on foreign oil, and lower transportation costs and greenhouse gas emission. Eating locally grown food is patriotic and good for the environment! Local foods are fresher. Fresher foods mean better taste and better nutrition. Plus, when you go to a farmer's market to buy your food, you get to meet the people who grow it. This builds relationships and strengthens our communities.

Avoid foods from developing countries that don't share our standards for growing, handling, labeling, or processing foods. A 2003 FDA study found three times more pesticide violations in imported foods than domestic foods. We don't have enough food inspectors to check more than 2% of shipments to the US. Imported foods may be contaminated with heavy metals, such as lead or mercury, toxic pesticides, illness-causing bacteria or fungi, misidentified plants, or even industrial chemicals, such as the melamine found in formula from China in 2007.

Avoid genetically modified foods. Farmers have practiced genetic *selection* for thousands of years, replanting seeds from their best crops, and promoting reproduction from their best livestock. This is smart farming. Genetic *modification* is vastly different. It inserts genes from one species into another, creating new-to-nature hybrid species. The long-term effects and unintended consequences of this practice are unknown. This is why many European countries are wary of genetically modified foods and stringently regulate labeling of edible products created this way; we should do the same.

Summary of Dietary Do's and Don'ts to Address ADD

Do	Avoid
Drink pure water	Carbonated, sweetened beverages with artificial colors, flavors, or sweeteners
Eat fruits and veggies (fried potatoes don't count)	Fast food
Eat whole grains to keep your blood sugar stable	Processed foods and junk food
Eat foods rich in high quality protein, which contains essential amino acids	Fried foods, foods with trans fats, and foods rich in saturated fats (whole milk, fatty meats)
Eat foods that contain omega-3 fatty acids, olive oil, and other healthy fats	Food dyes and preservatives, pesticides and other chemical additives
Eat locally grown foods	Food imported from developing countries
Eat organic foods rich in essential vitamins and minerals	Genetically modified foods

For easy steps to start and track changes to your child's diet, see chapters 9 and 10.

Optional Activities

Beyond reading, what else would you like to do to address a healthy diet? Here is list of possibilities. Consider doing one or more of the following:

1. Visit your farmer's market. Get to know a local farmer.
2. Plant a garden, or encourage your local school, neighborhood, community, and/or workplace to plant one.
3. Remove all the junk food from your pantry.
4. Keep a food log for one month to look for patterns in your responses to foods.
5. Read food labels.
6. Throw a party serving healthy foods and beverages.

7. Find out how much of your tax dollars go to subsidize corporate farms to produce the corn (high-fructose corn syrup) and soy (oil) that go into junk food. Compare that with subsidies for small farmers in your county who grow organic fruits and vegetables.
8. Sneak more fruits and veggies into your recipes. Check out Missy Chase Lapine's book *The Sneaky Chef,* or Jessica Seinfeld's book *Deceptively Delicious.*
9. Eat at least one more meal a week as a family.
10. Advocate for healthier food in your schools. If school food is not up to your standards, pack a lunch instead.
11. Carry dried fruit and nuts (unsalted) with you on errands so if you get hungry, you can snack on something healthy rather than driving through for fast food.

CHAPTER 5

Second Fundamental: Fitness and Sleep

> Olivia, a 15-year-old gymnast, loved to work out for three to four hours every afternoon. Unfortunately, her high school homework had escalated, and she was staying up until midnight every night just to keep up. The harder she worked, the more disorganized and unfocused she felt during the day. She found her mind wandering, making mistakes on the balance beam that almost ended in catastrophe. Olivia's friends offered her energy drinks to stay focused in the gym, and she drank cola in the evening so she could study, but then it was hard to fall asleep and hard to get up the next day. The first three class periods were a blur. Should Olivia start drinking coffee in the morning to help her through? Her aunt, Kim, asked me what I thought.

OLIVIA WAS WAY ahead of most Americans in terms of getting enough exercise. Most of us would benefit from both more exercise and more sleep. However, when it comes to exercise, more than enough is not necessarily better than just enough. Olivia had picked a great sport to build coordination and balance. However, she was overexercising, leading to an unbalanced life and far too little sleep.

For most of us, vigorous exercise during the day helps us get better, more restful sleep. Being well rested improves attention and the ability to stay organized, be efficient, and stay diligent and productive. How much exercise is enough?

Exercise

Anyone old enough to walk needs a minimum of 30 to sixty minutes of aerobic activity daily. Both young children and grandmothers know what many adults have forgotten: it's good to go outside and play! Exercise outdoors in nature is even better than exercise in a gym or urban setting.[1]

Benefits for Body and Brain

Exercise is good for the whole body. It battles obesity, optimizes blood pressure, and cuts the risk of heart disease, diabetes, cancer, and osteoporosis. Exercise enhances vitality yet makes it easier to sit still when the situation demands it. It improves sleep and serves as a buffer against psychological stress.

Exercise is also good for your brain. Exercise increases levels of brain-derived neurotrophic factor (BDNF), helps build new neurons, creates connections between neurons, and enhances overall cognitive function. Exercise improves mental focus, memory, and academic achievement.

Best Exercise

What kind of exercise is best? Whatever kind is fun, safe, and done often! Running, swimming, biking, skiing, tennis, dancing, and gymnastics are terrific. One of the world's leading experts on brain health, Dr. Daniel Amen, is fond of Ping-Pong. A 2009 study in children with developmental coordination disorder found that regularly playing table tennis was indeed helpful both for their coordination and their ability to sustain focus.[2] Walking the dog, raking leaves, and shoveling snow are not only good exercises, they can improve self-esteem by making a real contribution to the family too. If you feel it's really fun or really worthwhile, you're more likely to stick with it.

New scientific studies suggest that the cerebellum (the part of the brain involved in balance and coordination) is involved in ADD and ADHD. This has led to growing interest in activities that build balance and coordination, such as yoga, juggling, cross-midline exercises, the Interactive Metronome® method, and Brain Gym®. Quiet, mindful exercises such as tai chi and yoga encourage focus on the body as it moves, which make them great choices for people with ADHD. Practicing yoga can improve our ability to focus and be more deliberate and less impulsive.[3] Martial arts training promotes discipline. Try different activities to find out what is most interesting and enjoyable. Change it up to maintain interest and strengthen different skills, muscles, and parts of the brain.

ABCs: Activity Bursts in the Classroom

You don't have to do it all at once. Taking short breaks once an hour to stretch and move can help children and adults stay focused during long days. Dr. David Katz from Yale recommends the ABCs—Activity Bursts in the Classroom (or Corporation). I also favor the idea of Bursts and Breaks. Do work in brief bursts interspersed with breaks. Not enough time for a full game of baseball? Do a few push-ups, sit-ups, or jumping jacks. Organize a walking club at work. Urge your schools to ensure that recess is part of the daily schedule.

Safety

Impulsive, distracted people are particularly prone to injuries. Use your bike helmet when you bike and a ski helmet when you ski. Try small classes with close supervision and low student-teacher ratios (karate, tae kwon do, tai chi, or yoga) to help develop better body awareness and self-discipline.

> I advised Kim that it might be smarter for Olivia to cut back a bit on the gymnastics so she'd have time to finish her homework without so much caffeine. The caffeine was interfering with her sleep, which was making it difficult to focus during her morning classes.

Avoid overuse injuries. Even though exercise is a terrific way to improve attention and a great antiaging strategy, too much of a good thing may *not* be a good thing! Exercising more than two hours a day can interfere with other worthwhile activities such as homework, chores, and sustaining relationships. Exercising just before bed can interfere with sleep. Speaking of sleep . . .

Sleep

Welcome to the 21st century, a time when Americans sleep nearly 10% less than we did in the 19th century. Our bodies just don't adapt that fast. Adults are getting an average of 60-90 minutes less sleep than they need, and teens are often getting two hours less than optimal amounts of sleep. Compared with our ancestors (and our genetic programming), we are sleep deprived.

Effects of Sleep Deprivation

Sleep deprivation makes it hard to focus, to be organized, and to remain diligent and self-disciplined during boring tasks. Inadequate amounts of sleep and poor sleep quality impair attention and judgment, increases fidgeting, lowers performance, and lead to more mistakes, auto collisions, and injuries. Sound familiar? Many people diagnosed with ADD or ADHD find their symptoms resolving almost miraculously when they start sleeping better.

Strategies to Improve Sleep

The three best strategies to improve sleep are the following:

1. Optimize daytime activities,
2. Improve the sleeping environment, and
3. Develop a healthy sleep routine.

1. Optimize Daytime Routines

✓ Exercise vigorously early in the day; if you need an activity break in the evening, go for gentle stretching, yoga, or tai chi.

✓ Use bright lights early and dimmer lighting later in the evening to give your brain and its body clock the signals they need to stay awake and fall asleep at the appropriate times.

✓ Don't go to bed angry. Settle disputes and ask for forgiveness earlier in the day so your emotions don't keep you in turmoil when you should be turning over.

✓ Don't drink caffeinated beverages within six hours before bedtime. Some people need up to 12 hours to metabolize the caffeine. Think about when you want to go to bed and adjust your beverage schedule accordingly.

✓ Don't drink alcohol within three hours of your planned bedtime. Alcohol causes sleepiness initially, but two to four hours later, it leads to rebound wakefulness.

✓ Keep electronic work and entertainment (TV, Internet, or electronic games) under an hour a day.* If you must work at a computer, stop doing it two hours before you plan to go to bed. Studies in children show that the more TV, video games, and Internet surfing children do, the worse their sleep.[4-5]

---

* For most Americans, that's a huge decrease from current levels. School-age children spend on average more than seven hours daily with electronic media (TV, computer, video games, etc.)[4]. In contrast, they read for less than 45 minutes a day.

- ✓ Learn and practice a stress-management technique such as meditation, guided imagery, or progressive relaxation (see chapter 7). Keeping your stress levels manageable during the day will make it easier to fall asleep at night.
- ✓ Here's one of my favorite prescriptions: regularly get a massage or back rub from someone you trust. Massage can improve sleep and attention. Massage not only feels good; scientific studies support its use for improving ADD symptoms.[6-7]

2. Improve the Sleeping Environment

- ✓ Keep the room cool, dark, and comfortable. Night-lights interfere with deep sleep and melatonin production. Make sure the mattress and bedclothes are comfortable.
- ✓ Get the TV out of the bedroom, and do not listen to dance music or sing-along stations when you're trying to sleep. Instead, listen to soft, soothing instrumentals or nature sounds.
- ✓ Consider using relaxing fragrances, such as lavender, roses, or chamomile. Avoid artificial chemical fragrances; they can be irritating to some people.
- ✓ Pick up the clutter. Organize your desk or dresser so you aren't lying in bed thinking of all your chores instead of sleeping.
- ✓ Do not use your bed as a workplace, to talk on the phone, or play electronic games. Train your mind that the bed is for sleep.

3. Develop a Healthy Sleeping Routine

- ✓ Do the same things in the same order every night.
- ✓ Go to bed at the same time every night. If you never feel rested in the morning, try heading to bed an hour earlier than you usually do.
- ✓ Consider eating a light snack containing a protein (such as a handful of nuts) and a carbohydrate (juice or fruit) one to two hours before bed.
- ✓ Take a warm bath or shower before bed to relax your muscles.
- ✓ Consider having a cup of calming herbal tea, such as chamomile, lemon balm, hops, mint, or passionflower.
- ✓ Keep a journal. Draw, write down, or record any worries, anger, irritations, or other negative perceptions. Get them out of your head, then set them aside and let them wait until tomorrow.

- ✓ Relax. Read something soothing, reassuring, or inspiring. Count your blessings. Note the things you appreciate or for which you are grateful.
- ✓ Talk with your health professional about trying natural supplements, such as theanine (a calming amino acid found in green tea), valerian (an herbal sedative that smells like sweaty gym socks but works well), or a short trial of melatonin (one to three milligrams per night). Melatonin can help reset the biological clock for those suffering from jet lag or delayed-sleep-phase syndrome.

Review your medications (even nonprescription cold medicines). Stimulant medications (and coffee) frequently cause insomnia. On the other hand, suddenly stopping some medications can cause insomnia too. When in doubt, talk with your health professional.

> Olivia spoke with her coach about cutting back on her gymnastic workouts to two hours on school days so she could keep up with her homework without staying up until midnight. Although she was worried about losing her edge, Olivia's workouts actually became more productive with fewer missteps and falls, so she lost less time to injuries. It was easier to wake up in the morning, and she found new interest in her morning classes too.

For an easy way to start and track healthy fitness and sleep routines that work for *your* family, see chapters 9 and 10.

Optional Activities:

1. Play the I-like-to-move-it-move-it game at school. Tap fingers while spelling. Do jumping jacks while reciting multiplication tables. Play beanbag-toss games while playing question-and-answer games in social studies. Turn a spelling bee into a relay race.
2. Think of ways to incorporate movement into daily chores or activities.

CHAPTER 6

Third Fundamental: Friendship with Others—Communication Skills, Being a Good Role Model, and Behavioral Strategies

FRIENDSHIPS AND NURTURING family relationships are fundamental to physical and mental health. Clear communication and effective behavioral strategies are critical for creating greater attentiveness and self-discipline over the long term. Good communication includes being a good role model, listening and paying attention to others, and meaning what you say (following through). Consistent, clear, compassionate communication helps others to learn that you trust them, and they can trust you. It builds relationships. It demonstrates that you are a person worth paying attention to. It shows that you are a person whose attention is desirable, who deserves respect and emulation. Through your example, others can learn to manage their inner impulses, enhance self-discipline, and develop forethought. Compassionate communication is the gift that keeps on giving.

No Means No—Learning Limits and Managing Frustration

Skillful communication and consistent behavior helps others learn that *no means no*. No does not mean that if you whine, beg, negotiate, scream, threaten, or become violent, you will eventually get what you think you want right now.

Hearing no is frustrating and disappointing. As parents and teachers, we don't want to make life difficult for anyone. However, avoiding setting limits deprives children of learning how to develop internal discipline and deal effectively with frustration. We need to say no clearly and compassionately to help children master the skills they need to become responsible, thoughtful adults.

Those who hear no—who have not yet learned that it is a reliable limit—will predictably try to test that limit to get a less frustrating answer. Testing limits is an essential human task to learn about the world and how we can function in it. Learning about limits helps us learn self-discipline and the forethought to look before we leap. Let's look at several communication skills to help develop desirable skills such as self-discipline, forethought, and empathy.

Communicating Expectations, Rules, and Limits: Clear and Concrete

Rules and expectations are easiest to understand if they are clear and concrete. Look at the common tasks and two types of communication in Table 6.1. Which would be easier for you to follow? Specific, unambiguous expectations help focus attention. They also make it easier to identify and praise success or make a correction later.

Table 6.1 Communicating Expectations Clearly

Task	Unclear, Vague (Problematic because . . .)	Clear, Concrete
Bedtime	Go to bed. (*when?*)	Bedtime is 8:00 p.m.
Meals	Peas are really healthy for us. (*Information or expectation?*) I worked hard to make healthy food for you. (*Request for appreciation, assistance, or what?*)	Finish all the peas on your plate *or* eat three bites of each item on your plate.
Hygiene	Good girls brush their teeth. (*Information, value judgment, or expectation?*)	Brush your teeth and then floss before we leave for school.
Entertainment	You're watching too much TV. (*How much? Why? Specific action?*)	You can play a computer game for 20 minutes after you finish your homework and chores.
Shopping	What happened to the $50 I gave you last week for a new shirt? (*Request for accounting, advice, invitation to go shopping?*)	Here is $50 for you to spend on clothing, meals, and entertainment for the next two weeks.

Exercise	Exercise is good for you. (*Information or advice?*)	Go outside and play. Come back at 6:00 p.m. to wash up and set the table for dinner.
Chores	Try to help out. (*How? What? When?*)	Bring your clothes to the washing machine after you make your bed.

Use Authoritative Language

We like to be liked. For some of us, it sounds very harsh to be directive, and it is not always appropriate (e.g., with peers or colleagues when we are not in charge). Over the long run, our goal is cooperation, not blind obedience. However, if you're an authority in a situation in which you expect obedience (not a negotiation)—that is, if you are a parent or a teacher—it is helpful to use clear, authoritative language. Learning obedience helps children develop internal expectations and behave in ways that are consistent with those expectations. In the long run, authoritative language helps children develop a sense of self-mastery and self-esteem that promotes real cooperation.

Table 6.2 Authoritative Language

Avoid	Because	Authoritative Language
How about if you . . . ?

Would you . . . ? | This implies that the listener has a choice. It invites a *no!* | Give directions using positive action verbs: Clean up, pick up, study, write, put away, complete, turn in, finish, keep your eyes on your paper, keep your hands to yourself, etc. |
| If you get a chance, could you . . . | This implies choice, lacks a time frame, or contingency for behavior. | After you do X, we can all do Y. |

I wish you would . . . I hope you will . . . When I was a child . . .	This informs about your wishes, hopes, or history, not their behavior—implies choice.	It's time for you to . . . X is your responsibility. You need to . . .
Don't be foolish.	This labels child and doesn't tell them what *to* do.	Before you get in the car, make sure you have keys, license, and registration.

Be SMART—Make your Expectations Specific, Measurable, Achievable, Relevant, and Timely

Clear, authoritative language includes making requests *specific*. For example, asking her to put the clothes (currently on the floor) into the hamper (where they belong) is more specific than asking her to clean her room. Being specific helps you track or *measure* whether or not it was done. Be sure the request is something your child *can actually achieve*. You cannot expect most five-year-olds to practice the piano for 60 uninterrupted minutes. Focus requests on behaviors that are positive and *relevant* to the child's life. "Please play in the family room" is better than "Don't touch the papers on my desk." Including a *time* element helps improve specificity and measurement (e.g., "Spend 15 minutes on spelling" is much better than "Improve your grades." "Curfew is 11:00 p.m." is more measurable than "Get home at a reasonable hour.").

In his book *Parenting Children with ADHD*, Dr. Vincent Monastra lists the top things he's heard parents say they'd like their child to learn. They include home skills such as getting up in the morning without a battle, eating breakfast that includes some protein, making the bed, keeping the bedroom tidy, brushing teeth, and going to bed at bedtime. They also include school-related skills such as remaining seated when asked to do so, staying quiet unless called on, doing assigned homework, and keeping school materials organized. The last group of skills are related to social interactions and communication skills and solving disagreements peacefully without arguing with parents, listening respectfully, apologizing when appropriate, taking responsibility for behavior, offering to make amends for problems caused, and expressing thoughts and feelings without using obscenities or vulgarity.

How many of those sound worthwhile to you? All of them? Great! It's best to start by focusing on one or two top priorities. Remember, Rome wasn't built in a day. It typically takes three to six weeks to learn and establish a new behavior pattern. If the chore is too complex for him at this time or for his developmental stage, break it down.

Break It Down

Break down new or complex jobs into achievable smaller tasks. Over time, you can add the smaller pieces together into a complex task. For example, setting the table can start with putting the plates at each setting. Later, the napkins, cutlery, beverages, condiments, and serving dishes can be added step by step.

When Charles loaded the plates in the dishwasher for the first time, he went straight from the table to the nearest open space in the machine. Jill, a skillful mom, beamed and thanked him for helping. Then she asked, "Charles, do you think the machine would have an easier time cleaning these dishes if we scraped and rinsed them first? Or do you think it's strong enough to get them clean just the way they are? Let's do an experiment. I'll scrape and rinse one. See? Now you show me one. Good! Now let's see how it does with those two compared with the ones we didn't scrape. What do you think will happen? Which plates will be cleanest?" She didn't overwhelm him by making him scrape and rinse the whole lot or giving him her own special tips on optimal arrangements: how to add soap or set the timer. She engaged him in one question as a process of discovery they undertook together. Later that day, Charles asked her if the dishes were done yet. He wanted to see what happened! By engaging his curiosity in one part of the process, Charles was motivated to master the rest. Jill is a masterful mom, and she promotes responsibility and her child's sense of mastery. As a side benefit, the dishes were just as clean when they weren't rinsed first, so Charles' experiment eventually saved Jill time, water, and effort, too.

Try not. Do . . . or do not. There is no try.
—Yoda, Star Wars Episode V

The word *try* implies that there is some doubt about the outcome. Avoid saying, "Try to sit still for 15 minutes" or "Try to practice the piano." This implies you doubt that she is able to sit still or play the piano and sets her up for failure. If you really don't expect her to be able to sit still, don't ask her to! Give her a task she *can* master. For example, say, "Sit still while the dentist counts your teeth," or "Practice the piano for ten minutes, then come help me finish making dinner."

Managing Predictable Responses to Limits and Expectations

Are clear directions and authoritative language guaranteed to give you unquestioning obedience 100% of the time? No! They are definitely more effective than vague requests or *try* directions. As human beings with free will, most of us prefer our own ideas to someone else's rules. We also prefer to be invited, to be asked, and to voluntarily offer our cooperation as an appreciated gift. You can count on the fact that under some conditions, even the best-behaved children and youth will do one of the following:

Test Limits and Rules

When is a rule really a rule? A rule is really a rule when it has clear, concrete, predictable, reliable consequences. To find out whether rules are really rules or (as they say of the pirates' code in *Pirates of the Caribbean)* "they're really more like guidelines," people will test them.

Gravity rules. One-year-old Tonya drops her cup over the tray of her high chair. It falls. Her mom picks it up and puts it back on the tray. Tonya drops it. It falls. No matter how many times Tonya drops it, the cup falls. Eventually, Tonya's mom puts the cup out of Tonya's reach. But Tonya isn't finished yet. Next she drops her spoon! It falls too! Tonya is testing the rule of gravity. It is really a rule, not a guideline. No matter how often she does it or what object she drops, gravity keeps working. It does not get angry with her for repeating the experiment or changing on different days. By the time Tonya turns two years old, she has thoroughly tested the rule of gravity in relation to dropping objects from her tray. She stops testing it (at least intentionally); it still works even when she's not testing it intentionally (e.g., when she learns to ride a bike). Knowing that rules have consistent consequences gives a sense of order and predictability to the world and helps us find and nurture our internal organization.

Children Are Scientists: They Experiment

Children are small scientists. You may explain the theory of gravity, but they are not satisfied with this theory until they have run a few experiments on their own. Having tested gravity to their satisfaction long ago, most moms are soon bored with the dropping experiment. Eventually Mom says, "That's it. No more. I'm not picking it up again." What happens? Well, here's another theory to test: Mom means what she says. Is that theory true? Let's drop it again. Will she pick it up? If she picks it up, there is evidence refuting the theory. Mom does not always mean what she says. A no is not always a no.

What if Mom *is* reliable? She does not pick it up! Next the child will likely test the theory again in another way to find out just how reliable, predictable, and self-disciplined Mom is by the following:

Initial Limit-Testing Strategies: Looking Cute, Whining, Begging, or Crying

Human beings are very determined scientists when it comes to testing the rules of physics and human behavior. When Mom stops picking up the object, the infant will test her to see if she will change her mind. He may grin, try to look cute, or look down at the object and back at Mom. If he knows a few words, he may use them. "Pleeeeeeeease?" or "Again!" If that doesn't work, he may bang his tray, bang his head, cry, or scream. Is this a bad child? No, all of these are perfectly normal, predictable methods of testing whether the theory of Mom's reliability holds up under varying conditions. You can acknowledge what your child is doing without giving in. "I see you smiling, I hear you asking. I see that you are disappointed, frustrated, or angry. I love you, and I'm all done playing the dropping game."

Obviously, changing your mind once or twice does not scar your child for life or make him believe the world is an untrustworthy, unpredictable place or that you are easily manipulated. However, the more disciplined and consistent you can be, the less he will need to test you. You will be rewarded with less (not zero, but less) whining, begging, and crying later on. And your child can learn from you how to be reliable, consistent, and disciplined regardless of what happens externally. ("No, I really don't want that cigarette." "No, I really don't want to find out how thrilling shoplifting can be.")

If you get frustrated with his experiments and lash out with a loud, angry voice, threats, throwing something, or slapping him, he will learn that an adult response to frustration is anger or violence. This is probably not what you want him to learn. Reflect on how you respond to your child's limit testing. Consider how you can demonstrate desirable responses to frustration and help your child learn self discipline.

Give 'Em Three—Use an Early-Warning System

For toddlers and preschool children, when you want to get focus and attention quickly and prevent the testing response, count to three. Out loud. Slowly. Consistently using a standard count (as a warning that a consequence is about to happen if he does not respond) is an easy way of helping your child focus and plan his actions accordingly. Sometimes he may be wrapped up in his own world or may think your request was more like a suggestion or a game. Counting alerts him to the fact that you are serious, and it gives you an opportunity to remain cool and collected while you consider your options. If you get to three and he has not responded, there is an automatic penalty (time-out, loss of privileges). Counting to three is a very effective strategy with young children.

> Billy and his dad were building forts one evening when his dad realized it was nearly Billy's bedtime. "OK, Billy. Let's put away the toys and take down the forts now. It's time for you to get ready for bed." Billy jumped on his dad and started tickling. Dad remained calm, his face grew serious, and he lowered his voice. "One . . ." Pause. "Two . . ." Before Dad got to "three," Billy got down and started picking up toys. "That's great, Billy. I really like how quickly you paid attention and started helping me pick things up. Your mom and I are proud of how your listening has improved."

When you exhibit reliability, predictability, self-control, and self-discipline, you help your loved one learn those skills. When you observe his behavior and empathize with his feelings, he feels understood and doesn't need to escalate. Be as calm and consistent as gravity. If this is difficult for you, plenty of help is available from pediatricians, peers, psychologists, and counselors. Expect your child to test the rules. After all, she tested gravity. It's human nature. Testing rules and limits is normal, predictable, and healthy.

As they get older, children develop a broader repertoire for testing. As parents and teachers, we need to develop the skills to respond in ways that continue to support their mastery of self-discipline, self-control, patience, and forethought.

Advanced Limit Testing Strategies

Older children develop and use a variety of strategies to test limits. This is not bad; it is normal expected behavior. When you say, "No, I said all the peas, and I meant all the peas," you can expect (at least the first few times) bargaining, rationalizing, comparing, or attempting to distract you. The more often one of these strategies works, the more likely they will be used in the future.

> *"Eat all the peas on your plate before you eat dessert."*

Bargaining

> *"How about if I eat all the carrots and the rest of my milk instead of the peas?" "What if I eat double serving of brussel sprouts tomorrow?" "What if I wash the dishes instead?"*

Rationalizing

> *"But I hate peas. You really shouldn't have served them."*
> *"These peas are overcooked/undercooked" or, for some other reason, "are inedible."*

Comparing

> *"James's mom doesn't make him eat vegetables."*
> *"You never made me eat vegetables before."*

Distracting

> *"Maria is teasing the dog."*
> *"I have to go to the bathroom."*

KATHI J. KEMPER, MD, MPH

It's Not About the Peas!

Your child is not just learning your views on the value of eating peas, he is also learning to recognize and accept emotions and the self-discipline needed to handle frustration, disgust, fear, and disappointment. It's not about you; it's not about the peas. It's an opportunity to practice emotional self-awareness and self-discipline.

Remain as Calm, Emotionally Neutral, and Impartial as Gravity

You may notice aloud: "You feel mad when I remind you to eat the peas." By naming his emotion, you are helping him recognize and respond to his feelings. The next time he feels frustrated, disappointed, or some other unpleasant emotion, he can remember that it is possible to remain calm while observing his emotions. You don't need to avoid him or react impulsively in anger (flight or fight). Instead you can say, "I understand. We all feel mad sometimes when we have to do things we don't enjoy." He can learn that he also doesn't have to avoid or act on his emotions impulsively. The rule doesn't necessarily need to change, and he doesn't have to enjoy the rule. You are teaching him about something much more important than peas.

Demonstrate Compassionate Consistency, Not Fight or Flight

It can be stressful to watch someone feel frustrated, angry, scared, or sad. You may want to react to this stress with a flight (leaving the room or giving in) or fight (yelling, arguing, trying to make him feel guilty, or comparing him to other children) response. These are understandable reactions, but there are more skillful ways to coach him on how to handle negative emotions. He may not realize it, but testing a limit helps him learn to handle his frustration. He is giving you an opportunity to demonstrate a patient, self-controlled, calm, deliberate response to an unpleasant situation. When you show him that you can be consistent *and* loving, disciplined *and* accepting, he learns life's best lessons about empathy.

The Power of Empathy

A word of kindness and understanding can work wonders. We most need empathy and acceptance when we feel we least deserve it. By empathizing, you help him learn to respect himself and respond to his emotions with clarity and skill.*

Another way to show empathy is to paraphrase what you have heard and repeat it to make sure you've understood. If a child says he hates homework, you can say, "I understand that you really don't like homework." Just knowing that someone understands can decrease the stress. It also gives him an opportunity to elaborate before you jump in with a solution based on incomplete understanding.

Once he feels understood, he may offer the reason why he dislikes it. "Yeah, I hate homework because it takes too long." You might then respond, "So if it was shorter, you wouldn't mind so much?" If he agrees, you can suggest he do his work in short increments with built-in breaks and praise for working diligently. If, on the other hand, he says he hates it because he doesn't understand, you can offer to help him by listening to him read the directions out loud or reading them together or helping in some other way. By empathizing, you are building an alliance and helping him master problem-solving strategies.

Responding to Escalation, Threats, or Violence

Parents and teachers occasionally encounter children whose frustration and limit testing escalates to behaviors that may be disrespectful, dishonest, or dangerous. These include name-calling ("You are mean. You're not fair. You're a bad cook. You are stupid."); yelling; lying (hiding the peas or getting rid of them when your back is turned); threatening himself or you or an object ("If you make me eat these peas, I will gag myself and throw up."); or violent behavior such as breaking something, hitting, or biting.

As the adult, it's your job to decide which behaviors are unacceptable and what the consequences will be. You can remain as calm as gravity without behaving in ways that are inconsistent with your core values. Be prepared to deliver an immediate consequence of sufficient magnitude to discourage such behaviors in the future. John Rosemond, author of *The Well-Behaved Child*, calls this the Godfather Principle: make him an offer he can't refuse. Advance preparation will help you state and carry through with the consequence calmly and avoid demonstrating undesirable behaviors yourself.

---

*   For more information on the power of empathy and emotional coaching, see Dr. John Gottman's book *Raising an Emotionally Intelligent Child*.

KATHI J. KEMPER, MD, MPH

Stacy's son, Ryan, was a big 14-year-old who had struggled since first grade with impulsivity and hyperactivity. She had separated from his father when Ryan was 11, and Ryan had become increasingly disrespectful and defiant, calling her names and threatening to go live with his father if she didn't give him what he wanted. After reading about the benefits of a healthier diet and less television, Stacy decided to remove the television from his bedroom, stop buying junk food, and decrease the fast-food restaurant routine from three times a week to once a week. But she feared Ryan's reaction. So she planned ahead, prepared to follow through, and sought support. She called their pastor and Ryan's homeroom teacher, told them what she planned, and asked for their help. She also let his dad know so he'd hear it from her first. She removed the TV from Ryan's room and threw out all the junk food before he got home from school. And she prepared a Godfather Principle-type offer. After he'd had a snack, she told Ryan she had talked with a doctor, their pastor, his teacher, and his dad about ways to help him succeed in school. She empathized with him, noting that he probably wouldn't like it, but the changes in diet and TV were her decision as his mother. As Stacy expected, when Ryan heard the new deal, he blew his lid, calling her names and threatening to break her favorite porcelain doll unless she changed her mind. Stacy stayed calm and responded, "I know you don't like the situation, but it is not acceptable for you to call me names or make threats. You have now lost the privilege of watching any TV and playing any games on the PS3 for the next month. If you continue to argue, it will be two months. Three strikes and the TV and PS3 go to Goodwill. Now take a deep breath, count to ten, and go to your room for the rest of the night to think of how you might handle yourself in the future." Ryan was shocked. He went to his room grumbling. He tried calling his dad to complain, but his dad, anticipating the call, backed Stacy.

Prepare to follow through. He may storm off or return to bargaining, whining, apologizing, promising not to do it again, or crying. If he apologizes and promises not to do it again, accept his apology, praise his positive intention for the future, *and* follow through with the consequence. If you think you might forget the date privileges resume, jot a note on the calendar. "If Ryan calmly cooperates, he gets TV today."

Set the Stage for Success

When it comes to sports, enroll your youngster in individual or small-team activities with close adult supervision such as tennis rather than events involving large fields where attention easily wanders. If you go on a tour, encourage her to stand as close to the leader as possible to help her focus on the guide rather than wander off. Ask the teacher to seat her close to the front of the room and next to a child who models good behavior. Plan ahead, anticipate challenges, use your resources, ask for help, and make backup plans!

Avoid Forbidden Fruit

Humans find forbidden fruit much more tempting than any other kind. Just ask Adam and Eve. Even with a perfect Parent and garden full of delights, knowing that there was one thing they could not have led to the first episode of disobedience and denial of responsibility. The same thing happened later according to the Greeks when Pandora opened the forbidden box. As adults, there are things we must forbid to keep our children safe. We cannot allow them to put their fingers in sockets, take food away from a dog while it is eating, jump off a roof, etc.

How can we minimize the forbidden fruits problem? Here are three strategies: (a) modify the environment, (b) set standards, and (c) identify and enforce clear, consistent consequences.

A. Modify the Environment

This is the obvious strategy for protecting toddlers and young children. Putting safety gates across stairways, locks on cabinets, and pot handles turned toward the back of the stove protects youngsters from the damaging consequences of their natural curiosity. For older children and teens, modifying the environment is also effective. Remove the TV from the child's bedroom, put a lock on it, unplug it, or remove it from the house. If you've changed the environment, you do not need to forbid the behavior.

B. Set Standards

This is another useful alternative to forbidding. It makes the desired object or activity attainable, which decreases some of its allure.

KATHI J. KEMPER, MD, MPH

When Brianna hit her teenage years, she started staying up later and later and having a harder time getting up in the morning. Her mom, Michelle, grew exasperated. "She can't just stay up all night!" I replied that if someone told me I couldn't stay up all night, I'd probably want to try simply because it was forbidden. Was there another way she could tell Brianna what she thought was healthier and better for her school attendance? She thought a minute. "Yes, I can tell her that bedtime for a 14-year-old in our house is 9:30 p.m., and if she helps with the dishes, she can stay up reading in bed until 10:00 p.m." Brianna had one smart mom! Michelle had managed to turn a limit into a privilege.

You can set arbitrary standards (bedtime, curfew) as well as use legal standards (state law says you need to be at least 16 years old to drive on the highway); you can also set behavioral or financial standards (you can read whatever book you like after you finish your homework, or you can have the new game for your system when you've saved enough money to pay for it). Communicating standards instead of rules reduces the resistance you might encounter to *you can't*.

C. Anticipate Potential Consequences

This strategy helps us learn how to think things through before jumping in. "If you jump off a building, you will fall." This is an important strategy for minimizing impulsivity. Identify upcoming events. Anticipate possible decisions the child will face and how he can make the smartest choices.

One late summer day, Denise's son Dylan asked if he could go ride bikes down the street with his best friend, Nate. "Sure, you can go ride your bike with Nate until 7:30 p.m. Before you go, let's think for a minute. If you ride your bike without a helmet, what could happen?" Dylan answered, "Aw, Mom, you worry too much. I'm a great rider. I never fall. I'll be fine." Denise responded warmly, "Oh yes, I've seen you ride, and I know you're very good. I've also seen how fast cars can go on that street, and with the sun at this angle, it may be hard for them to see you. Even if you're the best biker in the world, you can't control the sun or those crazy drivers. You can control the steps you take to protect yourself and play smart by using a helmet every time you ride." Dylan agreed. When he found Nate, he told Nate to get his helmet too. "It's just the smart thing to do," he explained.

Anticipate common situations in which your child has been impulsive or distracted. *Imagine* together what the consequences would be like for different kinds of behavior. *Practice* the scenario in advance of the real event. For example: "Let's pretend we are going to the grocery store." If you plan to help your child learn to stop picking up candy at the check-out counter and the consequence is to leave without buying her favorite cereal, practice together in your imaginations first. You can reinforce the imaginary practice with a real but brief practice trip to the store just for the cereal. This will make it easier to *follow through* on the consequence than if you have a huge load of groceries and expect company for dinner soon. *Anticipate the situation, imagine together different behaviors and consequences, practice, and follow through.*

Table 6.3 Anticipating Activities, Behaviors, and Consequences: ABCs

Activity	Behavior (what will happen if . . .)	Consequence
Grocery store with candy at check-out counter.	A. Hannah picks up candy and starts to eat it without permission.	Leave without buying cereal.
	B. Hannah looks at the candy but doesn't touch it even though she wants it.	Hannah and Mom are proud of her self-control. She gets to pick cereal.
Abigail comes over to play with Hannah playing at your house.	A. Fighting over toys.	Hannah and Abigail are asked to solve it themselves. If not, Abigail goes home immediately.
	B. Both children want the same toy. What else can they do?	Each take turns for two minutes. Parents are proud.
Playing ball in backyard.	A. Break a neighbor's window.	Apologize to neighbor. Pay for window. (May need to do extra chores to earn money.) Wash the windows on our house. No ball for two weeks.
	B. What can you do to prevent injury or damage?	B. Play in park. Play a different game in backyard. We are proud of ourselves.

Anticipating potentially challenging situations and identifying consequences for different kinds of behaviors helps us overcome impulsivity. Imagining a scenario out of the heat of the moment develops the capacity to plan ahead and prevent problems. It also dramatically reduces whining, begging, and bargaining. It is much easier to be as calm and reliable as gravity if you have planned and practiced in advance.

An ounce of practice beforehand is worth
a pound of preaching after.
(Proverb)

Anticipating challenging situations, possible behaviors, and their consequences can also be very helpful in later life. Teenagers and adults are beset with numerous temptations: sex, smoking, drinking, drug use, shoplifting, and other risky behaviors. An excellent form of immunization against these risks is anticipating them, imagining how they might unfold, the consequences of different choices, and role-playing with parents or peers.

Make Backup Plans

Making backup or contingency plans helps us learn to think ahead and anticipate challenges, reducing impulsive actions induced by stress. For example, if your family is planning a picnic for the weekend, ask your child for ideas about what to do if it rains. If the store doesn't carry brand X, what might be a good second choice? If traffic might cause delays, will we leave earlier than usual to make sure of getting there on time, or should we just hope for the best? If Dad can't pick you up, will you walk home, or ask Mr. Smith for a ride? If tickets are sold out, what else could we do? Engage your active child or adolescent in making the plans, preparing for backups, and anticipating the consequences if things don't unfold as hoped.

The Power of "Let's"

Let's play. Let's run. Let's go to the store. Let's visit the park. Whenever we use the word *let's*, we're inviting someone to join us. Inviting is much easier to hear than commanding, and it demonstrates our connection and support. Even chores are more pleasant when we do them together. "Let's fold the laundry. Let's make dinner. Let's walk the dog." Let's be sure that when we invite someone to join us, we don't abandon him or her to finish the chore alone. Let's be trustworthy!

KATHI J. KEMPER, MD, MPH

Reduce Resistance, Build Cooperation

Equal to the allure of forbidden fruit is resistance to coercion: "If I hafta, I don't wanna." Good communication can help reduce resistance and build cooperation. Providing information, predictability, and options helps others feel part of and invested in the process. Asking questions or involving them in a task also reduces resistance. Practicing these skills together is another great way of helping someone learn to anticipate events, pay attention, and act deliberately and cooperatively.

Table 6.4 Communicating to Encourage Cooperation and Positive Anticipation

Encourage Cooperation	Example: Doing Errands Together
Give information.	First we're going to the post office, then to the bank, and then the grocery store.
Ask a question.	Do you think the postal worker will be a man or a woman? Do you think we'll see someone we know at the grocery store, or will we meet a new friend?
Involve them in the task.	When we're at the grocery store, please help me find the ripest tomatoes and the best bunch of bananas. Tell me when you have to use the restroom so I can take you.
Give choices in which you can accept either outcome.	We need to get two fresh vegetables for dinner. Which two would you like? We need to get a loaf of whole wheat bread; please read the ingredient list on these three loaves and pick the one that looks healthiest to you.

Use Solution-Focused Language

Asking questions helps children learn to solve problems responsibly. The key to these kinds of questions is to focus the child's attention on the goal or solution rather than the problem. For example, rather than ask "Who left these socks on the floor?" ask "Are you going to put these socks in your laundry basket or in the washing machine?"

Be careful how you ask the questions. *If you don't want to deal with a no, don't ask a question that can be answered with* no. I learned this the hard way as a young pediatrician. If I said, "I'd like to look in your ear, OK?" and the child said no, I was stuck! I either had to skip the ear exam and be incomplete, or override their choice and get help holding them down as they struggled. Finally I learned in a hypnosis workshop the power of choices. "Left or right ear first? Sitting on Mommy's lap or up on the table? Leaning against Daddy's chest or sitting up straight on your own?" Learning to give choices has made physical exams much easier for me and my patients.

Table 6.5. Solution-Focused Questions

Problem Focused	Solution-Focused questions
What's wrong?	What's your goal?
Isn't that too much?	What is a reasonable first step? What else do you need to get started?
What caused it?	How can you fix it?
Who is to blame?	What can you do to correct it?
Will you fail?	What will it take to succeed?
Can't you ever get it right?	What did you learn from this to help you do better next time?
Why are you telling me this?	Would you like me to do something, offer a suggestion, or just listen as you work through it out loud?
Why didn't you ask me?	How would you like me to help?

Repeating and Writing

You can build rapport and confidence by repeating what you heard him choose. Express confidence in his plan, your willingness to support him, and your parameters or constraints. "I heard you choose to do your math homework first, then spelling. Great choice! I can help you from 6:30 to 7:00 p.m." For older children, teens, and adults, you can strengthen their commitment by having them jot down what they have agreed to do; writing also helps us remember when we're distracted by other activities to get back on track with commitments we've made to ourselves.

I keep a whiteboard in my kitchen so we can jot items for the grocery list, chores that need to be done, and phone calls to make. At work we keep a giant to-do list with all our team's activities and projects, key coworkers on each project, deadlines, and what each of us is working on this week and this month, as well as recurrent tasks. Our team reviews the list weekly to help us stay organized and anticipate areas where we can help each other.

Communicating Organizational Skills

One of the hallmarks of having ADD is having trouble organizing stuff. Stuff means times, tasks, things, thoughts, and emotions. That's a lot of stuff to organize!

To help manage time, keep a calendar handy, noting important family, work, school, and community events. Place clocks (set to the same time) all over the house. Create routines and predictability. For example, identify one day each week as grocery day, another day as bill-paying day, one night as family-game night, one night as friends-time night, etc. Put them on the calendar every week. Make bedtimes, mealtimes, toothbrushing, homework, reading, phone calls to distant family, and other events routine.

To help manage tasks, keep a grocery list or list of chores where everyone in the family can see them. Consider making a chart or wheel of household chores. Help your child learn to anticipate when a test is coming up, what's needed to prepare, and make a list of tasks needed for test prep for the week before the test. Congratulate your child on each task completed. Focus on accomplishments.

Organizing the Day

Consider making a chart of a typical day's activities (with separate charts for weekend days or holidays), and post it where your child will see it. Some people make sticker charts to provide concrete rewards for completing each task on time. Here's a sample schedule for a child who goes to bed at 9:00 p.m. and gets up at 6:45 a.m. on school days. Notice that homework is divided into several fifteen-minute segments.

Time	Activity
6:45 a.m.	Wake up, go to bathroom, get dressed
7:00 a.m.	Breakfast
7:15 a.m.	Brush teeth, gather school materials
7:30 a.m.	Leave for school
8:00 a.m. to 3:00 p.m.	School
3:15 p.m.	Home, snack
3:30 p.m.	Play outside
4:15 p.m.	Homework
4:30 p.m.	Chores
4:45 p.m.	Homework
5:00 p.m.	Activity, play, or practice
5:15 p.m.	Homework
5:30 p.m.	Chores, practice, or activity
5:45 p.m.	Activity
6:00 p.m.	Help with dinner, eat, clean up
7:00 p.m.	Homework or chores, put schoolwork into book bag, get all permission slips signed and into book bag
7:30 p.m.	Play quietly
8:00 p.m.	Start getting ready for bed, lay things out for tomorrow, check calendar and to-do list
9:00 p.m.	Lights out

Organizing Homework, Chores, Practice, or Tasks

It may be helpful to divide things into smaller time intervals or to make separate checklists for more complex activities.

For example, homework might involve the following:

— Take homework out of book bag and put it on the table.
— Review assignment sheet and deadlines.
— Pick one subject to do first. Put other materials away.
— Do work.
— Double-check work. Make sure name is on top of paper.

— Put homework in homework folder and replace in book bag.
— Check clock to plan next activity—more homework or break for activity, chores, snack, or something else?

Here's a practice plan for piano.

Sample Piano Practice Plan

— Sit down at piano bench; set timer for _____ minutes.
— Get out books for assigned pieces. Decide what order to play them.
— Play through first piece slowly with both hands.
— Play right hand only.
— Play left hand only.
— Repeat difficult or challenging parts of piece very slowly.
— Repeat difficult measures or sections again, slightly faster.
— Play through first piece again with both hands.
— Play something fun as fast or slow as you like.
— Repeat.
— Make notes to ask for help or fingerings as desired—in pencil—on the book or paper.
— Play scales, chords, or other practice pieces.
— Play something fun as fast or slow as you like.

Congratulations!
You are mastering the piano—a skill to enjoy your whole life!

Organizing Transitions

Transitions from one activity to the next may be very easy for impulsive children, but often, children dislike ending activities such as playing with friends, ending a game, leaving a party, or turning off the television. Faced with a transition, it is helpful to give some advance notice. Here's an example of leaving a party or playdate: "We will be leaving in ten minutes. Time for you to take last turns, tidy up, and find your coat." Here's an example for ending TV time: "TV time ends in five minutes." A few minutes later, remind him, "TV time is over in one minute." Or if you're trying to get everyone ready to leave the house, say, "We will leave in ten minutes. Time to use the restroom, wash hands, brush your teeth." A few minutes later, say, "We will leave in five minutes. Time to get your coat, shoes, and backpack." Then say,

"We are leaving in one minute. Get what you need and get in the car now." This makes it easier for the child to hear: it's time now to finish, leave, stop, turn off, put away, etc. It also helps children learn to organize their time and expectations and begin to internalize the process of preparing for a transition. In my experience, setting an arbitrary ending time and giving two to three specific advance notices (with one to three specific directions for how to spend the remaining time) dramatically reduces the resistance to the transition.

Organizing Possessions

A place for everything and everything in its place.
—Benjamin Franklin

Set aside some time each day and each week to organize possessions. For example, you may set aside 15 minutes as part of the bedtime routine to put toys in their box or on their shelf, put all homework in a folder in the book bag, put all dirty clothes in the laundry, and set out clothes for tomorrow. You could set aside 30 minutes every Saturday morning as tidy-up time to move all the things from the table, couch, and floor to the places they belong. Setting aside one day a month as clean-the-garage day or clean-the-closets day can also help reduce the piles and disorganization that tend to creep into dark corners.

Set Aside Some Planning Time

Since organizing tasks and time is so challenging, be sure to set aside some time just for planning. Many families set aside time on Sunday nights to review the calendar to find out what's on the calendar and plan the week ahead. Some families also set aside time for giving allowances, planning a budget, balancing checkbooks, reviewing current saving and spending patterns, and paying bills.

I like the old African proverb about elephants: "An elephant in the distance looks small, but an elephant up close can crush you." This means that a task or deadline that isn't due for a while doesn't seem like a big deal, but as the deadline approaches, it is stressful. Help your child anticipate deadlines for school projects, and break them down into smaller pieces to accomplish each week.

To minimize my elephant/deadline stress, when I take on a new task (especially one with a deadline more than a month away), I block out time on the calendar for the days and weeks prior to the deadline to complete the task in plenty of time to reduce the stress of last-minute rushes and inevitable unforeseen complications. Before agreeing to a shorter deadline, I consult my calendar to make sure there are open spaces to complete the required tasks. I set aside time every Friday afternoon to review the next week's task with my team, reflect on, and revise priorities as needed. Every morning, I review my to-do list and calendar for the day to anticipate what's needed and make sure I have materials ready for clinics, meetings, seminars, and lectures.

Narrate and Involve to Promote Planning

When you narrate your chores, your child learns what is involved in being a responsible adult. It helps children see you as a role model of self-discipline and self-control. Consider narrating what you are doing and involve your child in the process.

"I'm writing checks to pay for our utilities. They need go in the mail before we go to the park. Please put one stamp on each envelope in the upper right corner. Tell me when you're finished."

"I'm doing laundry so we have clean clothes. Please help me carry them outside so we can hang them on the line to dry."

Managing Mistakes

A person who never made a mistake, never tried anything new.
—Albert Einstein

Everyone makes mistakes. It took Thomas Edison over 25,000 attempts to make a lightbulb. When asked if he was discouraged by all those failures, he responded, "No. I learned 24,999 ways *not* to make a lightbulb." Learning from our mistakes helps us learn to take responsibility for our actions.

Mistakes are bound to happen, and they are terrific learning opportunities. Make the most of mistakes by managing them constructively.

Table 6.6. Managing Mistakes Constructively

Do	Don't
Recognize the mistake.	Ignore or cover up an error.
Recognize a learning opportunity.	Engage in name-calling (e.g., idiot, moron, loser, terrible person, awful parent) or faultfinding.
Remember that all human beings have needs, values, and goals.	Tell yourself what you *should* have done.
Reflect on your resources.	Dwell on deficiencies.
Pick one small, concrete, measurable, achievable behavior to improve.	Be overly ambitious or vague.
Plan to celebrate your successes.	Take success for granted.

Practice reframing mistakes as learning opportunities. Avoid turning one mistake into a belief that she'll never get it right. Instead, focus on how well she's practicing and learning to master a new skill. Things don't have to be perfect. Mistakes are to be expected.

Communicating Responsibility—I Statements

It's challenging to learn to take responsibility for our behavior, thoughts, and feelings. One good way to practice is to play the "I think/feel/want message" game. Pick one or more of the phrases below on the left column and rephrase them using an I message from the right column. Try starting your sentences with "I think," "I feel," "I want," or "I'd like" and observe what happens with the conflict and esteem levels in your home.

Table 6.7 Communicating Responsibility

Blaming or Judging	I Think/Feel/Want
That's just careless.	I think you could get a better grade if you double-checked your work.
Baseball is boring.	I think hockey is an exciting sport.
You are too wound up.	I'm tired and need a break for a few minutes.
You hurt her feelings.	I felt sad when you said that. I'd like you to apologize.
She's always such a sourpuss.	I feel cheerful when I spend time with cheerful people.
You are too noisy.	I would like it to be quieter while I do homework.
You are lazy.	I want some help with the chores.
She always gets to pick what we play.	I'd like a turn.
You never show me any respect.	I'd like you to listen to me and say "Yes, sir" when I've finished.

Ultimately, none of us can control others' behaviors. But we *can* notice our own thoughts, feeling, and desires, and express them. This is being responsible for ourselves and is far more effective in getting our needs met than blaming or judging others. Try it. If you grew up in a very critical family or culture, you may want to ask a counselor or psychologist for some coaching as you practice these new skills.

Powerful Praise—Catch 'Em Being Good

Children crave parental approval. Praise desired behavior, and you will see more of it. "You sat still for five minutes. That's great." "Thanks for using your inside voice." "I noticed that you were quiet throughout the concert. I'm proud of you." "Thanks for carrying in the groceries." "The dog likes it when you walk her." "I'm proud of you for eating all those peas without complaint. That's a sign of growing maturity." "Great job of taking turns with the toys." "Even though you made a mistake, I'm glad you were honest about it. That takes courage." Recognize her strengths, such as enthusiasm and creativity, and find constructive outlets for those gifts. Recognize his adaptability and his ability to shift his attention quickly; this may help him become a great salesperson or race-car driver. Praise what you like, and you will see more of it.

When you praise him, be specific. Say, "I admire how diligently you worked on your math homework," or "I'm happy to see you trying new foods at dinner," or "Even though your team lost, I admire how much effort you gave and how much you improved on your forehand serve this week." If you simply say, "You are a good boy/girl," or "You're a good sport," you have really conveyed your own judgment rather than helping identify and reinforce the desired behavior.

Avoid following praise with a *but*. For example, avoid, "You did great on the test, but you missed three questions," or "You really helped clean the garage, but next time I don't want to have to tell you five times to take the trash out." Ending praise with a *but* sets the child up for not really trusting the praise. Let him enjoy the praise without worrying that a criticism will follow. If there are aspects of the performance that need improvement, give that feedback immediately. "You still have time to double-check your work." Or you save it for the next time. "This time, when we clean the garage, let's put the garbage cans right next to the door to help us remember to take them out."

We tend to get more of whatever we focus on. Focusing on what you don't want leads to discouragement, despair, and more of what you don't want. Focus on what you want, what you like, what you enjoy, and what makes life easier or more pleasant for your child or others; and you will find your child working hard to earn more praise.

Communicate Confidence

Build a successful mind-set by communicating confidence. Focus on your child's talents, strengths, and interests. Remember her successes. Help her find the things she enjoys doing and is good at. Support her interests and reward her curiosity. Asking her for help gives her the message that she is capable of helping. Remind her of her achievements. Read stories about successful adults who overcame the challenges of ADHD. Building on strengths and accomplishments is like putting money in the bank of confidence. When she faces challenges that seem insurmountable, you can draw on those reserves to help her develop winning strategies.

How Did I Get Here?

Planning is a valuable skill. Although most of the time we start from the beginning of a project, sometimes it is helpful to work backward. Ask your child or youth what he'd really like to be when he grows up. Help him imagine himself being great and successful in this adult role. Now you can pretend you're a news reporter and ask him three or four of the following questions:

- Why did you want to become a _____ (firefighter, explorer, teacher, athlete, musician, or whatever)?
- Who inspired you?
- Who or what helped you the most?
- What were your biggest challenges?
- When did you get started?
- How did you do it?
- What advice would you give to someone who wanted to do what you've done?
- What do you enjoy most/least about this job?

The Hope of "Yet"

The inspiring physician and author Rachel Naomi Remen taught me the power of the word *yet*. I've never been athletically gifted, and I felt a bit embarrassed about it. But now when someone asks me if I play golf, windsurf, water-ski, or snowboard, I answer, "Not yet." Now the door to possibility and hope remains open.

Sometimes our slow progress discourages us. This is exactly when we need the hopeful power of *yet*. For example, a child might say, "I got another D on my math test. I'll never be any good at math." Use the power of *yet*: "Two years ago you couldn't add, and now adding is easy. You may not have mastered long division *yet*, but you are making progress, and I'm proud of you." Or a youth might say, "Another girl turned me down. I'll never get a date." And you can respond, "I've seen you make new friends at camp. You haven't got a date *yet*, but you haven't had a lot of practice. I'm confident that just as you learned to make friends, you will learn to make dates too."

Optional Activities

What can you do to promote positive communication and implement effective behavioral strategies? Here are list of possibilities. Consider picking one or more of the following:

1. Play the "can you hear me now?" game. Speak very softly and ask if your child can hear you. Try using sign language or using an unusual accent. Using a variety of strategies helps maintain interest and attention. And it's fun!

2. Play the patience game. For example, ask a four-year-old if he'd like to have two blueberries now or five blueberries in three minutes? Ask a ten-year-old if she'd rather have $1 million dollars now or $10 million in five years. What if it was $1 million now or $10 million in 15 years? Talk about what makes it easier or harder to wait and the benefits of waiting. Share examples from your own life of the benefits of waiting. For example, by waiting to buy my first car until I was in my twenties, my insurance rates were much lower than if I'd bought it as a teenager. I saved a *lot* of money.

3. Make a praise-correction-praise sandwich. Identify some behavior you would like to correct. Now find two positive things to praise about your child's intention or behavior. Say one positive thing, then state a specific, measurable, timely correction followed by the praise. Ask someone you trust to do this for you. Notice how much easier it is to swallow the suggestion when it surrounded by some nice tasty praise!

4. Make your own daily, weekly, or monthly activity chart.

5. Look for Barbara Sher's book *Attention Games* and pick one or more to play.

6. Go to the library and check out *How to Talk so Kids Will Listen & Listen so Kids will Talk* by Adele Faber and Elaine Mazlish. Look at the cartoons with your child. Discuss whether some of those ideas might work for you too.

7. Talk with your family about your favorite ways to celebrate or reward yourself for mastering a new skill or changing an old habit.

For easy ways to start and track your new skills, see chapters 9 and 10.

CHAPTER 7

Fourth Fundamental: Friendship with Self-Building Attention and Self-Discipline while Managing Stress and Frustration

Christian was nearing the end of the third grade in a new school. His teacher told Chris's mom, Vicky, that she was concerned about his attention, but Vicky had attributed it to all the changes they'd gone through with the move, the new house, new school, and then the holidays. By April, she'd found a new gym for herself. She'd seen the yoga and tai chi classes offered for families and wondered if those might be helpful for Chris. Besides the benefits of exercise, do practices with meditative movements have any evidence for improving attention or decreasing impulsivity?

ALTHOUGH ADD AND ADHD are modern diagnoses, human beings have learned many strategies over hundreds of years to build attention, self-discipline, and patience while managing frustration. Although they have largely developed within the context of religious communities, in the 20th century, a variety of meditation practices became popular secular strategies to enhance cognitive and emotional well-being.

Learning to manage frustration and stress are important lifelong skills. Offering clear communication, being a good role model, and using proven behavioral strategies can all help children learn self-discipline and self-control in the face of daily frustrations and temptations. However, life occasionally hands out major stressors, such as divorce, moving, loss of a job or house, serious health challenges, war, and loss of a loved one. Stress requires internal skills (friendship with self) as well as support from others.

Stress

Stress interferes with concentration and focus and can wreak havoc with self-discipline. When stressed, it is easy to fall into temptations of poor eating (junk food or comfort food), using drugs or alcohol to seek relief, or acting on angry or self-indulgent impulses. Learning to manage stress skillfully is a fundamental life skill, not only for those with ADD, but also for those who are stressed by living with someone with ADD! Fortunately, there are a variety of successful strategies for managing stress—some are commonsense, and some require training and practice.

Commonsense Stress Management

The commonsense strategies my grandmother taught me have stood the twin tests of time and experience: (1) take a deep breath, (2) count to ten, (3) count your blessings, and (4) know yourself.

Take a Deep Breath—Take Three

Taking a deep breath (or two or three) helps reduce reactivity in the autonomic nervous system, which reduces our distress. Deep breathing is relaxing and gives us time to reflect before we act. It requires no special equipment, costs nothing, and can be done anywhere under any circumstances. It has no side effects. Facing a stressful event such as a talk with the principal or boss, or child's resistance, forgetfulness, or opposition? Remember to breathe!

Count to Ten

Counting is another effective (and free) way to calm down before reacting to a stressful event. Did someone cut you off in traffic? Call you a name? Start an argument? Refuse to obey? Omit part of an assignment? Make a mess? Count to ten before you respond. Counting to ten allows your brain to hit the reset button. This helps you avoid impulsive responses that will be regretted later. If you are a parent or teacher, count out loud to model this behavior.

Count Your Blessings

When something stressful happens, it is easy to fall into a downward spiral of self-pity. Although self-pity is occasionally a delicious self-indulgent treat, it often has a bitter aftertaste, is easily overdosed, and can lead to anxiety, depression, and a sense of impotence, anger, self-righteousness, or doom. Besides, at a pity party, the food is terrible (can of worms), and no one else wants to stay for long.

An excellent antidote to prevent poisonous pitiful states is appreciation. To make it easier to switch into the gratitude gear, it is helpful to make mental lists of *things I am grateful for*. This can also be done as a game—take turns naming something mundane, sublime, outrageous, or practical for which you are grateful (e.g., electricity, nature, feather boas, or can openers). Or think of as many things as you can that start with the letter *S* (or any other letter) for which you are grateful (e.g., sunsets, snowplows, screen doors, strawberries, school vacations, etc.).

> To help him establish a calm routine before bed, I used to ask my toddler to name three things he was grateful for before he went to sleep. One night, as he dozed off, he replied, "Blue." Not sure I heard him correctly, I asked him to repeat it. "Blue," he said, "and orange and yellow and red and purple and green. I'm grateful for all the colors of the rainbow." Based on this wonderfully inventive response, we created Grateful for Blue, a small book with colorful drawings that his preschool used to share the gratitude game. When one of us hears the other start to lament, all we have to do now is say "What three things are you grateful for right now?" to turn things around.

Know Yourself

It's easier to manage stress if you arrange your schedule and activities to suit your individual needs. Morning people may want to get up earlier to tackle challenging tasks whereas night owls may want to save perplexing problems until later in the day when their brains are finally awake. Avoid forcing yourself to be a lark if you're really an owl or vice versa! Learn whether you understand and learn better by seeing, hearing, or feeling new material. This helps you learn whether to ask for material in books, CDs, or MP3s and whether to review by reading silently or out loud. Do you work best when it's absolutely silent or with background music? Do you learn best while sitting still or walking? Are you most efficient when working in the kitchen, the den, or the library? Do you like to learn on your own at your own pace or as part of a group? Know yourself and plan to meet your unique needs in ways that lower the stress in your life.

Early-Warning System

Another commonsense strategy is to develop early-warning systems about stress, especially about strong negative emotions. Feeling overwhelming anger makes it easy to blurt out something impulsively that we regret later. What are your early-warning signs that you're starting to feel impatient, frustrated, scared, stressed, or annoyed? If you catch it early, you can take a breath, count to ten, or switch to feeling gratitude. An early-warning system acts like a lighthouse to keep you clear of the rocks of imminent negative impulses. Here are some common early-warning signs of stress:

- ✓ Breathing faster than usual
- ✓ Heart pounding or racing
- ✓ Tight muscles in the face, shoulders, neck, belly, arms, legs, or back
- ✓ Body leaning forward more than usual
- ✓ Feeling hot, especially in the face, chest, or belly
- ✓ Wrinkled forehead
- ✓ Pinched lips
- ✓ Tight throat
- ✓ Voice getting higher-pitched or louder
- ✓ Feeling a sense of time pressure, urgency, or hurried
- ✓ Feeling impatient, frustrated, sorry for yourself, like no one else understands

Learn to notice these early-warning signs in yourself and your loved ones. Recognizing stress symptoms early can help you take commonsense measures to counteract stress before it leads to an impulsive, regrettable action. In addition to common sense, you can also practice skills such as meditation.

Meditation

Just as there are many kinds of sports, all of which improve physical fitness, there are many kinds of meditation, all of which can improve attention and focus. Just as some kinds of sports involve rackets, bats, or balls, meditation can be done with eyes open or closed, while sitting still or moving, in silence or not, while visualizing or not, and alone or in groups. Prayer, chanting, extending compassion, and offering forgiveness can also be forms of meditation.

Concentration-based meditation practices involve focusing on a word, sound, object, idea, emotion (such as gratitude or compassion), or movement. When other thoughts, sensations, or emotions arise, they are gently placed aside, and the mind returns to its object of concentration. *Mindfulness* meditation is the moment-to-moment practice of nonjudgmental awareness of sensations, thoughts, emotions, and experiences. When the mind wanders to past or future concerns, it is also gently returned to the present.

Scientific Studies about Meditation's Benefits

Scientific studies suggest that most meditation practices slow the body and mind down. They lower heart rate and blood pressure and lead to calmer, more focused EEG patterns. Meditation also reduces stress reactions in our brain and endocrine system, resulting in a state of calm coherence.[1-2] Just as regular physical exercise can build up muscle strength and size, regular meditation practice changes blood flow in the brain and increases the size of the parts of the brain dealing with attention, focus, planning, emotional self-regulation, and mood.[3-8]

Meditation practice improves attention, creativity, mental clarity, and reduces errors, aggressiveness, anxiety, and depression, particularly in the face of stress or distractions. A number of studies in school settings show that mindfulness-based meditation training can improve attention, emotions, and behavior, with fewer fights and better grades.[9-15] Similarly, students who practiced concentration-types of meditation had fewer problems with absenteeism and suspension for behavioral problems,[16] less distractibility and anxiety with better creativity,[17] and better cognitive function and grades.[18-19]

It may be especially helpful for active children to learn mindful moving meditation, such as yoga, tai chi, or qigong.[20] Regular practice reduces test anxiety and improves academic achievement. As with most activities, those who practice the most reap the greatest rewards.[21]

Meditation Safety

Meditation is very safe. Although there have been rare reports of problems for patients who have schizophrenia who start meditation training, there have been no reports of serious side effects in studies of meditation training for children or adults with ADD or ADHD who do not have pre-existing thought disorders like schizophrenia.

Meditation—How Much?

The need for formal training and the intensity, duration, and frequency of practice vary for different types of meditation and different people. Just as national guidelines recommend 30 to 60 minutes daily of physical exercise to maintain physical health, recommendations for meditation practice typically range from just a few minutes for young children to ten minutes twice daily for school-age children to 40-60 minutes daily for older adolescents and adults. Those with greater needs or higher aspirations may engage in longer practices and seek formal training or guidance. A variety of books, CD recordings, and Internet sites offer training. See the Resources section for more information.

Meditation Training

Some psychologists and other mental health professionals have undergone specific training and certification to provide specific kinds of meditation training (e.g., mindfulness-based stress reduction, mindfulness-based cognitive behavioral therapy, or dialectical behavior therapy). Nevertheless, due to the absence of consistent state or national certification for mind/body training, it is prudent to ask about a provider's training and experience. Even licensure and certification do not ensure a perfect fit, so it is helpful to ask for recommendations from your physician and friends. Ask how many sessions are standard, the duration of training, expectations for home practice, what the costs are, how many patients or students they have taught in the past year, and whether they work individually, in groups, or by telephone or Internet.

As with other clinicians, look for those who are welcoming, warm, empathetic, and show genuine interest in people, not just their favorite techniques. The most effective teachers and trainers offer steadfast acceptance and positive regard. They create an atmosphere of safety and trust while fostering independence and acknowledging students' strengths and capacities.

Meditation Costs and Insurance

Aside from care provided by licensed psychologists or counselors, meditation training is unlikely to be covered under most insurance plans. Some flexible medical spending programs will cover the costs if your physician writes a letter indicating the condition being treated and the rationale for training. Some trainers and teachers of meditation and yoga take a percentage of patients with limited means as part of their community service. Reduced-price classes may be available from student/trainee teachers.

Students and trainees who offer these services are generally idealistic, compassionate, diligent individuals who receive ongoing supervision and feedback from experienced mentors.

Isabella "Bella" was a 14-year-old girl who enjoyed writing fantasy stories, but had poor grades, rumpled clothes, and hadn't washed her hair recently. She had notebooks full of stories and sketches, but few friends. Her mother was frustrated with Bella's spaciness, sloppiness, and poor attention to schoolwork. She wondered if there was something Bella could do to promote better focus and help her reconnect with the everyday world. Since Bella loved writing, I asked her about character development. She told me she preferred to focus on plot. I could empathize. However, I said, "To be a really great writer, you need to develop characters and settings too. Sometimes it helps to be really present in your body and in your environment to notice those details that might help a story." I suggested she try an online-mindfulness class. Bella's mom noticed that she seemed to pay more attention to the food as she ate, and she enjoyed it more. Bella reported that her class practiced really feeling and experiencing the shower and shampoo, and she enjoyed it enough to start making it part of her daily routine. She began to pay attention to how her body felt as she gazed around her room and how she felt when she was in more organized clean spaces. Over time, mindfulness practice enriched Bella's life and helped her become a better writer.

Although it is possible to learn to meditate by reading a book or listening to a CD, studying with an experienced teacher, reading books devoted to meditation, or joining a group can be invaluable assets in mastering these subtle practices. Please see the Resources section for additional information.

Reflect, Reassure, and Rehearse

Reflect

One of the best strategies to help a child learn to manage stress is to reflect on a stressful situation at a calmer time. Many families find that taking a few minutes at bedtime to review the day's highlights or unresolved issues helps settle a child for sleep, builds relationships, and consolidates stress-management skills. For example, a parent might reflect that he noticed his daughter seemed sad or withdrawn after school, inviting her to share her experience.

> Father: I noticed that after school today, you seemed quieter than usual and a little sad.
>
> Meaghan: Well, the other girls were talking and laughing on the bus, and Teri said that Jackie's new shoes were cute, but I said they were ugly because they are, and Teri said she wouldn't talk with me anymore because I was mean.
>
> Father: I understand that you felt sad because you want to be included, and you don't want them to think you're mean.
>
> Meaghan: Yeah, I'm such a big mouth. I'll never have any friends. Sometimes things just pop out of me.

By reflecting and empathizing, Father has set the stage for a stronger relationship, enhancing Meaghan's own ability to reflect and articulate a problem rather than just blaming the other girls for excluding her. Once she states the problem, "things just pop out of me," Father can offer reassurance that this is a problem that can be solved.

Reassure

> Father: Meaghan, I'm proud of you for taking responsibility. You did a great job of saying how you felt and what you'd like to change. You have so many excellent skills already, I'm sure you'll be able to improve on things popping out of your mouth. What ideas do you have for tackling that?
>
> Meaghan: I'm not sure. What would *you* do?
>
> Father: Here's a saying that's been really helpful for me. Before speaking, ask yourself three questions: Is it true? Is it kind? Is it necessary? If the answer to all three is yes, go ahead and say it, but if any one of them is no, hold your tongue. What do you think? Would that work for you?
>
> Meaghan: I'm not sure. I don't understand how that works.

KATHI J. KEMPER, MD, MPH

If Meaghan liked the first suggestion, understood it, and was ready to adopt it, they could make a specific plan. If not, Father now has an opportunity to *rehearse*. Rehearsing helps prepare Meaghan, builds her confidence, and by decreasing anxiety, makes it easier to fall asleep.

Rehearse

> Father: OK, let's pretend I'm one of the girls. I say that Jackie's new shoes are pretty, but you think they are ugly. Would you say something? Remember the three questions. Is it true? Kind? Necessary?
>
> Meaghan: Well, it's true that I think her shoes are ugly. But it may hurt her feelings, so it's not kind, and it's really not necessary for her to know how I feel if she didn't ask me. So I guess I don't say anything, right?
>
> Father: Great job. It sounds like you really do understand. Want to try another one?
>
> Meaghan (yawning): No, I'm good. 'Night, Dad. I love you.
>
> Father: Good night, Meaghan. I love you too.

Practicing the skills of reflection, reassurance, and rehearsal can also be a game.

The Triple R (Reflect, Reassure, Rehearse) Game

> *Step 1. Reflect. Ask one question that requires the child or youth to reflect on events or circumstances that trigger emotions. Examples: What makes you really, really mad? Which scares you more: monsters under the bed or snakes in the grass? What superpower would make you happier: invisibility or flying? What you make you more proud: discovering a new planet or a new source of clean energy? Which is more frustrating: waiting for your turn to talk or waiting at a stoplight?*
>
> *Step 2. Reassure the child that you might have those feelings under those circumstances too. "I understand. If that happened, I'd probably feel mad, scared, happy, proud, or frustrated too. In fact, let's pretend!"*
>
> *Step 3. Rehearse. Pretend that the child or youth is the parent, teacher, or coach, and you are the child. "This (event from step 1) has happened, and I feel really (emotion from step 1)." Exaggerate. Make a face. Make*

it fun. "What do you say to me?" Repeat as often as desired. Vary the questions. Occasionally use a situation that occurs in real life (such as having to sit quietly, wait a turn, share, clean up, tempted to take a risk, apologize, etc.) that has led to an emotional meltdown or a problem. Keep the game fun by interspersing realistic, difficult situations with silly, imaginative scenarios.

When you practice the Triple R game, the child learns to do the following:

a. recognize events that can trigger emotions,
b. accept feeling emotions as normal, and
c. understand and rehearse alternative ways to manage those emotions.

> Christian and Vicky started practicing the gratitude game before bed to help him settle down and sleep better. During the day, Vicky asked Chris whether he preferred yoga or tai chi. He chose tai chi. As he practiced, he felt calmer and was able to focus better. His coach was a terrific role model of calm, capable self-discipline who taught him to breathe deeply before undertaking a difficult challenge. Christian learned he could focus on his breathing at school too. Vicky started spending five minutes at night reflecting on the day with Christian to help him consolidate his new skills and rehearse challenges before they arose. By the time he started the fourth grade, Christian was well settled. He had developed several strategies for successfully managing stress and improving his focus, both in tai chi and in his classroom. He was calmer and more respectful too.

Transform Negative Self-Talk with Positive Insights

Given all the negative feedback children and youth with ADD or ADHD have received about their behavior and academic performance, it's not surprising that they have internalized many of these messages. Negative self-labels are sometimes projected onto others, leading to blaming rather than constructive problem solving. By recognizing, questioning, and transforming negative self-talk, you can build confidence and problem-solving capacities.

Table 7.1

Negative Statement	Positive Insight
I am so stupid. I might as well quit.	Sometimes I feel stupid when I'm trying to learn something new too. But we are not stupid; we are learning. Learning takes time and practice. I'll bet we can think of some things together that will make this more fun.
School is stupid. Teachers are dumb.	It sounds like you are frustrated with school. Let's take a break, stretch, and then think of one thing we could do to make things better.
I can't do this homework. It's too hard, and I just don't get it.	It's frustrating not to understand part of the directions. I'm going to take a big breath and feel my forehead relax and my belly loosen so I can listen better. Let's start with the parts you do understand. How is this like a problem you've already solved? What parts do you understand? What did you do to get this far? How could you find out what the rest of it means?
Everybody hates me.	It sounds like you feel really lonely and would like to have some friends who like you for who you are. Let's go for a walk with Skipper (dog). We can think of what we like best about the people in our family and our neighborhood.
I'm really clumsy, and I always get picked last for sports.	I know it hurts to get picked last like you did today. Everyone has different talents. I'm impressed by your amazing ability to figure out those computer games and to come up with so many creative ideas for stories. Let's think of what kind of activity would be fun for you (and help improve coordination): Ballet? Brain Gym? Yoga? Tae kwon do? Juggling? Ping Pong? Drawing? Sculpture? Piano?

Positive insights are easiest to hear when they're preceded with empathetic understanding. Reframing moves the discussion toward positive goals, skills, talents, and interests that can mobilize energy toward problem solving instead of giving up or getting angry. Imagine yourself as a coach encouraging your star player to overcome a challenge in her technique. Empathize, praise, and ask questions to help her see the answer herself. Give her choices and suggestions to empower her and encourage her problem solving.

Optional Activities

1. Develop a family or classroom early-warning-signal system. Create a verbal signal so family members or classmates can safely alert each other if they notice someone sliding into stress. For example, you might say, "Looks like clouds moving in, do we have an umbrella?" to let someone know you notice their mood and ask if they are ready to address it.
2. Teach your child to take a deep breath when stressed.
3. Practice taking a deep breath together when you are cut off in traffic, have to wait a long time in a line, or in some other frustrating or annoying situation.
4. Teach your child the benefits of counting to ten by doing it out loud yourself the next time she frustrates you.
5. Keep a gratitude journal.
6. Play the gratitude game at mealtimes or before bed.
7. Take a meditation class.
8. Enroll in a yoga, tai chi, or qigong class.
9. Spend five minutes at night reflecting, reassuring, and rehearsing challenging situations.

Help your child identify his own strengths, preferred learning strategies, and skills so he can maximize his potential and minimize his stress.

CHAPTER 8

Fifth Fundamental: Fields—A Healthy Habitat

Lindsay was a 28-year-old mother of two who had moved north after Hurricane Katrina destroyed her home. After the stress of the hurricane, she had started smoking more and was up to a pack a day. To calm her nerves at night, she'd drink a six-pack while sitting on the porch with her mom, watching the kids—Destiny and Dakota—play outside. Both children had had difficulty in school before and after the move. Dakota's new teacher had suggested having him tested for ADHD. Lindsay wondered whether living in the FEMA trailer for three months before they moved might have caused his behavior problems. His grandmother said he seemed to pay attention just fine to the video games and TV shows he watched after school while waiting for Lindsay to come home from her job in a furniture factory. Lindsay was pregnant with her third child; she asked what she could do to help the next child do better in school.

OUR PHYSICAL AND social environments affect our ability to focus and maintain self-control and self-discipline. Modern American advertising culture fosters impulsivity (Buy now!), impatience (Limited time offer!), peer pressure (Don't be the last one on your block! Thousands of others have used our product!), and self-indulgence (You deserve it. It's easy!). Electronic media demand and reward rapid changes in attention; instant replays reinforce the notion that we need not pay close attention the first time because we'll get it again in a minute.

Furthermore, many modern chemicals in the environment, food, and household products can disrupt brain function. These chemicals are called neurotoxins. For example, pregnant women who smoke transfer the chemicals in tobacco to their babies. Babies born to smokers have about twice the risk of developing ADD as babies of nonsmokers, even after controlling for other factors.[1-2]

Reduce Negative Influences

Parents and teachers naturally want the best for their children. Most want to know how to avoid exposing themselves and their children to known chemical and physical toxins that affect the brain. Which toxins are most important, and how can we avoid them?

✓ *Stop smoking. Do not allow your child to spend time with adults who smoke.* Support tobacco-free policies in public places. Regulations restricting smoking and taxes that increase the cost of cigarettes are also effective deterrents. Maternal smoking during pregnancy accounts for more than a quarter of a million cases of ADHD in the US every year.[3]

> One of the best things Lindsay can do for her health and for Destiny and Dakota, as well as her future child, is to stop smoking now. I advised her to quit smoking, to set a quit date, and to sign up for the free smoking-cessation classes at the community center so she'd have some support. I offered to call her in a month to see how it was going. I encouraged her mom to quit at the same time so they could support each other and get all the temptations and smoking reminders out of the house.

✓ *Do not misuse alcohol.* Do not use alcohol as a stress-management strategy; it can backfire and lead to poor judgment, poor sleep, accidents, injuries, poor communication, and a host of medical problems. There are more effective, less damaging stress-management strategies to practice as role models for our children (see chapter 7). Anticipate that your child will be tempted to drink during adolescence; imagine together the severe penalties (including injury, death, and imprisonment) for drinking and driving or riding in a car with someone who has been drinking. Set your own family rules and consequences. For example, if he gives you any reason to think he has been drinking and driving, he loses driving privileges until he is 21 years old.

Lindsay's beer drinking posed a risk of her baby and could impair her judgment while watching her kids. I asked her what kinds of health habits she'd like Destiny and Dakota to have when they grew up and if she'd like them to learn some easy, skillful stress-management strategies. She was afraid they might become alcoholics like her uncle but wasn't sure how to prevent it. Her uncle had finally joined AA. He had been sober for two years and encouraged her to join him for a meeting. I asked what she thought of that option, what she saw as the pros and cons of attending a meeting, and what barriers she might face if she decided to try it. It really helps to think things through with someone else before making a decision about a big behavior change, and it gave Dakota a good example to hear his mom take an organized, thoughtful, deliberate approach to her decision.

✓ Avoid food and water that contain excessive amounts of *heavy metals* such as lead, arsenic, and manganese. They are toxic to the brain and contribute to ADHD symptoms and learning difficulties. Exposure to lead and tobacco together is even worse than either one alone[2]. If you have well water, have it tested regularly. Remove lead from your home; it can be found in older paint, batteries, toys, ceramics, and even some folk medicines from Mexico, China, and India. Check with your local public health department about lead-abatement programs in your community.

✓ Avoid exposure to environmental chemicals such as PCBs, PBBs, and PBDEs;* they can interfere with thyroid function essential for normal brain function. Advocate for their elimination from the environment. See the Resources section for information about groups working on environmental issues.

---

* PCBs are polychlorinated biphenyls, PBBs are polybrominated biphenyls, and PBDEs are polybrominated diphenyl ethers used like PBBs. These compounds are used in a variety of industrial processes and found in many household products. Read labels. For more information, see the US government Web site for the Agency for Toxic Substances and Disease Registry at the Centers for Disease Control and Prevention (atsdr.cdc.gov). For additional information, see the US Environmental Protection Agency (epa.gov) fact sheets.

✓ Avoid exposure to *formaldehyde*, which can cause irritability and problems with sleep and memory. Formaldehyde is present in some building materials, such as particleboard and plywood.

> Formaldehyde is thought to be the agent responsible for health problems in people living in FEMA trailers after Hurricane Katrina in 2006 and the Iowa floods of 2008. It is also found in pressed-wood products in some furniture. Most often it causes respiratory problems such as irritated eyes, stuffy noses, and cough. I printed for Lindsay the HESIS (Hazard Evaluation System and Information Service) fact sheet on formaldehyde from the California Department of Health Services, which is available free online. Formaldehyde is a toxin, which could add to the risk for Lindsay's children posed by exposure to tobacco and alcohol.

✓ Avoid exposure to *persistent organic pollutants* (POPs) such as *dioxin* (a byproduct of the process used to bleach paper products). Avoid pesticides such as *dieldrin and atrazine*, which increase the rate of learning disabilities and ADHD.[4]

> Although it is prudent to reduce exposures to POPs and neurotoxic pesticides, these compounds were less of an immediate threat than tobacco and alcohol for Lindsay.

The physical environment is not the only source of toxic exposures in our environment. Numerous studies have shown a significant link between more TV and impaired attention, worse school performance, and more aggressive, sexual, and violent behavior.[5-9] Minimize exposure to electronic media, including TV, video games, computer games, and handheld electronic games.

✓ Remove the television, computer, and electronic games from your child's bedroom. Contrary to what they might tell you, children do not need electronics in their bedrooms; evidence suggests worse behavior and ADHD problems in children who have them there.[10]

✓ Consider removing them from the house entirely. For the first several months, your child is likely to consider this a draconian measure not in keeping with the 21st century. Parents may also suffer from withdrawal. However, parents in my practice who have taken this step have reported remarkable improvements in the child's attention, demeanor, sleep, behavior, and grades.

✓ Reduce the use of electronic media to less than one hour daily. Spend your time instead reading, learning, walking, or other activities, interactive family games or hobbies, or social activities or clubs.

> I asked Lindsay's mother what she and her siblings had done for fun after school when she was a girl. "Oh, we played imaginary games in the woods, tag, things like that." I suggested she might share some stories from those times with Dakota and Destiny and offer to take them to a park to play after school when the weather was nice rather than spending all afternoon indoors. She smiled. "That's just what my grandma would have said. I believe it would do them some good!"

The environment may also exert *favorable* influences on attention and behavior. Use natural daylight and music to your advantage. Spend more time in nature. Go for a walk in the woods.

✓ *Natural daylighting* in schools can improve attendance and academic performance while lowering energy costs. Talk with your school board about school designs for future buildings.

✓ *Clean up clutter and develop an organized schedule* (see chapter 6). Clean designs and a neat, well-organized environment can help improve concentration and clarity and reduce distractions.

Table 8.1

Sample Weekly Chore Schedule for a 10-year-old

Time/Activity	Mon	Tue	Wed	Thu	Fri	Sat	Sun
Morning							
Brush teeth	√	√	√	√	√	√	√
Gather homework	√	√	√	√	√		
Feed and walk dog	√	√	√	√	√	√	Dad does it
Bring in newspaper							√
Help put groceries away			√			√	
After school							
Homework	√	√	√	√			√
Garbage out		√					
Recycling out				√			
Tidy room		√		√		√	
Clean bathroom						√	
After supper							
Load dishwasher	√		√		√		
Empty dishwasher		√		√			
Check garbage and recycling, move to bins in garage		√		√		√	
Brush teeth	√	√	√	√	√	√	√

✓ Listen to *music and sing along or make up your own songs*. It's easier to memorize the ABCs when you learn them with a song. Rhythm and pitch help enhance learning and recall, and silly songs for learning are fun! You can even use rhymes or poetry as memory aids. Music can also be used to reward desirable behavior; allow your child the privilege of listening to music after he studies or does chores. Avoid listening to distracting music during tasks that require concentration. Keep the volume down to avoid ear damage.

✓ Spend more time in *nature*. More time in green outdoor settings can reduce symptoms of hyperactivity and attention deficits and improve self-discipline.[11]

> Lindsay and her mom decided that as a treat after a long visit to the doctor's office, they'd take the children to a park they hadn't yet explored. Just breathing the fresh air and smelling the pine trees helped them feel better about their decision to stop smoking.

Optional activities

1. Read the book *Last Child in the Woods* by Richard Louv about the benefits of nature on children's behavior and health.
2. Go on a TV-free diet for a week.
3. Have your well water tested.
4. Read the labels on your household cleaning agents and pesticides.
5. Check out the government fact sheets from ATSDR on your workplace chemicals.
6. Advocate for smoke-free schools, workplaces, restaurants, and public buildings.
7. Offer to monitor high school parties to ensure that no alcohol is allowed.
8. Develop a "go outside and play before dinner" habit.
9. Make up a song to help remember something important.
10. Organize your kitchen and living room and make a plan to keep them organized.
11. Make a family calendar of events and hang it in a prominent place.
12. Visit a county, state, or national park.

CHAPTER 9

Making a SMART Plan

IN CHAPTERS 4-8, you read lots of great ideas for improving lifestyle fundamentals for improving attention, self-discipline, and social skills. You probably want to get started, but there are so many options. What's the best way to start? The best plan is a SMART plan.

What is a SMART Plan?

A SMART plan is
Specific
Measurable
Attainable
Relevant
Trackable and time related

A *specific* plan is the opposite of a vague idea. A lot of people have vague ideas of doing better, being more responsible, paying better attention, or being successful. While these are great goals, they are not very specific. The more specific the goal is, the easier it will be to measure the outcome and assess whether it is realistically achievable in the available time.

Table 9.1 Specific Goals

Vague Goal	Specific Goal
Do better	Improve social studies grade from C to B over the next semester.
Be more responsible	Get up by 7:00 a.m. to get ready for work.
Pay attention	Write down assignments each day at the end of each meeting or class.

Be successful	Submit ten applications and get hired for a full-time summer job.
Be safer	Put the phone away while driving.
Stop blurting out and interrupting.	Carry a notepad today. When I feel the urge to blurt or interrupt, I will jot down a note at last twice today. I will wait until it's my turn to talk, and then decide if I want to share my idea or not.
Exercise more	Walk at least 30 minutes a day at least five days a week for the next 21 days.
Eat better	Make a salad as part of dinner at least four nights this week; take an apple and a quarter of a cup of nuts to eat as a snack four days this week.
Be more self-disciplined	Turn off the TV at 9:00 p.m., take a hot shower, and write in my journal five nights a week.
Control my temper	Practice imagining myself in a situation that usually triggers anger. Practice breathing slowly and counting to ten. Breathe slowly and count to ten tomorrow morning if someone cuts me off in traffic.
Communicate more compassionately	At least once this week when my daughter complains that I'm not being fair, I will listen until she's finished, empathize with her, noting that I might feel the same way if I was in her shoes. For one week I will empathize without arguing, telling her life isn't fair, telling her a story about my adolescence, or judging her as spoiled and ungrateful.
Reduce my stress	I will write five things for which I am grateful on six out of seven nights this week before I go to bed.

Did you notice how many of the examples of specific goals were also *measurable*? Measuring a grade, a wake-up time, an assignment calendar, or a behavior, such as writing a note, is much easier than measuring success. One of the nice things about plans with measurable goals is that a plan can be revised to suit the changing needs and resources of a specific situation. Include the amount you will do, how, when, and how often you will do it.

Some people might object that "not everything that matters can be measured, and not everything that can be measured matters." This is true. It is hard to measure characteristics like love and understanding. You might be pleasantly surprised to learn that when we aim for a specific, measurable, behavioral goal rather than vague ambitions such as "Be a better listener," "stop interrupting," or "be more compassionate," we are more likely to actually attain them. Having a specific behavior in mind helps us imagine it, practice it, and achieve it.

It is also true that you could plan to achieve a specific measurable goal that is *not* worthwhile ("I plan to eat one of every kind of pastry in the bakery tomorrow."). Use common sense. When in doubt, ask for help from someone you trust and respect, such as a family member, friend, professional counselor, or clinician.

Did you notice that the specific goals in table 9.1 were also realistic and *attainable*? None of them aimed for perfection every day forever. It's perfectly OK to have one day a week that is the designated "veg-out, stay up late, and eat whatever you want" day. Having a day like that helps you see how much better you feel when you follow your plan and helps you feel less deprived or overwhelmed with excessive expectations. It helps you avoid cheating on the other days too.

Start with baby steps and build on success. Know in advance that you may want to revise a goal once you've had a week or two of experience with it. For example, if you find that it is easy to eat salad for dinner but that the challenge is avoiding the drive-through on the way to work, set a new goal accordingly. If it is unrealistic to get a full-time job in the midst of a recession; you might revise your goal to finding part-time work and a part-time volunteer position. Review and revise the plan regularly.

Relevance means the goal is right for you. A plan that works for a second grader is probably not the same as the plan for a high school sophomore. The plan for a working parent is different than a plan for a college student. None of us lives a perfectly healthy life. We all have unique opportunities for improving our lifestyle or our community. Aim for an achievable improvement that fits your priorities and your situation.

Track your success. It really helps to write things down every day to track success. Be honest with yourself. There is no point in cheating yourself! If you don't like writing, consider looking at one of the growing number of applications for mobile phones to track behavior. For a new behavior, I like to review progress weekly at first to see if the plan needs a little tweaking. Once it seems about right, the progress review can happen every two to three weeks.

Baby Steps

Divide each difficulty into as many parts
as is feasible and necessary to resolve it.

—Rene Descartes

Take baby steps. It is much better to take tiny steps in the desired direction than to fail at an overwhelmingly difficult goal. Build on positive momentum of small daily victories and use every opportunity to celebrate mastery. For example, if your long-term goal is for your child to graduate from high school, but he's in the fourth grade, consider a shorter-term goal (e.g., passing this quarter by spending 20 minutes a night on homework and reviewing progress with a teacher). If your daughter's goal is to be a professional ballerina by the time she's 17, and she's ten years old, talk with her teacher about the number of classes she should take each week and how many minutes a day she should practice for the next three months.

You may want to break it down into even smaller steps. For example—for the homework challenge—for the next week, each evening we will read the assignment for each class out loud, and you will explain what you think it means. Then tell me what you need to do to complete it. Do you need a paper and pencil, a calendar or computer? How long do you think it will take? If it's more than 15 minutes, let's work on it for 15 minutes, take a five-minute activity break, and then complete it. Shall we set a timer? Where will you put your work when you're finished? What will you do to remember to turn it in? How will you feel when you turn it in? What will we do to celebrate? If this sounds like it would be a big challenge in your household, find one small thing that is achievable. Plan it, do it, and celebrate success.

Make it simple. Nothing succeeds like success. And nothing fails more often than a plan that is too complex, too challenging, seems irrelevant (why do we have to do this? I don't have a problem!), or one that lacks built-in rewards on a regular basis.[1] By exhibiting realism, patience, positivity, and persistence, you are helping your child internalize those same characteristics. Remember how many times you repeated "mama" before your child repeated it back to you? Remember how happy he was to see you smile when he said it? Repetition and rewards are key parts of learning any new skill, not just with vocabulary, but also with more abstract skills like organization, patience, diligence, and attention.

Tracking Success

Most people find it useful to make plans that involve a daily or weekly activity and tracking success using a calendar. Just about any behavior improves when we track it daily. For example, dieters typically "cheat" less when they write down everything they eat in a diet diary. Joggers run more consistently when they keep a written or electronic log.

> Last year I decided to get back to my college weight, which meant losing 13 pounds. To make it more enjoyable, I downloaded an application for my iTouch and started logging my daily activity and dietary intake. I was tempted to cheat! But I knew I'd just be cheating myself. Just knowing that I was going to enter it in the log made me think twice about what I ate. And logging my activity made me compete with myself to see if I could do more this week than last. The device automatically calculated the calories burned with each activity and the calories, carbohydrates, protein, and fat from each food. I learned a lot! I rewarded myself with a new application or song for every pound I shed. It took six months, but I did reach my goal, and I'm pleased to say I've maintained it too. By now there are dozens of applications to help us achieve our health goals. Please let me know which ones you've found work best for you!

Charts, calendars, diaries, logs, and activity lists are especially important for those struggling with attention and organizational challenges. If your child struggles with daily responsibilities, consider making a wall chart together like table 8.1 on page 113. Across the top, list the days of the week. As each activity is completed, allow the child to make a checkmark or add a sticker. Decide in advance how you will celebrate success.

Remember, Rome wasn't built in a day, but it was built and continues to be rebuilt. Show your child how small steps can add up to larger success. Make it vivid and memorable. For example, you could use a measuring cup and a tablespoon. How many tablespoons does it take to fill half a cup? If you added one tablespoon a day to the cup, how many days would it take to fill the cup? Now think about homework. If you read ten pages a day, how many days will it take to finish a 70-page book? If you read one book a week, how many books can you read during a nine-week summer vacation? If you memorize four bars of music a day, how many days will it take to memorize the whole piece? Share stories with your child about how you accomplished something big by taking small steps. Read stories together about people who overcame great challenges through focus, persistence, and dedication.

Praise and Gratitude

> *A spoonful of honey will catch more flies*
> *than a gallon of vinegar.*
> —Benjamin Franklin

Praise, praise, praise steps in the desired direction. Reinforce the image of your loved one as responsible, patient, focused, diligent, thoughtful, deliberate, and successful. If your child remembered to make his bed and get dressed but forgot to brush his teeth, give him a praise sandwich (praise for bed making, constructive question or suggestion about the teeth, praise for getting dressed). Tell him how proud you are that he is being so responsible. Tell him that *when* (not "if," which implies possible failure) he finishes brushing his teeth, you will be even prouder of his diligence. The more we tell someone how happy we are with an aspect of their behavior, the more they will try to live up to that image. Keep praising small steps in the desired direction.

As a perfectionist who constantly sees opportunities for improvement, it has been a challenge for me to incorporate praise when there is so much room to do better. If you're like me, you may find it easier to focus on gratitude than on praise. I have learned that I'm far happier and more effective if I regularly review our team's progress with gratitude before considering the next goal and the next tasks. I have more energy and feel clearer and less overwhelmed when I take the time to reflect and appreciate accomplishments, and the team is energized by appreciation too. I've also realized that the people I most enjoy being around are those who express gratitude for the people and experiences in their lives rather those who find fault with things that fall a bit short.

Focus on what you like, and you will find more of it; you will also feel more enthusiastic and energized. Those who focus on faults are sure to find them, making themselves and those around them miserable and draining the energy available to make further improvements. Take a moment to be grateful to yourself for taking the time to read this book and for this day's opportunity to live a better, healthier, more attentive, calm, compassionate, joyful, and wise life.

Imagine Success Vividly

Vividly imagine success. What will it look like when you organize the kitchen? How big will Mom's smile be when she sees you doing your homework? What will the completed chore chart look like? What will he hear Dad say when he gets home before curfew? How will it taste and smell when you bake homemade cookies to celebrate? Get as many senses involved as possible in imagining your desired outcome. Going for graduation? Pretend you are walking across the stage, shaking hands with the principal, taking the diploma, waving to your family. Trying to win a tournament? Make a clay model of the trophy. Whatever your goal, make it as real and vivid as you can.

Anticipate Challenges and Use Resources

Anticipate challenges. If you are tempted to text while driving, plan to turn it off and put it away out of sight before turning the key in the ignition. If your child is tempted to watch TV or play electronic games instead of doing homework, make sure the TV is off when he gets home from school, and do not put a TV or electronic-gaming system in his bedroom. If your daughter tends to oversleep, make sure she gets to bed early with a sound sleep routine to allow her to get enough hours of rest before the alarm goes off in the morning.

Use your resources. Remember, it takes a village. We are stronger together than we are alone. If you need help making a plan, ask for it. Find a friend, a support group, counselor, or clinician who has experience with the challenges you face. Check out chapter 13 and the Resources section at the end of this book.

Your Plan

Consider the strategies from the previous chapters to achieve it. For your first step, do you want to improve nutrition, exercise, sleep, communication skills, stress management, or your environment? Pick just *one* SMART change.

Even a SMART change is challenging. Before you get started, review your motivation for wanting to make a change, realistically review the challenges you anticipate, and consider the resources you can use to help you and your loved one succeed with your strategy for achieving your goals.

Maximizing Motivation for Making a Change

How Important Is It?

1. On a scale from 0 to 10, how *important* is it to you to make a change to help your loved one achieve your goal (goal:_____)? Pick a number.

| 0 | 1 | 2 | 3 | 4 | 5 | 6 | 7 | 8 | 9 | 10 |

0 = not important   10 = very important

Why Is It Important?

If you picked any number greater than 0, reflect on your reasons for picking your number rather than a lower number. For example, if you picked 8, why did you pick 8 instead of 5? What are the three most important reasons you want to make the change?

| *Sample* | Three important reasons for change |

a. Better concentration   a._____
b. More complete homework   b._____
c. Better test scores   c. _____

Challenges

Whether you want to change your lifestyle or seek professional help, a new behavior or habit can be challenging. Consider your confidence, resources, and barriers to changing to your new strategy.

On a scale from 0 to 10, how *confident* are you that you can make this change?

0   1   2   3   4   5   6   7   8   9   10
0 = not at all confident   10 = very confident

If you are already a 10, congratulations! If your confidence is something less than a 10, what would it take to move you up a point or two on this scale? What do you need to succeed? What are *barriers* to your success? What are *resources* to help you succeed?

Lindsay Decided to Stop Smoking within 30 Days

Resources	Barriers
1. Motivation to help her children be healthy and successful	1. Addiction to nicotine
2. Physician support	2. Mom smokes and friends smoke
3. Community support group	3. Need to consider whether or not to use a medication to help quit
4. Medications available to help with cravings	4. Fear of failure, fear of being embarrassed, or guilty if unable to quit the first time

Can you think of a few ways to start overcoming those barriers? If you are really stuck, you may want to consider another strategy.

My Resources and Barriers for My Plan _____

Resources	Barriers
1.	1.
2.	2.
3.	3.

KATHI J. KEMPER, MD, MPH

On the other hand, if the barriers can be met but you are still *ambivalent*, it may be helpful to weigh the pros and cons of making a change.

Pros and Cons

What are the pros and cons of your new strategy? For example, let's say Janey plans to eat breakfast at home four days a week, bring nuts and raisins as snacks, and pack her own lunch three days per week, with Mom matching funds saved from buying school lunches.

Pros and Cons Worksheet for Janey's New Diet

CHANGE	Pros—Benefits (Reasons to Do It)	Cons—Risks (Reasons Against It)
Making Changes	Better attention during second and third period Less sleepy after lunch Better grades Less risk of overeating at lunch Skin may be better from healthier food More money for shopping	Takes time in the morning Hard to get up earlier Takes time to make lunch the night before Have to remember to bring the snacks
Not Changing	Get to sleep later Predictable morning routine More time to do usual things	Poor attention during classes Continued struggle with grades We'll never know if it would have helped; feel guilty for not even trying

My Pros and Cons Worksheet for _____

CHANGE	Pros—Benefits (Reasons to Do It)	Cons—Risks (Reasons Against It)
Making a Change		
Not Changing		

Now that you've discovered the benefits of a SMART plan, decided to take a baby step in the desired direction, maximized your motivation, realistically assessed your challenges, and in and track your success. That's what chapter 10 is all about.

CHAPTER 10

Tracking Success

Aaron and his mom decided he would start taking a multivitamin and fish oil daily. They decided this would be an easy first step and had discussed different kinds of fish oil products (he went for capsules instead of liquid) and times of day (at breakfast). They weighed the pros and cons and were ready to start tracking his success.

YOU'VE MADE A SMART plan. You've established a clear goal, picked a specific strategy, vividly imagined success, weighed the pros and cons, and realistically assessed the barriers and resources that will help you and your loved one succeed. Now it's time to track your success.

What you track depends on the specifics of your SMART plan. The more specific, the better. If you're going to exercise, how many days a week will count toward success? How many minutes per day? How many miles? If you're going to take supplements, which ones? What form? How many? How many days a week? What time of day? If you plan to practice a new communication skill, how will you practice? How often will you try it in real life? With whom? At what time of day? Where? If you're starting a new stress-management behavior, what is your deadline for beginning a new class? Seeking new information? Calling a support person, coach, or health professional?

If I'm going to focus first on a new exercise routine, I will set specific goals for this week and how I will celebrate. Writing down your goals helps you make a commitment, and that makes it easier to follow through and succeed.

Tracking Success

My Exercise Goal for Week One	Goal
Type of exercise (walking the dog)	Walking the dog for at least 20 minutes or at least half a mile total in the evening.
Number of days I will do it this week	Four
I will celebrate success by seeing a new movie next Saturday.	

Aaron planned to take two fish oil capsules at breakfast when he was at home (not on sleepovers or trips to Grandpa's house). Four times a week was enough to celebrate, five was great, and seven was awesome.

Aaron's Nutritional Plan

Aaron's Plan for Week One	Goal
Specific amount, time, help, and plan to track	*Two fish oil capsules at breakfast. Mom will set them out. Aaron will take them before brushing his teeth. Aaron will mark on the calendar when he takes them.*
Number of days Aaron will do it.	*5 days per week*
Aaron will celebrate success by having buckwheat pancakes for breakfast on Sunday.	

Aaron's Success Calendar for Taking Fish Oil—Week One

	Mon	Tues	Wed	Thurs	Fri	Sat	Sun	TOTAL
Fish oil Two caps at breakfast	√	√		√	√	√		5

Aaron sure enjoyed those pancakes, and his mom was happy to make them.

Now try it with your own goal. To start, pick just one strategy that you feel confident about improving.

Tracking Your Success

My Plan for This Week	Goal
Type of change and amount of time or number of times each day	
Number of days I will do it in the next seven days	
I will celebrate success by	

Your Success Calendar for the First Week:

Goal	Mon	Tues	Wed	Thurs	Fri	Sat	Sun	TOTAL

Celebration: _____

How did it go? After reviewing your week, would you like to modify your plan? Keep using the weekly calendar until you're satisfied that this plan is ready to use for four weeks in a row.

Use one of the examples below (feel free to make as many copies as you like), or your own calendar, diary, or electronic spreadsheet to track your success. Remember, *the more you track a behavior, the more it tends to improve.*

Be honest with yourself. Tracking is for you, not your teacher, your boss, or your permanent record! If your accomplishments fall short of your goals, use the log to identify a more achievable target.

Be sure to vividly imagine and write down how you plan to celebrate your success. You can write it, draw it, or paste a picture of your success and the celebration you plan.

Sample Log for Tracking Success for Exercising 20 Minutes Five Days a Week for Four Weeks

	Mon	Tues	Wed	Thurs	Fri	Sat	Sun	TOTAL SUCCESS
Week 1	+ 10	+		-10	+	+ 10	+ 10	5
Week 2		+		-10	+	+	-10	3
Week 3	+10	+	+		+	+ 10	+	6
Week 4	+10	+		-10	+	+ 10	+	5

Notes:

+ means I did the 20 minutes.

+ # numbers indicate additional minutes beyond my goal (exceeded expectations)

—# numbers indicate that I did fewer minutes than my goal, but I still did some

Review the four-week log. What do you notice? For the sample, Tuesdays and Fridays look pretty consistent. It looks like Wednesdays have some barriers, and Thursdays aren't working so well. Saturdays and Mondays are really great. Maybe we can set the bar a bit higher for those days and stretch a little. Reviewing helps us see patterns, identify barriers, and revise plans. Here's yours:

My Log for Tracking Success for Four Weeks for _____

Activity	Mon	Tues	Wed	Thurs	Fri	Sat	Sun	TOTAL SUCCESS
Week 1								
Week 2								
Week 3								
Week 4								

I will celebrate my success by _____.

After four weeks, I notice that _____.

Next month I plan to _____.

After four weeks, review the entire month. What are you most proud of? What other changes have you noticed in your life? Would you like to try something different for the next four weeks to keep things fresh and interesting? Feel free to copy this page to keep charting your goals and progress.

Making and Tracking Multiple Changes

I strongly advise you to just make one change per week. OK, I know that some of you won't be content with that and may even see it as a dare to do more. Quit smoking *and* drinking? Eat breakfast *and* go to bed at 10:00 p.m. *and* start a gratitude journal? If you want to try to challenge yourself by making several changes at once, here's another tracking sheet for you to monitor a week at a time. Take it easy. Be realistic. Remember to set yourself up for success.

Sample Daily Change Tracker for Several Changes

Plan to be asleep by 10:00 p.m. four days a week.
Eat breakfast five days a week.
Write in my gratitude journal three times the first week.
Volunteer at the soup kitchen once.
I will celebrate my success by buying a special beautiful blank book to track my success and keep my gratitude journal and a novel to relax.

Activity	Mon	Tues	Wed	Thurs	Fri	Sat	Sun	TOTAL SUCCESS
Asleep by 10:00 p.m.	X	X	X	X				4
Eat breakfast	X	X				X	X	4
Gratitude journal	X		X			X		3
Volunteer						X		1

After one week, I notice that Mondays are easy, but by the end of the week, I'm staying up later. It's hard to eat breakfast on weekdays. What might make that easier? The volunteering was fun. I really slept well the nights I wrote in my gratitude journal. I'm going to aim for four days of that next week, although I fell a little short of my goal for breakfast. I will celebrate with that new novel.

If you want to try multiple changes (and I'm not suggesting you do):

Daily Change Tracker for Several Changes

Improvement 1: _____

Improvement 2: _____

Improvement 3: _____

Improvement 4: _____

I will celebrate my success by _____.

Activity	Mon	Tues	Wed	Thurs	Fri	Sat	Sun	TOTAL SUCCESS
1.								
2.								
3.								
4.								

On review, I notice that _____.

Next week, I plan to _____.

Tell Someone You Trust

Tracking changes can be even more effective if you tell someone you trust. Tell someone who cares about, supports, and encourages you. Avoid telling naysayers or someone who will sabotage your efforts. This means sharing your plans with a family member, friend, a blog, or a health professional.

KATHI J. KEMPER, MD, MPH

I'm confident you can succeed. This is a learning experience. You are gathering more information and experience to make better, SMARTer plans. What worked? Were there other barriers you hadn't anticipated? Do you need other resources? Do you need more time to settle into a new habit pattern? *The only failure is the failure to learn from experience.* Remember to focus more on what you want and what you like than what you don't. Reward yourself for the effort of planning and trying something new. Remember to use the resources at the end of the book. Rest, reflect, revise, and restart.

Ready to move beyond the fundamentals?
Here you go.

CHAPTER 11

Beyond the Fundamentals—
Safety First

E VEN WITH OPTIMAL practice of the fundamentals of a healthy lifestyle and environment, some people with ADD and ADHD benefit from additional interventions. Dietary supplements, medications, psychotherapy, counseling, biofeedback, support groups, massage, and acupuncture may be helpful for specific individuals. None of them replaces a healthy lifestyle.

When considering which therapies to try next, keep safety in mind.

First, do no harm.
—Hippocrates

While there is no contraindication to a good night's sleep and very few for massage and acupuncture, there *are* contraindications to many drugs and supplements. Furthermore, some medications and supplements decrease sleep and appetite or interfere with the absorption or metabolism of essential nutrients. If you use them, pay extra attention to the fundamentals of nutrition and sleep.

Cost is another concern. Most support groups and some training schools offer free or low-cost services. Professionally provided therapies, on the other hand, are often costly and may not be covered by your insurance. Check your policy carefully, and if there is any doubt, ask the clinician and insurance carrier to verify their practices and standards in writing. And remember, fundamentals first!

The therapy most people use to improve attention and decrease impulsivity is biochemical therapy (i.e., pills, both medications and natural supplements).

Supplements and Safety

In the US, the Food and Drug Administration (FDA) regulates herbs, vitamins, minerals, and other dietary supplements. Supplements are regulated more like food than like drugs. This means that supplements, like coffee or tea, may vary in their quality depending on the growing, harvesting, manufacturing, distributing, and storing conditions. The FDA allows supplement manufacturers to claim their products can support healthy mental function or optimize focus, but they cannot legally claim to prevent or treat ADD (unless they want to go through all the studies and regulatory processes required of medications).

The US Federal Trade Commission (FTC) regulates marketing. It enforces rules that say that manufacturers cannot lie or substantially mislead the public. The FTC has to detect lying or misleading advertising before they can prosecute a company for it.

Trustworthy Sources

Most European countries and Canada regulate supplements more stringently, so their products are forced to conform to stricter standards. Due to concerns about variations in quality, I recommend that you (or ask your health professional) compare brands using information from independent-testing organizations such as ConsumerLab (www.consumerlab.com), the US Pharmacopeia (www.usp.org), or the National Sanitation Foundation International (www.nsf.org).

Beware of Imports from Developing Countries

Be particularly cautious about using supplements imported from developing countries. Remember the scandals involving Chinese imports (e.g., melamine-tainted milk). In May 2007, the *Washington Post* reported mushrooms laced with banned pesticides, bacteria contaminating scallops and sardines, and dried apples preserved with cancer-causing chemicals—all imported from China. There are also numerous reports of heavy-metal contamination in supplements imported from India and Mexico.

Interested in learning more about the effectiveness of medications and supplements? That's what chapter 12 is all about.

CHAPTER 12

Pills and Plants

Jason was a nine-year-old boy whose teacher had suggested his mom get him evaluated for ADHD. Jason's behavior certainly met the standard criteria for the diagnosis, but his mother wanted to avoid medications. She didn't think they would help, and she wanted to try ginkgo, Saint-John's-wort, or megavitamins instead. I spent some time with her exploring her interest in these remedies and her reluctance to try medications.

Pills—Part 1: Medications

MEDICATIONS IMPROVE SOME symptoms, at least over the short term, for about 2/3 to 3/4 of people with ADD. Sometimes one medicine will work when another has not. Most medicines for ADD and ADHD start to work quickly, and the effects wear off soon after they are discontinued. The best way to determine whether a particular medication is helpful for a particular person is to do an N-of-1 trial.

What is an N-of-1 trial?

An N-of-1 trial is an experiment conducted for just one person. It is an elegant way to determine whether the pill is more potent than a placebo (sugar pill) and has become a widely used method to determine whether or not a child will benefit from a stimulant medication.[1] This trial can also help determine whether someone who has been on a medication continues to benefit in subsequent years (i.e., to make decisions to stop medication).[2]

When we do N-of-1 trials for stimulant medications such as methylphenidate, we involve the patient, the parents, the teachers, and our friendly neighborhood pharmacist. The trial typically takes four weeks. Week 1 is a baseline without any medication. Parents and teachers (and sometimes coaches or others who spend a lot of time with the child) rate his behavior on a Tuesday, Wednesday, or Thursday (avoiding the first and last days of the school week and school holidays). We use the standard Vanderbilt rating scale for parents* and teachers.** Over the next three weeks, the child receives either (a) a low dose of a medication, (b) a higher dose of the same medication, or (c) a placebo. Neither the parents, the patient, the teachers, nor I know which week the child receives each product. Only the pharmacist knows for sure.

Each week, parents and teachers rate the child's behavior using the same standard scale. At the end of the month, we gather all the evaluations and assess which week was best for the child. The child gets to vote too! Then we call the pharmacist and find out what the child received each week of the trial. If the best week was the higher dose of stimulant medication, we agree to use that medication for the next three months and monitor growth and sleep. If there was no clear best week or if the best week was the placebo week, we avoid starting that medication, though we may decide to do a trial of a different kind of medication.

For those who benefit from medications, we repeat the N-of-1 trial every year or two to determine whether there is continued benefit or if another medication or another strategy might be in order. By repeating trials on a regular basis, we stay in closer touch, monitor side effects and benefits regularly, and avoid thinking that medication is a lifetime burden. There is always another evaluation in sight.

Medication Options

Over the past forty years, there has been an explosion in the number of medications available to treat ADD and ADHD. The primary distinctions are between stimulant and nonstimulant medications. Stimulant medications, combined with behavioral therapy, remain the first-line treatment for youth with ADD and ADHD in the US, though the long-term effectiveness of any type of medical intervention is unclear.[3] Stimulant medications may sound scary, but they help many people. They are not addicting, and using them as advised by a physician does not lead to addiction (grinding them up and snorting them or injecting them can definitely cause problems).

---

*   For parents www.vanderbiltchildrens.org/uploads/documents/DIAGNOSTIC_PARENT_RATING_SCALE(1).pdf

** For teachers, coaches or others: www.brightfutures.org/mentalhealth/pdf/professionals/bridges/adhd.pdf

Stimulant medications include methylphenidate (Ritalin and Methylin); amphetamines, such as Adderall; the old diet pill, dextroamphetamine (Dexedrine, Dextrostat); and the newer lisdexamfetamine (Vyvanse), which breaks down to dextroamphetamine. Related compounds include dexmethylphenidate (Focalin) and extended release methylphenidate and amphetamine (Adderall, Metadate, and Concerta). The patch medication (Daytrana) provides a controlled release of methylphenidate. Like coffee, most stimulants start working within about 20 minutes. There are short, medium, and long-acting medications.

Short, Medium, and Long-Acting Stimulant Medications

Short (Three to Six Hours)	Medium (Four to Eight Hours)	Long (More than Eight Hours)
Ritalin	Ritalin LA	Concerta
Methylin	Ritalin SR	Focalin XR
Focalin	Metadate CD	Daytrana (patch)
Metadate	Methylin ER	Adderall XR
Adderall		Vyvanse

Stimulant medications generally improve attention and reduce activity levels, but they do not affect oppositional or defiant behaviors much. They have little overall effect on quality of life, and initial benefits seen in the first year or two of use may not be sustained over long-term use.[4] This means that regular reevaluations are important to determine the ongoing need for medication in those who benefit initially because symptoms improve over time for many children even without medication. In fact, recent rigorous research done by scientists without conflicts of interest* showed that stimulants were little better than placebo treatments.[5] The prestigious British National Institute for Health and Clinical Excellence (NICE) guidelines for treating ADHD recommend stimulant medications as a first-line therapy for adults with ADHD but only for children with severe symptoms, not mild or moderate ADHD.[6]

---

* Some earlier research that suggested benefits of stimulants was conducted by people with financial conflicts of interest.

Nonstimulant medications used to treat ADHD and ADD include atomoxetine (Strattera), Modafinil (Provigil), clonidine (Catapres), guanfacine (Tenex and extended-release Intuniv), buproprion (Wellbutrin), and several types of blood pressure, antidepressant, and antiseizure medications. Atomoxetine is the most commonly prescribed nonstimulant medication for ADHD. In adults, studies show that atomoxetine is much better than placebo for improving the ability to focus, be organized, regulate attention and emotions, and remember things over the short term.[7] Atomoxetine has also proven beneficial for children with ADHD, but side effects such as sleepiness and decreased appetite limit its appeal.[8] Many of the other medications are prescribed off-label, that is, they have not been approved by the FDA for treatment of ADD or ADHD but are approved for other medical problems, and prescribers use them to try to help patients with ADD who have not been helped by stimulant medications.

In addition to not working for some people, there are several problems with medications:

1. *Side effects.* The most common side effects of stimulant medications are decreased appetite, poor growth, and insomnia. Less-common side effects include nausea, headaches, stomachaches, sweating, jitteriness, tics, dizziness, a racing heart, and—paradoxically—drowsiness. Of greater concern, stimulant use is linked to psychosis, hallucinations, heart arrhythmias, and even sudden death.[9-10]

2. *Failure to work* when they are not taken. Medications are not a cure for ADD. When a dose is missed, the medicine cannot work. If someone stops taking the medicine, it stops working. For a variety of reasons, more than half of patients stop taking stimulant medication without being advised to do so by their physician.[11-12] In one of the largest studies ever undertaken comparing the benefits of medications alone, medications combined with intensive behavioral therapy, and behavioral therapy alone, there were significant improvements in those treated with medications for the first year or so. After about 14 months, the differences between treatment groups were not significant.[3]

3. *Relying on medications* instead of making healthy changes in lifestyle and environment. When people rely on medications, they may not make more challenging improvements in nutrition, exercise, sleep, the environment, communication, stress, or behavior.

4. *Long-term costs.* Continuous dependence on medications is costly for individuals and society. Stimulant use has increased from 0.6% of children under 19 years old in 1987 to 3.4% in 2003. In terms of overall costs of medications, of the top five drugs prescribed for children, three were medications for ADD and ADHD, ahead of antibiotics.*

5. *Long-term effects* of chronic medication use or using multiple medications at once are unknown. Although stimulant medications have been used for decades, there are no long-term studies evaluating the effects on developing brains (or bodies) of using these medications daily for 30 years. Short-term use has been evaluated for one drug at a time, but the effects and side effects of taking multiple medications simultaneously are unknown.

6. *Misuse, diversion, and abuse.* As the number of prescriptions for stimulant medications has grown, so has the number of reports of them being diverted or sold to people who do *not* have ADHD. A 2009 study reported a 76% increase in the number of calls to poison control centers related to adolescent abuse of prescription ADHD medications.[13]

Given these concerns about medications and the fact that my clinic focuses on natural therapies, I rarely recommend them. When I do recommend medications, I suggest that we do an N-of-1 trial to determine the short-term benefits and risks for a particular child. I also suggest that this trial be repeated annually to assess the ongoing need for medications. *And* I stress the importance of treating the whole child: treating ADD involves more than medications, even when medications are helpful.

---

* The US Agency for Healthcare Research and Quality reported in 2007 that the top five drugs (based on spending) for children were: Singulair (an asthma medicine), Concerta (ADD drug), Strattera (ADD drug), Zyrtec (allergy medicine), and Adderall (ADD drug). Over $2 billion was spent on these five drugs in 2004, accounting for nearly 1/4 of all prescription medication costs for children in the US.

> Jason's mom was willing to do an N-of-1 trial for a month to see if a stimulant medication might help him, so we did. Jason's behavior was a bit better at school and at soccer, but not at home. His mom remained concerned about side effects and asked if there were any natural products, like homeopathy, megavitamins or herbs that might help him.

Pills—Part 2: Homeopathy

Homeopathic preparations are extremely dilute. In fact, many homeopathic practitioners believe the more dilute the preparation, the more potent it is. This is not how most scientists think about biochemical remedies.

Case studies suggest that long-term follow-up by a homeopathic practitioner can help some people with ADHD. However, rigorous randomized controlled trials have had inconsistent results: some suggest it is helpful, while others find no effect.[14] Although homeopathy is safe, I do not routinely recommend it for treating ADD symptoms.

Pills—Part 3: Vitamins, Minerals, Herbs,
and Other Dietary Supplements

Pills, even natural products such as herbs, do not replace a healthy diet. However, in the face of constant advertising and the low cost of junk food, most American children do not meet their brain's needs for essential nutrients.[15-16] Therefore, as much as I encourage families to adopt healthy food habits, selected supplements have become part of my routine recommendations for ADD. I routinely recommend a *multivitamin/mineral* and an *omega-3 fatty acid* supplement. I sometimes recommend other supplements and herbs to address specific concerns or related health issues. Let's look at the most commonly used supplements in a little more detail.

Vitamins and Minerals

The best way to get essential vitamins and minerals is through locally grown food raised on healthy soil. Due to widespread depletion of soils and the length of time required to transport many foods from across the country to stores and tables, the foods we commonly consume lack the levels of minerals and antioxidants present in locally grown foods a hundred years ago.[17-18]

This is why I generally recommend a daily multivitamin/mineral supplement. This recommendation is based on studies showing the importance these essential nutrients in making neurotransmitters and improved behavior in adults and children who receive them.[19-20] B vitamins are particularly important for proper brain function; supplements can improve ADHD symptoms.[21-25] Most general multivitamins contain plenty of B vitamins for most children. Two favorite supplements of pediatricians and psychiatrists who specialize in natural therapies include Juice Plus® and EMPower Plus®.

However, most multivitamins contain only trace amounts of minerals.

If your child eats an excellent diet rich in essential minerals, he may not need supplements. Ask your doctor to check a ferritin level (this is more sensitive than getting a hemoglobin level for iron) and an RBC zinc level (this is better than getting a serum or plasma zinc level).

The minerals most often deficient in people with ADD are iron, magnesium, and zinc.[26-28] For example, *iron deficiency* interferes with memory, concentration, behavior, and school performance;[29-30] supplementing iron-deficient teenagers can improve their learning, memory, and test scores. *Magnesium* supplements have been used successfully in combination with vitamin B6 to improve behavior in children with ADHD and autism;[31] other studies have shown that six months of magnesium supplements alone helped improve behavior in children with ADHD.[32] Several studies have also shown benefits from *zinc* supplements for children with ADHD;[33] most of the studies on zinc were done in countries where nutritional deficiencies are common. There are no compelling studies showing that mineral supplements improve symptoms for people with ADD who are not deficient.

Remember that it can take weeks or months to restore optimal mineral levels throughout the body. You cannot take a mineral supplement in the morning and expect to function with greater clarity, focus, or patience in the afternoon.

What About Megavitamins?

Supplementation with large individual doses of vitamins A, C, E, and K or the minerals calcium, chromium, copper, iodine, and selenium has not proven helpful for people with ADD. Restoring optimal vitamin D levels through supplements may help improve mood but has not been tested as a remedy for ADD. Excessive intake of any mineral may cause imbalances and side effects. Taking a daily multivitamin/mineral is safe for most people; those with genetic conditions such as hemochromatosis, Wilson's disease, or similar conditions should check with their health professional before starting any kind of supplement.

Jason's mom was already working on reducing their trips to fast-food restaurants and doing healthier cooking at home. Because Jason had been eating so poorly for so long, we tested his blood for ferritin, a marker of iron levels, and started him on a multivitamin. His iron levels were normal, so he did not need iron supplements. Because he also suffered from constipation, we added one tablespoon of milk of magnesia (magnesium hydroxide) daily for two weeks to help both problems.

Amino Acids

Many of the brain's messengers are made from amino acids, but there is little scientific evidence that amino acid supplements improve symptoms of ADD. Two small European studies suggested that *carnitine* supplements could help improve attention and behavior in school-age boys, but an American study of acetyl-L-carnitine supplements showed they were not any better than placebo for most children with ADHD. Although they are generally safe, I do not routinely recommend carnitine or acetyl-L-carnitine supplements. In a small open study in adults, supplementation with *s-adenosylmethionine* (SAM or SAM-E) improved ADHD symptoms,[34] but these benefits have not been verified in larger controlled trials nor in children.

Essential Fatty Acids

Fish oil supplements are excellent sources of EPA and DHA, important long-chain fatty acids for optimal brain function (see chapter 4). Unless they are already eating fatty fish such as wild salmon, herring, or sardines several times a week, I generally recommend that patients with ADD take omega-3 fatty acid supplements. This is because omega-3 fatty acids found in fish are important parts of brain-cell membranes and because studies suggest that supplements can improve attention.[35-36] Omega-3 fatty acid supplements can also improve mood, decrease anxiety, diminish aggressive behavior, and improve school performance.[37-39]

Good vegetarian sources of omega-3 fatty acids include flaxseed, certain kinds of algae,* and walnuts. For those who prefer fish oils, my usual dosage recommendations range from 500 milligrams to 2000 milligrams daily of the combination of EPA (eicosapentaenoic acid) and DHA (docosahexaenoic

---

* Algae are the sources of DHA added to most infant formula in the US.

acid) combined; smaller doses for smaller people, larger doses for larger people. If in doubt, ask your health professional.

Omega-3 fatty acid supplements are generally free of the mercury, dioxins, and PCBs that contaminate many fish. Check with www.consumerlab.com to see a recent comparison of commonly used brands. (Note: access to complete information requires a subscription, so you may want to ask your physician or librarian to subscribe.) Also, see our Internet site for the Center for Integrative Medicine at Wake Forest University Baptist Medical Center for my recommendations about omega-3 fatty acid supplements. You can print it out and take it to the store with you: www.wfubmc.edu/cim (look for the link to the page on dietary supplements).

> Jason's mom started serving salmon once a week. To boost Jason's intake of fruits and vegetables, she made him a smoothie after school with frozen fruit, yogurt, water, and a tablespoon of flaxseeds.

Melatonin

Melatonin does not improve daytime symptoms of ADD, but it can help improve sleep.[40-43] This is important because many people with ADD have trouble falling asleep.[44] Those most likely to be helped are those who work different shifts and those who tend to fall asleep and wake up later and later each day. The typical adult doses of melatonin are 0.3 to 5 milligrams one hour before the desired bedtime. Melatonin is not a substitute for a healthy sleep routine. Melatonin does not cause a morning hangover; however, it may interact with other medications and may make depression symptoms worse. One study followed children with ADD who had started taking melatonin as part of a clinical trial on sleep. Nearly four years later, over 2/3 of them were still using melatonin because it was helpful and had no serious side effects.[45]

> Sleep was not a particular problem for Jason, so we did not start any melatonin. However, his mom remained interested in herbal remedies that might help him. Her cousin's grandmother swore by ginkgo, and she wondered if it might help Jason too.

KATHI J. KEMPER, MD, MPH

Herbs

Herbal remedies have been used for thousands of years before anyone had an official diagnosis of ADD. Research about modern uses for ancient herbal remedies is ongoing. The National Library of Medicine (NLM) has a Web site, Medline Plus, with great information about medications, supplements, and herbs. Check with your clinician or ask your library to subscribe to an independent database (such as Natural Medicines Comprehensive Database, Natural Standard, or ConsumerLab) so you have access to the latest studies from reputable scientists.

Historically, some herbs have been used to promote calm and decrease agitation, while others have been used to promote increased focus. None replaces a healthy lifestyle. In general, herbal remedies are gentler and safer than most medications. But do not assume that just because something is natural that it is safe. Even commonly used herbal products like coffee and tea can cause jittery feelings, insomnia, and a racing pulse.

Calming Herbs

Calming herbs such as chamomile, hops, kava, lavender, lemon balm, passionflower, and valerian may promote sleep or reduce agitation, but they are not usually helpful for calming daytime hyperactivity, inattentiveness, or impulsivity. Remember, most medications used to treat ADD are stimulants, not sedatives. It makes sense to use an herbal tea with chamomile, lemon balm, or passionflower in the evening to make it easier to fall asleep. If stimulant medication is making it difficult to relax and fall asleep in the evening, it may also be worthwhile to try a combination of valerian and lemon balm, which was shown in one German study (which used a product called *Euvegal forte*) to improve sleep and reduce restlessness.[46]

Stimulating Herbs

Herbs like coffee and tea that contain caffeine are natural stimulants (see chapter 4 for more detail on coffee, tea, and other foods we love). Green tea also contains an antioxidant, EGCG, and theanine, which can be calming, offsetting some of the unpleasant side effects of caffeine.[47-50] Caffeine helps promote focus and enhance attention in both children and adults. I often recommend green tea and coffee to help promote focus and attention, and I drink them myself. I prefer coffee and tea to artificially colored, flavored, and sweetened beverages to minimize my brain's exposure to potentially toxic chemicals. To minimize the risk of insomnia from caffeine, do not drink caffeinated beverages within six hours of planned bedtime.

> Jason's mom started giving him a cup of green tea at breakfast and iced tea after school.

Other Herbal Products

Ginseng is traditionally used as a tonic for older or debilitated people in Asia. For them, ginseng can improve abstract thinking, arithmetic skills, learning, memory, and reaction times. However, there are no studies showing the ginseng alone helps children, adolescents, or young adults improve ADD symptoms. Similarly, *ginkgo biloba* is widely used to improve memory and cognitive performance in the elderly who suffer from impaired blood circulation to the brain. A pilot study from Italy indicated that ginkgo might help improve ADD symptoms.[51] A 2001 study showed benefits for a Canadian product (AD-fX) that combines ginseng and ginkgo for patients with ADD or dyslexia.[52] Given the large variations in the quality of ginseng and ginkgo products and the relatively few studies suggesting they might be helpful, I do not routinely recommend them. When I do, I suggest the Canadian product AD-fX.

Pycnogenol or European *pine bark extract** is the name for a group of powerful antioxidants (oligoproanthocyanidins or OPCs) that have proven significantly better than placebo pills in improving attention and concentration and decreasing hyperactivity in children in several European studies (some of which were funded in part by Pycnogenol producers).[53-55] Given the variability in product quality and the lack of US data, I do not routinely recommend Pycnogenol supplements, but if families want to try them, I do not object.

Neither *evening primrose oil* (which contains the mildly anti-inflammatory fatty acid, gamma linoleic acid or GLA) nor *Saint John's wort* supplements have proven any more useful than placebo pills for ADHD. I do not recommend them.

---

* Pycnogenols are also found in grape seed extract.

Although I don't recommend ginkgo for children, Jason's mom really wanted to try it. I helped her identify a reliable product using ConsumerLab, and she agreed to monitor his response using the same forms we had used for the N-of-1 trial of stimulant medication. By the end of the month, his constipation had markedly improved, but she had not seen any real benefits of the ginkgo. However, she was pleased with the process because she could tell her cousin that she'd tried it, and she felt more confident rating Jason's behavior and how his focus, attention, and self-discipline were affected by other events in his life.

Summary

1. Remember, pills are not a substitute for healthy habits and a healthy habitat, but they can help decrease distractibility while reducing impulsivity.
2. Talk with your health professional about doing an N-of-1 trial before making a long-term commitment to a medication. If you or a loved one is already taking medication, consider doing an N-of-1 trial every year or two to make sure it is still providing a meaningful benefit that outweighs its costs and side effects.
3. If you're not getting essential brain nutrients from your diet, consider taking a multivitamin/mineral supplement.
4. If you're not eating flaxseed or fish several times a week, consider changing your diet or taking a supplement that provides 500 to 2,000 milligrams of the combination of EPA+DHA daily.
5. If your child has trouble falling asleep, consider using melatonin or a calming herbal tea to help while you optimize your sleep routine.
6. Use reliable evidence-based resources like Medline Plus, and buy only brands that have undergone rigorous reviews for quality.

CHAPTER 13

A Village:
Counseling, Biofeedback, School, and Support groups

> After reading more about ADD, Taylor's dad, Jack, thought he might have some symptoms too. He wanted to get some coaching, along with Taylor, to help learn some new strategies for reframing thoughts, managing behavioral problems, and helping her succeed better in school. It sure would be nice if he could find other parents like him who could tell him what worked (and what didn't) for them. The Internet seemed overwhelming. He even read about something called neurofeedback. What was that, and would it be useful? Where should he start?

Professional Counseling

LARGE STUDIES SUGGEST that, at least in the short term, the most effective treatment for children with ADHD is an integrated strategy behavioral therapy and stimulant medication.[1] Behavioral therapies, guided by professionals, take a little longer to show a benefit than medications do. But while the effects of medication end when the pills stop, the skills learned in behavioral therapy can persist for years after the therapy officially ends.[2] Although it may appear to be more expensive in the short-term, behavioral therapy can be an excellent cost-effective investment.

Many psychologists, social workers, teachers, school counselors, pediatricians, and family physicians are trained to provide effective behavioral advice and support for families facing ADD, including parent training. Professional counseling may be particularly helpful for those who have coexisting conditions, such as anxiety or depression, or for families whose parents were not fortunate enough to have good role models for effective parenting skills. Psychological or neuropsychological testing and advice help identify and treat children with specific learning disabilities.

For adults with ADD, a novel type of psychological therapy called metacognitive therapy can help teach skills such as time management, organization, and planning. This kind of training promotes significant improvements in daily living skills and job performance.[3] Given the impressive improvements in initial studies, it is likely that this kind of therapy will be incorporated into standard behavioral therapy for children and adolescents as well.

Insurance policies often cover professional testing and counseling services. Check with your insurance carrier to make sure what kind of clinician is covered, what percentage of the visit is paid, and how many sessions are covered under your policy. If you have questions about specific learning problems, ask the school to conduct testing to see if your child qualifies for special services. Schools in the US are legally required to do so, but parents may need to advocate persistently for it to be done because many schools have more requests than resources.

> Given Jack's interest and intelligence in considering counseling, I referred him to our pediatric psychologist, Dr. Gail. Pediatric psychologists are used to working with families and used to working with busy family schedules. Dr. Gail and Jack decided to meet weekly at first to get things moving in the right direction. Dr. Gail also offered to do neuropsychological testing for learning problems and sensory-processing problems because the school had a ten-month waiting list and would accept her findings and recommendations based on their previous work together. Dr. Gail also helped answer Jack's questions about neurofeedback and called her colleagues who offered those services to get Jack and Taylor an appointment to try it. What is neurofeedback?

Biofeedback and Neurofeedback

Electroencephalographic (EEG) biofeedback (also known as neurofeedback) provides information about current EEG levels, allowing the user to alter brainwave patterns. It can significantly improve behavior, attention, and IQ scores.[4-16] In fact, neurofeedback has proven as effective as more standard therapies.[10, 17-19] EEG biofeedback has even been helpful for children with Aspberger's syndrome and those with mental retardation.[20-21] To achieve sustained improvements, most studies provided at least 20 EEG biofeedback-training sessions with a professional trainer. Typical costs range from $75 to $200 per session—about what you'd pay for weekly psychotherapy or family therapy.

EEG biofeedback training develops a skill. Unlike medications, whose effects stop when the pills stop, EEG biofeedback-training benefits can be expected to persist if the skill is mastered, and practice continues.

EEG biofeedback training may not be covered by your insurance yet because the studies supporting it are so recent. On the other hand, most professionals who offer EEG biofeedback are psychologists, and their professional services may be covered by insurance. Check your policy and ask your clinician to assess your unique situation.

Another form of biofeedback for hyperactive children is providing feedback about activity levels. Modern devices about the size of a wristwatch (e.g., the BuzzBee® Actigraph) can keep count of movements and provide feedback about physical activity levels. Providing positive verbal feedback when a child attains the desired (lower) level of activity has resulted in startling improvements in behavior.[22-23]

> Jack called the neurofeedback therapist and found out that his insurance wouldn't cover it, but his flexible medical spending plan (or medical savings account, available through his employer) would. Taylor was really curious about the machines and hit it off right away with the therapist. Jack decided that he'd take Taylor for ten sessions to see if they noticed any improvement. If yes, they'd continue, and he'd plan on trying it himself next year.

School

Help teachers and school administrators recognize your child's unique gifts and challenges. Advocate for your child to receive the public services to which he is legally entitled. A 1999 addendum to the US Individuals with Disability Education Act (IDEA) says that children and youth whose disabilities adversely affect their educational performance should receive special services or accommodations that address their problem (e.g., ADHD) and its effects. Section 504 of the US federal Vocational Rehabilitation Act prohibits discrimination against any person with a disability. Under Section 504, students may receive services such as a smaller class size, tutoring, modification of homework assignments, help with organizing, and other assistance.

Check with your health-care professional and your school to learn about the latest policies and regulations. You can also find the federal regulations on the Internet at www.ideapractices.org or from the US federal government at www.ed.gov.

At the very least, schedule regular meetings with your child's teachers to monitor progress and advocate for seating arrangements that put the child near the front of the classroom. Experienced teachers are real experts on child behavior and development. They can offer lots of helpful advice and insight. Not only have they observed hundreds of children who are the same age as your child, they spend many hours a day with them, watching them under a variety of circumstances.

If your child has been diagnosed by a qualified health professional with ADD or ADHD and has not received sufficient services or accommodation within six months of asking the teacher and/or principal, consider writing to your school district's director or chairperson for special educational services. Your letter should specifically request an evaluation for specific learning disabilities and a functional assessment to determine how his disabilities are affecting his classroom performance. These evaluations are required to develop an Individual Educational Plan (IEP) or a 504 Accommodation Plan. Middle school and high school students diagnosed with ADD or ADHD are also entitled to these evaluations and, if appropriate, an IEP or accommodation plans. For help with letters, see the Web site for the National Information Center for Children and Youth with Disabilities.

With an IEP, your child may qualify for extra help, special classes, extra time for tests or projects, having an extra set of books for home study, being able to take notes on a computer keyboard rather than with handwriting, extra breaks in the day, fewer classes, and other accommodations. For more information, see the Resources section at the end of the book.

Your child spends a large part of his early life in school. Advocate for schools as healthy environments that serve healthy food and encourage healthy physical activity. Urge schools to include daily recesses, optimally use music to promote learning and positive behavior, and incorporate physical activity in lessons. Support teachers and administrators who offer creative, effective strategies to promote your child's strengths. Encourage your school board to use daylight* and natural spaces in designing new buildings and green cleaning and pesticide management practices to reduce toxic exposures. Work with local parents and physicians and with national advocacy groups such as Jamie's Food Revolution (www.jamieoliver.com/campaigns/jamies-food-revolution) to promote healthier school lunches (avoiding artificial colors, sweeteners, and flavoring agents while promoting fresh, local ingredients prepared on site).

Homework

Historically, homework didn't really start until high school. Nowadays, in an effort to prepare kids for high school, schools give homework for children as early as kindergarten. While finishing one worksheet or picture may not present much of a challenge, larger projects (such as a review for a test) may require additional assistance. Help your child with organizational skills for planning homework, making sure necessary resources are on hand, and having a special folder for completed work so it's more likely to get back to school intact before "the dog eats it." Here are some tips:

- Get on the same side of the issue. Connect with your child and the teacher. Set goals and develop strategies together.
- Set aside homework time every Monday to Thursday.
- Pick a special homework place (e.g., kitchen table or desk).
- Stop working if it's unproductive. Use bursts of work interspersed with breaks to keep things fresh and interesting. Sometimes a new solution or insight will appear when you take a walk, sing a song, or set the table.
- Get organized. Set aside a certain amount of time for each subject. Have extra materials (pencils, paper, calculator, dictionary, computer, etc.) on hand. Consider asking for an extra set of textbooks to keep at home.
- When the homework is reading or reviewing, develop a strategy:

---

* A study from the 1970s showed that the flickering light associated with fluorescent lights was associated with worse behavior than was seen with incandescent lighting, at least in the six children with autism who were studied.[24]

1. Read the chapter title and section headings to get an overview.
2. Ask yourself what the most important information is likely to be; verify by reading the questions or problems at the end of the chapter.
3. Look at the highlighted, bold, or underlined words and make notes about their definitions.
4. Read the material; consider using a computer program or other device to read the material out loud if there are problems with visual processing. Consider using colored highlighters or take notes on colored cards to organize the material.
5. Answer the questions, or do the problems. Ask for help if needed.

> Taylor's school was really backed up on doing learning evaluations but said they'd be happy to work with Dr. Gail, meet with her and Jack, and implement a plan based on Dr. Gail's findings. Jack bought two DVDs about food and gave them to the principal who could share them with teachers and then give them to the local library. Jack also asked his parent-teacher organization (PTO) rep to add a discussion about school lunches and snacks to the next PTO meeting. The rep was delighted to have another parent's active participation, and the principal was grateful for the new resources.

See chapter 6 for more tips on developing organizational and time management skills.

Other Activities

School is not the only thing kids do! Other activities provide a terrific way to explore interests, talents, and possible lifelong passions or vocations. When choosing activities, consider the adult-child ratio. Music, art, tutoring, and individual language lessons may offer more individual attention than soccer leagues. Consider scouting, volunteering, church groups, and civic organizations. Be flexible. Your child is trying things out. Do not invest in an expensive instrument before he's shown serious interest over some time. Look for consistency. A class that meets every Tuesday is easier to schedule and attend than a sports team that has inconsistent practice and game schedules requiring frequent changes in the family driving routine.

Support Groups

There is nothing that can help you feel saner and supported than knowing you are not alone in facing a challenging situation. Support groups can be enormously helpful for parents and families struggling with a loved one with ADHD. Here are a few national groups that may be helpful for you.

All Kinds of Minds (AKOM) is a nonprofit organization that aims to help individuals with learning differences achieve success in school and in life. Their Internet site has toolkits and other resources for parents, schools, and health professionals: www.allkindsofminds.org

Children and Adults with Attention Deficit Hyperactivity Disorder (CHADD) is a national nonprofit organization that works to improve the lives of those affected by ADD and ADHD through education, advocacy, and support. Their home page offers links to local chapters as well as international activities: www.chadd.org

The National Federation of Families of Children's Mental Health is a parent-run organization to support families caring for children and youth with emotional, behavioral, or mental disorders. The Web site provides links to publications, research, and state chapters: www.ffcmh.org.

Learning Disabilities Association of America (LDA) was founded in 1963 to support people with learning disabilities, their families, teachers, and health professionals. It sponsors an annual conference. The Web site provides resources, legislative updates, and links to state chapters: www.ldanatl.org.

Mental Health America, formerly known as the National Mental Health Association, is the national's oldest and largest community-based network dedicated to promoting mental health, preventing mental disorders, and achieving victory over mental illness through advocacy, education, research, and delivering programs and services. They strongly supported the Mental Health Parity law that became effective in 2010 and continue to provide updates, action alerts, and advocacy to ensure effective implementation. Their Web site provides links to local affiliates and a wealth of advocacy information: www.nmha.org.

Even before their first appointment with Dr. Gail, Jack went online to the CHADD and found a monthly support-group meeting that was only 20 minutes away. The Web site also provided more details about Taylor's rights at school under the US IDEA, Section 504 and gave him information about a regional conference where he could meet hundreds of others like him and Taylor. CHADD has been holding conferences for more than 20 years, and they've accumulated a wealth of practical experience in knowing how to support families and encourage effective advocacy.

Summary

Professional and peer support can be invaluable for families facing ADD and ADHD. Fortunately, there is plenty of high-quality, experienced support available for personal services, conferences, and online information.

1. Professionals such as psychologists, social workers, and physicians can offer counseling, education, behavioral strategies, and training in cognitive-behavioral skills and communication skills.
2. Psychologists and other licensed health professionals can also offer newer therapies such as neurofeedback. Check your insurance to find out how these services are covered for you.
3. Schools are full of dedicated experts on child development and behavior. Get to know your child's teacher. Ask for testing and accommodations if appropriate.
4. Peer support is available through national education and advocacy groups via their Internet sites, local meetings, newsletters, and regional and national conferences. These groups include All Kinds of Minds, Children and Adults with Attention Deficit Hyperactivity Disorder (CHADD), the National Federation of Families of Children's Mental Health, Learning Disabilities Association of America, and Mental Health America.
5. Additional resources are listed in the Resources section.

CHAPTER 14

Other Professional Therapists: Massage, Acupuncture, and Chiropractic

> Jennifer received a gift certificate for a massage for Mother's Day. As she felt the tension melt away, she wondered whether massage might help her son, Austin, whose medications for ADD were making it difficult for him to fall asleep. She brought it up at our next visit. Does massage do something more than relax muscles temporarily?

Massage

YES! MASSAGE DOESN'T just help muscles; it has powerful effects on blood flow and brain messengers that affect our focus and clarity.[1-2] It reduces stress, improves mood, decreases pain, and alleviates anxiety—all of which can improve concentration, deliberation, and self-discipline.[1, 3-7]

Although some people might worry that massage could make it harder to pay attention because the recipient would become so relaxed, studies suggest that massage therapy benefits people diagnosed with ADD, improving anger control, sleep, and behavior.[8] Even a 15-minute chair massage can improve speed and accuracy on standard tests.[9] Students diagnosed with ADHD who received regular massage (twice weekly for one month) had better moods and classroom behavior than similar students who did not get massage. Teens with ADD who received massage therapy were less fidgety, less hyperactive, and more attentive than teens trained in relaxation techniques. In another study, adults who received a 15-minute chair massage were more relaxed, alert, and better at standard tests, with lower levels of stress hormones than adults who simply rested for 15 minutes.[9] All these studies suggest that massage can be helpful for those with ADD. However, additional studies would be useful to help determine the best type of massage, the duration and frequency of treatments, and whether massage provided by friends or family members is as helpful as care from a licensed professional.

Massage—Safety and Licensing

Massage is safe. Use commonsense precautions, and avoid rubbing skin rashes or infections, bruises, or burns. Do not force massage therapy on someone who has suffered from physical or sexual abuse or who is very shy. Respect adolescents' desires for privacy.

In the US, massage therapists are licensed or certified as health professionals in 40 states; elsewhere, cities or counties license them. Check with your state health board or local health agency to find a licensed provider. You can also find a licensed professional through the American Massage Therapy Association's locator service.

Massage—Costs and Insurance

Getting a professional massage regularly can get expensive, and the cost of massage is not yet routine for most insurance policies. The cost of professional massage may be covered as physical therapy services under some insurance plans; however, you will probably need a referral from your physician or nurse practitioner. Insurance policies vary; check with yours to be certain of what is covered before you assume anything.

While professional training to become a massage therapist takes years, it is not difficult to learn some simple techniques using readily available books, videos, and instruction from a licensed therapist. Training a trusted family member or close friend to provide massage can make massage a financially viable therapy for those with ADD. Furthermore, massage benefits those who give it as well as those who receive it.[10-11] So do yourself a favor: learn to provide simple massage and offer it regularly to someone you love.

Jennifer found several books about massage for children at her local library. She also found information and demonstrations on the Web sites eHow.com and wikiHow.com; she also asked her new best friend, the massage therapist, to give her some tips on working with children. Jennifer was pleased to know there were pleasant things she could do as a mom to help Austin sleep better and be more relaxed and focused. When she mentioned her new interest to her neighbor Tiffany, she asked if acupuncture might help ADD too. Can it?

Acupuncture

Attention deficit disorder is a modern medical diagnosis that does not fit a traditional Asian model. Many scientific studies confirm acupuncture's benefits in treating people with anxiety, depression, and sleep problems—all of which impair concentration, self-discipline, and other elements of executive function that are important for organization and planning skills.[12-25] This means that acupuncture can help correct underlying problems that contribute to ADD and ADHD symptoms.

Acupuncture—Safety and Licensing

Acupuncture is generally safe. In two studies including over 30,000 acupuncture treatments, no serious adverse events were reported;[26-27] serious side effects are possible, but they are extremely rare.

The US has more than 11,000 licensed nonphysician and 3,000 physician acupuncturists. Acupuncturists certified by the American Association of Oriental Medicine typically receive about five times as many hours of training in acupuncture as physicians who provide acupuncture (1,500 versus 300 hours). Insurance policies vary in their coverage of acupuncture services. In general, service provided by a physician is more likely to be covered than service by a nonphysician licensed acupuncturist. Go figure.

Acupuncture—Bottom Line for ADHD

Although acupuncture is safe and widely available, there are no research studies that conclusively that it offers specific benefits for people with ADD or ADHD. Until such research is published, I do not recommend acupuncture as a treatment for ADD or ADHD, but I do recommend that those suffering from anxiety, depression, or insomnia consider trying acupuncture if healthy lifestyle alone has not solved the problem.

> Jennifer told Tiffany that acupuncture didn't seem beneficial for Austin. They were already having a good experience with massage two to three times a week. Tiffany asked if she'd ever tried chiropractic.

Chiropractic

Chiropractors are licensed as health-care professionals in all fifty states in the US. While most people seek chiropractic care for help with sore backs, necks, and other joints, some people use it for other problems too. Using chiropractic for non-joint problems is based on the belief that pinched nerves from malalignment of the spine or joints can affect all kinds of organ function, including brain function. Many chiropractors also offer advice to promote a healthy lifestyle.

Although some people swear by the benefits of chiropractic, osteopathic, or craniosacral adjustments for ADD and ADHD (you can find a lot of testimonials on the Internet from satisfied customers and clinicians alike), there are very few studies that have systematically compared the effects of these therapies to other therapies such as massage, medications, or a healthy lifestyle.[28-30] One ongoing study is a randomized controlled trial of a branch of chiropractic therapy called Neuro Emotional Technique.[31] This study was well designed, and its results will help guide evidence-based practice. Until more studies like this have been reported, I do not recommend these therapies as a primary treatment strategy to treat people for ADD symptoms, but it may be very useful in helping accident-prone ADD sufferers to recover from injuries to the head, neck, or joints.

Chiropractic Safety

Chiropractic care is generally safe. Minor side effects include headache, fatigue, and temporary discomfort in the joints being manipulated. Major side effects (fractures, dislocations, and strokes) are rare. People who have tumors of the bone, spinal cord, or brain and those who have had scoliosis surgery should be cautious about seeking spinal manipulative therapy.

> Jennifer decided to hold off on the chiropractic treatments until more definitive research showed it was useful for someone like Austin. In the meantime, her husband decided to learn some massage techniques so he could provide them for Austin and maybe save a little money on next year's Mother's Day gift by providing Jennifer's massage himself.

CHAPTER 15

Bottom Line

H ERE'S A QUICK checklist of the main points we've covered. For more details, see the individual chapters.

Summary

- ☐ 1. Make sure it's really ADD or ADHD and not some other problem. See your health professional to check for physical factors that can interfere with learning, concentration, patience, and planning. Ask for a referral to a neuropsychological specialist if you are concerned about special problems like auditory or visual processing disorders or learning disabilities (see chapters 1, 2, and 12).
- ☐ 2. Keep your eye on the prize. Focus on your goals and the strengths, talents, and interests your loved one has to achieve those goals. Reframe problems as goals and learning opportunities rather than labels that limit. Coaching and hope-oriented counseling or therapy may help you master these skills more easily (see chapters 2 and 13). Consider different options. Start with baby steps in the right direction to establish a pattern of success. Track your experience. Assess your success. Stay flexible. Keep practicing. Celebrate mastery.
- ☐ 3. Focus on the fundamentals of healthy habits in a healthy habitat. Which of these will you include in a SMART plan to improve your family's health?

  - ☐ *Food.* Eat nutritious food at least three times a day to keep blood sugar and brain nutrient levels stable. As Michael Pollan advises in *Food Rules*: "If it comes from a plant, eat it; if it's made in a plant, don't." Maintain a stable energy supply by eating whole grains, beans, seeds, whole fruits, and vegetables. Grow it yourself or buy from a local farmer if you can. Avoid artificial colors, flavors, preservatives, and pesticides. Drink plenty of pure water. Consider therapeutic green tea or coffee. If you suspect that certain foods impair thinking or concentration, keep a food diary or work with a nutrition expert to try an elimination diet. Eat fish rich in omega-3 fatty acids (e.g., sardines, salmon, or mackerel) at least twice weekly. Take a multivitamin/multimineral daily to avoid deficiencies of B vitamins, iron, magnesium, and zinc. Unless you eat fatty fish such as salmon or sardines two to three times a week, take an omega-3 fatty acid supplement such as fish oil or krill oil. Consult with a clinician with expertise in nutrition to plan major dietary changes or if you're considering an elimination or few foods diet (see chapter 4).

- *Fitness and sleep.* Exercise at least 30 to 60 minutes daily (perhaps one 45-minute intense stretch with three five-minute activity breaks during the day); try yoga, tai chi, or other kinds of mindful movement; consider juggling, dancing, gymnastics, and other activities that promote balance and coordination on both left and right sides of the body. Sleep—seven and a half to nine hours for adults and more for growing children. Use healthy routines and optimize the sleeping environment (see chapter 5).

- *Friendship with others.* Promote positive communication and build supportive relationships. Catch 'em being good. Let your compliments outnumber criticisms by five to one. Manage mistakes constructively. Set clear, specific, measurable expectations and provide consistent, fair, timely, and sensible consequences for behavior. Avoid yelling, name-calling, labeling, humiliating, and hitting; they do not work in the long term and can make things worse. A physician, psychologist, or licensed counselor can be very helpful in learning and practicing new ways of communicating compassionately while fostering self-discipline (see chapter 6).

- *Friendship with self.* Manage stress, cultivate a calm mind, and practice sustaining attention and building organizational skills. Offer positive behavioral strategies. Reframe negative experiences—turn stumbling blocks into stepping stones (see chapter 7).

- *Foster a positive environment and minimize exposure to toxins.* Spend time in nature. Use music mindfully as a reward or incentive or to help organize tasks or improve memorization. Keep work spaces brightly lit. Reduce clutter. Organize time and tasks clearly (e.g., calendars, clocks, charts posting chores and activities); include planning time in the weekly schedule. Foster predictability and make backup plans routine. Avoid exposure to environmental brain toxins such as tobacco smoke, alcohol, and illicit drugs as well as heavy metals like lead, arsenic, and manganese. Advocate for elimination of PCBs, PBBs, and PBDEs, persistent organic pollutants, BPA, and formaldehyde in the environment. Don't use dieldrin or atrazine pesticides, and ask your school and workplace not to use them. Limit electronic (and TV) entertainment to less than 30 minutes a day (see chapter 8).

- ☐ 4. *Make a SMART plan* to prioritize your plans, weigh the pros and cons, evaluate your resources and the barriers to improvement, and track your success (see chapters 9 and 10).
- ☐ 5. *Seek and use additional help.* Which of the following have you already tried? What has worked well for you? What else would you like to try next?

  - ☐ See a qualified professional, such as a clinical psychologist, social worker, physician, or licensed counselor, for more insight and evaluation of special concerns such as learning disabilities, mood disorders, auditory or visual processing problems, counseling, cognitive-behavioral therapy (to help learn to reframe negative thinking), strengthening supportive communication skills, or a careful N-of-1 trial or monitoring of medication (see chapter 13).
  - ☐ For those who tend to fall asleep later and later and wake up later and later, or those who travel across several time zones, consider melatonin supplements (see chapter 12).
  - ☐ Talk with your health professional about a supplement trial of multivitamin/minerals and omega-3 fatty acids; also discuss short trials of herbal remedies such as ginseng, ginkgo, or pine bark extract (see chapters 4 and 12).
  - ☐ Talk with your health professional and insurance company about referrals for EEG biofeedback and massage services (see chapter 13).
  - ☐ Be part of the village. Meet regularly with colleagues, teachers, and counselors for a strength-focused, mastery-oriented team approach to achieving success. Advocate for your family member to receive legally mandated evaluations and services from school. Encourage your child to join groups such as Scouts, church youth groups, civic organizations, or enroll in small classes for art, music, painting,

sculpture, yoga, or martial arts to explore diverse interests and talents while building friendships and support.

☐ Consider other therapies. Try a month of massage therapy. Give acupuncture a try to address related concerns, such as anxiety and depression (see chapter 14).

☐ Advocate for improvements in your school and community to support healthy attention and intentionality and reduce distractibility and impulsivity.

☐ 6. Use your resources (turn the page).

RESOURCES

Family, Peer, and Educator Support Organizations

Association on Higher Education and Disability (AHEAD) is a professional membership organization for professionals who develop policy and for persons with disabilities in higher education. www.ahead.org.

Attention Deficit Disorder Association support and provide information for patients and families faced with ADD. See www.add.org/.

Attention Deficit Disorder Resources Organization's mission is to help people with ADD achieve their full potential through education, support, and networking opportunities. Founded in 1993, ADD Resources is a membership-based nonprofit organization serving adults and children with ADD/ADHD. See http://www.addresources.org.

Children and Adults with Attention Deficit/Hyperactivity Disorder (CHADD) helps you find local chapters, training opportunities, and resources. See www.helpf4adhd.org or www.chadd.org

Council for Exceptional Children (CEC) is the largest international nonprofit professional organization dedicated to improving the educational success of individuals with disabilities and/or gifts and talents. CEC advocates for appropriate governmental policies, sets professional standards, provides professional development, advocates for individuals with exceptionalities, and helps professionals obtain conditions and resources necessary for effective professional practice. http://www.cec.sped.org.

Council for Learning Disabilities is an international professional organization that promotes evidence-based teaching, collaboration, research, leadership, and advocacy to enhance the education and quality of life for individuals with learning disabilities and others who experience challenges in learning. http://www.cldinternational.org

International Dyslexia Association is a nonprofit organization of professionals and parents that provides a comprehensive range of information and services to address the full scope of dyslexia and related difficulties in a way that creates hope, possibility, and partnership. http://www.interdys.org/.

Learning Disabilities Association of America has links to state chapters, training opportunities, and legislative updates. See www.ldanatl.org/

National Center for Gender Issues and ADHD is a nonprofit organization, founded by Dr. Patricia Quinn and Dr. Kathleen Nadeau to raise awareness of the impact of ADHD on girls and women and to disseminate information about ADHD in females to families, medical and mental health professionals, educators, the media, and women of all ages. http://www.ncgiadd.org/about/index.html

National Dissemination Center for Children and Youth with Disabilities provides information for families and educators on disabilities in infants, toddlers, children, and youth; IDEA, the law authorizing special education in the US; and research-based information on effective educational practices. See http://www.nichcy.org

National Institute for Learning Development assists schools, organizations, and individuals in the development of programs for students with specific learning disabilities. http://www.nild.net/

National Resources Center on AD/HD is a program of CHADD (see above). http://www.help4adhd.org/

Physician Organizations

American Academy of Child & Adolescent Psychiatry can help you find a qualified child psychiatrist. See http://www.aacap.org/cs.

American Academy of Family Physicians can help you find a licensed family physician. Most family physicians can provide family or individual therapy. See www.aafp.org/.

American Holistic Medical Association can help you find a physician who emphasizes natural therapies. See http://www.holisticmedicine.org/.

American Academy of Pediatrics (AAP) can help you find a licensed pediatrician. Many pediatricians have special training in behavioral therapies. Since 2008, the AAP has had a section on Complementary and Integrative Medicine, which maintains a list of integrative pediatricians. See http://www.aap.org/sections/chim/ParentResources.html.

Institute for Functional Medicine can help you find a health professional interested in using nutrition, supplements, and other natural approaches to achieve your health goals. See www.functionalmedicine.org.

Other Health Professional Organizations

American Dietetic Association offers referrals to members, most of whom are professional registered dietitians and some of whom have specific interests in using dietary support to promote mental health. See www.eatright.org/.

American Psychological Association provides information about psychology and various kinds of psychotherapy. It also offers a psychologist-locator service. See www.apa.org/.

National Board for Certified Counselors—most states have licensure laws about professional counselors. National certified counselors have met these professional standards. See http://www.nbcc.org/.

Environmental Health

Collaborative on Health and the Environment see http://www.healthandenvironment.org/.

Environmental Defense Fund provides information about food and products that minimize artificial colors, flavors, pesticides, and other harmful chemicals. See http://www.edf.org.

The Green Guide provides information about food and products that minimize artificial colors, flavors, pesticides, and other harmful chemicals. See http://www.thegreenguide.com/.

US Environmental Protection Agency (EPA) provides news about fish advisories (see http://www.epa.gov/fishadvisories/) and has a program on environmental design (see http://www.epa.gov/dfe/); the Superfund sites (see http://www.epa.gov/superfund/sites/index.htm) map provides information about toxic areas in the US.

US National Institute of Environmental Health Sciences Centers for Children's Environmental Health & Disease Prevention Research. See http://www.niehs.nih.gov/ and http://www.niehs.nih.gov/research/supported/centers/prevention/.

US National Library of Medicine Household Products Database (What's in all that stuff under your sink?) See http://householdproducts.nlm.nih.gov/.

US National Library of Medicine TOXMAP (reports of toxic chemicals released into the environment in the US). See http://toxmap.nlm.nih.gov/toxmap/main/index.jsp.

Exercise and Activity Resources

American Tai Chi and QiGong Association can help you locate certified teachers: http://www.americantaichi.org/forConsumers.asp

Brain Gym is committed to the principle that moving with intention leads to optimal learning. http://www.braingym.org/.

Interactive Metronome therapy provides a structured, goal-oriented process that challenges the patient to synchronize a range of hand and foot exercises to computer-generated reference tones heard through headphones. http://www.interactivemetronome.com.

Yoga Alliance is a national education and support organization for yoga in the US and can help you locate a certified yoga teacher. http://www.yogaalliance.org/teacher_search.cfm.

Herbs and Other Dietary Supplements

American Botanical Council has information about herbs and their medicinal uses; some information is free, but in-depth reports require a subscription. See www.herbalgram.org/.

American Herbal Pharmacopoeia promotes the responsible, knowledgeable use of safe and effective high-quality herbal products; some information is free, but in-depth reports require a subscription. See www.herbal-ahp.org/.

ConsumerLab.com compares the quality of different brands of vitamins, minerals, fish oil, herbal products, and other dietary supplements; some information is free, but in-depth reports require a subscription. See http://www.consumerlab.com/.

MedLine Plus (from US NIH) has free independent information about herbs and supplements derived from Natural Standard. See http://www.nlm.nih.gov/medlineplus/druginformation.html.

NSF is a nonprofit, nongovernmental organization that develops standards and certifies products for a number of products, including water, food, and dietary supplements. See http://www.nsf.org.

US Government Resources

Educational Resources Information Center is funded by the US Department of Education to provide a comprehensive, easy-to-use, searchable, Internet-based bibliographic and full-text database of education research and information that also meets the requirements of the Education Sciences Reform Act of 2002. http://www.eric.ed.gov/

National Institutes of Health's National Library of Medicine MedLine Plus provides information about nutrients and commonly used dietary supplements. See http://www.nlm.nih.gov/medlineplus/druginformation.html

National Institute of Mental Health at the US NIH has information about diagnosis and treatment using medications and behavioral therapy for ADHD. See www.nimh.nih.gov

Substance Abuse & Mental Health Services Administration provides publications and links to treatment locations. See http://mentalhealth. samhsa.gov/

Books—Generally ADD/ADHD Related Books
Classics (printed before the year 2000)

Barkley, Russell A. *Taking Charge of ADHD: The Complete, Authoritative Guide for Parents.* Rev. 2000. Guilford Press, 1995. ($19.95)

Copeland, Lori A. *Hunter and His Amazing Remote Control: A Fun Hands-on Way to Teach Self-Control to ADD/ADHD.* YouthLight, 1998. ($14.95)

Faber, Adele, and Elaine Mazlish. *How to Talk so Kids will Listen & Listen so Kids will Talk.* 20th anniversary ed. Avon Books, 1999. ($15.99).

Gottman, John M., Joan DeClaire, and Daniel Goleman. *Raising An Emotionally Intelligent Child.* Simon & Schuster, 1998. ($15)

For Parents

Amen, Daniel G. *Healing ADD: The Breakthrough Program that Allows You to See and Heal the Six Types of Attention Deficit Disorder.* Berkley Books, 2002. ($15.95)

Bernstein, J. *10 Days to a Less Distracted Child.* DeCapo Press, 2007. ($14.95)

Dawson, Peg,. and Richard Guare. *Smart, but Scattered: The Revolutionary Executive Skills Approach to Helping Kids Reach Their Potential.* Guilford Press, 2009. ($15.95)

Hallowell, Edward M., and John J. Ratey. *Delivered from Distraction: Getting the Most Out of Life with Attention Deficit Disorder.* Ballantine Books, 2005. ($15)

Honos-Webb, Lara. *The Gift of ADHD: How to Transform Your Child's Problems into Strengths.* New Harbinger Publications, 2005. ($16.95)

Honos-Webb, Lara. *The Gift of ADHD Activity Book: 101 Ways to Turn Your Child's Problems into Strengths.* New Harbinger Publications, 2008. ($14.95)

Kemper, Kathi J. *Mental Health, Naturally.* American Academy of Pediatrics, 2010. ($19.95)

Monastra, Vincent J. *Parenting Children with ADHD: 10 Lessons that Medicine Cannot Teach.* American Psychological Association, 2005. ($14.95)

Shannon, Scott, and Eric Heckman. *Please Don't Label My Child: Break the Doctor-Diagnosis-Drug Cycle and Discover Safe, Effective Choices for Your Child's Emotional Health.* Rodale, 2007. ($25.95)

Sher, Barbara, and Ralph Butler. *Attention Games: 101 Fun, Easy Games that Help Kids Learn to Focus.* Jossey-Bass, 2006. ($16.95)

For Children and Youth

Cook, Julia. *My Mouth is a Volcano.* National Center for Youth Issues, 2009. ($9.95)

Kraus, Jeanne. *Cory Stories: A Kid's Book about Living with ADHD.* Magination Press, 2004. ($9.95)

Nadeau Kathleen G., and Ellen B. Dixon. *Learning to Slow Down and Pay Attention.* Magination Press, 2004. ($12.95)

Quinn, Patricia, and Judith M. Stern. *Putting on the Brakes: Understanding and Taking Control of your ADD or ADHD.* Magination Press, 2008. ($12.95)

Taylor, John F. *The Survival Guide for Kids with ADD or ADHD.* Free Spirit Publishing, 2006 ($13.99)

Wood, Trish. *80HD: A child's perspective.* Tate Publishing, 2008 ($9.99)

For Teachers and Clinicians

Caselman, Tonia. *Impulse Control: Activities and Worksheets* (versions are available for teachers of elementary students and middle school students). YouthLight Inc., 2009. ($27.95)

Reiff, Michael I., and Sherill Tippins, eds. *ADHD: A Complete and Authoritative Guide*. Elk Grove Village, IL: American Academy of Pediatrics, 2004.

Rief, Sandra F. *How to Reach and Teach Children with ADD/ADHD*. Jossey-Bass, 2005. ($32.95)

Books on Specific Topics
Communication Skills

Patterson, Kerry. *Crucial Conversations: Tools for Talking When Stakes are High*. McGraw-Hill, 2002. ($16.95)

Rosenberg, Marshall B. *Nonviolent Communication: A Language of Life*. 2nd ed. Encinitas, CA: PuddleDancer Press, 2003. ($19.95)

Stone, Douglas, Bruce Patton, and Shiela Heen. *Difficult Conversations: How to Discuss what Matters Most*. Penguin Books, 2000. ($16.00)

Meditation

Guides for Parents and Teachers to Use for Children

Fontana, David, and Ingrid Slack. *Teaching Meditation to Children: A Practical Guide to the Use and Benefits of Meditation*. Watking Publishing, 2007.

Lantieri, Linda, and Daniel Goleman. *Building Emotional Intelligence: Techniques to Cultivate Inner Strength in Children*. Sounds True Inc., 2008.

Rozman, Deborah. *Meditating With Children-The Art of Concentration and Centering: A Workbook on New Educational Methods Using Meditation*. Planetary Publications, 1994.

Books for Children and Youth

Biegel, Gina M. *The Stress Reduction Workbook for Teens*. New Harbinger Publications, 2009.

Garth, Maureen. *Starbright-Meditations for Children*. HarperCollins, 1991.

Garth, Maureen. *Moonbeam: A Book of Meditations for Children*. HarperCollins, 1993.

Gordhamer, Soren. *Just Say Om!: Your Life's Journey*. Adams Media Corporation, 2001.

MacLean, Kerry Lee. *Moody Cow Meditates*. Wisdom Publications, 2009.

MacLean, Kerry Lee. *Peaceful Piggy Meditation*. Albert Whitman & Co., 2004.

Vallely, Sarah Wood. *Sensational Meditation for Children*. Satya International, 2008.

Weierbach, Jane, and Elizabeth Phillips-Hershey. *Mind Over Basketball: Coach Yourself to Handle Stress*. Magination Press: American Psychological Association, 2008.

CDs for Children and Youth

Salzman, Amy. *Still, Quiet Place: Mindfulness for Young Children*, 2004.

Biegel, Gina. *Stressed Teens: Mindfulness for teens—Meditation Practices to Reduce Stress and Promote Well-Being*. 2009.

Online Training or Practice Guides for Meditation

eMindful provides online interactive courses for a fee, including courses specifically for children and teens and others focused on specific physical or mental health challenges: http://www.emindful.com/schedules/

Learning Meditation. Patsy Gray has developed this site which provides *free* audio files and printable scripts for children to use to learn simple techniques. http://www.learningmeditation.com/children.htm

Meditation Society of Australia. This site has guided meditations for children that can be downloaded; a few introductory scripts are *free*, but access to others requires an online subscription (about $8 for access): http://children.meditation.org.au/. The site also has pages for adults: http://download.meditation.org.au/

Meditations for the Constantly Connected. This site offers audio files for a *fee*: http://www.sorengordhamer.com/Homepage_1.html

Amy Saltzman offers *free* online guided meditations: http://www.stillquietplace.com

Mindfulness in Education. http://www.mindfuled.org/innerkids/

ACKNOWLEDGMENTS

I AM DEEPLY grateful to the staff, supporters, members, and volunteers of the Center for Integrative Medicine at Wake Forest University Baptist Medical Center, particularly Paula Stant and Lauren Azevedo for their help with manuscript preparation. Special thanks also to Julie Milunic for her friendship and her steadfast support of the center's mission and for publishing my preliminary article on ADHD in *Natural Triad* magazine. Thanks to Jeff Feldman for his constructive suggestions on the text. Without the philanthropic support of Dr. Caryl Guth and the Kohlberg Foundation as well as the understanding of my colleagues in the Department of Pediatrics and the School of Medicine, this book would not have been possible. Thank you.

I am also grateful to the members and staff of the American Academy of Pediatrics, particularly Teri Salus and the members of the steering committee of the Section for Complementary and Integrative Medicine for leading the way for respectful, practical, evidence-based integration of natural therapies into the professional pediatric care for children and youth. I am especially grateful to Dr. Jane Foy who is not only a colleague at Wake Forest and the leader of the Academy's Task Force on Mental Health but a dear friend (you too, Miles).

Thanks are also due to the leaders of the Consortium of Academic Health Centers for Integrative Medicine, including the working groups on Pediatrics and Mental Health for pioneering science and education in integrative medicine. Thanks to James Lake for kindly writing the foreword. Thank you to Scott Shannon for being a model of a holistic child psychiatrist.

Thank you to BestHealth, the Children's Hospital Medical Group of Los Angeles, the North Carolina Pediatric Society, and others who have invited me to talk on this topic, and whose audiences and their questions, comments, stories, and suggestions have helped me make the points here more clearly.

Thanks to the professional staff at Xlibris who helped turn a manuscript into a book.

Special thanks to the Messicks for their patience and help with meals, chickens, cats, and general moral support as I worked odd hours completing the text.

Most of all, thank you to Daniel for your presence, humor, and love—you are my true north who makes it all worthwhile.

REFERENCES

Foreword

1. Canino, G., et al., *The DSM-IV rates of child and adolescent disorders in Puerto Rico: prevalence, correlates, service use, and the effects of impairment.* Arch Gen Psychiatry, 2004. 61(1): p. 85-93.

2. Newcorn, J.H., M. Weiss, and M.A. Stein, *The complexity of ADHD: diagnosis and treatment of the adult patient with comorbidities.* CNS Spectr, 2007. 12(8 Suppl 12): p. 1-14; quiz 15-6.

3. Biederman, J. and S.V. Faraone, *Attention-deficit hyperactivity disorder.* Lancet, 2005. 366(9481): p. 237-48.

4. Wallis, D., H.F. Russell, and M. Muenke, *Review: Genetics of attention deficit/hyperactivity disorder.* J Pediatr Psychol, 2008. 33(10): p. 1085-99.

5. McCann, D., et al., *Food additives and hyperactive behaviour in 3-year-old and 8/9-year-old children in the community: a randomised, double-blinded, placebo-controlled trial.* Lancet, 2007.

6. Swanson, J.M., et al., *Etiologic subtypes of attention-deficit/hyperactivity disorder: brain imaging, molecular genetic and environmental factors and the dopamine hypothesis.* Neuropsychol Rev, 2007. 17(1): p. 39-59.

7. Brennan, A.R. and A.F. Arnsten, *Neuronal mechanisms underlying attention deficit hyperactivity disorder: the influence of arousal on prefrontal cortical function.* Ann N Y Acad Sci, 2008. 1129: p. 236-45.

8. Berman, S.M., et al., *Potential adverse effects of amphetamine treatment on brain and behavior: a review.* Mol Psychiatry, 2009. 14(2): p. 123-42.

9. Lerner, M. and T. Wigal, *Long-term safety of stimulant medications used to treat children with ADHD.* Pediatr Ann, 2008. 37(1): p. 37-45.

10. Findling, R.L., *Evolution of the treatment of attention-deficit/hyperactivity disorder in children: a review.* Clin Ther, 2008. 30(5): p. 942-57.

11. Miller, M.C., *What is the significance of the new warnings about suicide risk with Strattera?* Harv Ment Health Lett, 2005. 22(6): p. 8.

12. Nissen, S.E., *ADHD drugs and cardiovascular risk.* N Engl J Med, 2006. 354(14): p. 1445-8.

13. Chan, E., L.A. Rappaport, and K.J. Kemper, *Complementary and alternative therapies in childhood attention and hyperactivity problems.* J Dev Behav Pediatr, 2003. 24(1): p. 4-8.

Chapter 1

1. Weiss, R.E., M.A. Stein, and S. Refetoff, *Behavioral effects of liothyronine (L-T3) in children with attention deficit hyperactivity disorder in the presence and absence of resistance to thyroid hormone.* Thyroid, 1997. 7(3): p. 389-93.
2. Nikolas, M.A. and S.A. Burt, *Genetic and environmental influences on ADHD symptom dimensions of inattention and hyperactivity: a meta-analysis.* J Abnorm Psychol. 119(1): p. 1-17.

Chapter 4

1. Isaacs, E.B., et al., *The effect of early human diet on caudate volumes and IQ.* Pediatr Res, 2008. 63(3): p. 308-14.
2. Mahoney, C.R., et al., *Effect of breakfast composition on cognitive processes in elementary school children.* Physiol Behav, 2005. 85(5): p. 635-45.
3. Muthayya, S., et al., *Consumption of a mid-morning snack improves memory but not attention in school children.* Physiol Behav, 2007. 90(1): p. 142-50.
4. Craig, W.J. and A.R. Mangels, *Position of the American Dietetic Association: vegetarian diets.* J Am Diet Assoc, 2009. 109(7): p. 1266-82.
5. Van Oudheusden, L.J. and H.R. Scholte, *Efficacy of carnitine in the treatment of children with attention-deficit hyperactivity disorder.* Prostaglandins Leukot Essent Fatty Acids, 2002. 67(1): p. 33-8.
6. Arnold, L.E., et al., *Acetyl-L-carnitine (ALC) in attention-deficit/hyperactivity disorder: a multi-site, placebo-controlled pilot trial.* J Child Adolesc Psychopharmacol, 2007. 17(6): p. 791-802.
7. Antalis, C.J., et al., *Omega-3 fatty acid status in attention-deficit/hyperactivity disorder.* Prostaglandins Leukot Essent Fatty Acids, 2006. 75(4-5): p. 299-308.
8. Hibbeln, J.R., T.A. Ferguson, and T.L. Blasbalg, *Omega-3 fatty acid deficiencies in neurodevelopment, aggression and autonomic dysregulation: opportunities for intervention.* Int Rev Psychiatry, 2006. 18(2): p. 107-18.
9. Amminger, G.P., et al., *Omega-3 fatty acids supplementation in children with autism: a double-blind randomized, placebo-controlled pilot study.* Biol Psychiatry, 2007. 61(4): p. 551-3.

KATHI J. KEMPER, MD, MPH

10. Lindmark, L. and P. Clough, *A 5-month open study with long-chain polyunsaturated fatty acids in dyslexia.* J Med Food, 2007. 10(4): p. 662-6.

11. Sinn, N., J. Bryan, and C. Wilson, *Cognitive effects of polyunsaturated fatty acids in children with attention deficit hyperactivity disorder symptoms: A randomised controlled trial.* Prostaglandins Leukot Essent Fatty Acids, 2008. 78(4-5): p. 311-26.

12. Sinn, N., *Physical fatty acid deficiency signs in children with ADHD symptoms.* Prostaglandins Leukot Essent Fatty Acids, 2007. 77(2): p. 109-15.

13. Sorgi, P.J., et al., *Effects of an open-label pilot study with high-dose EPA/DHA concentrates on plasma phospholipids and behavior in children with attention deficit hyperactivity disorder.* Nutr J, 2007. 6: p. 16.

14. Garland, M.R. and B. Hallahan, *Essential fatty acids and their role in conditions characterised by impulsivity.* Int Rev Psychiatry, 2006. 18(2): p. 99-105.

15. Buydens-Branchey, L. and M. Branchey, *Long-chain n-3 polyunsaturated fatty acids decrease feelings of anger in substance abusers.* Psychiatry Res, 2008. 157(1-3): p. 95-104.

16. Olsen, S.F., et al., *Fish oil intake compared with olive oil intake in late pregnancy and asthma in the offspring: 16 y of registry-based follow-up from a randomized controlled trial.* Am J Clin Nutr, 2008. 88(1): p. 167-75.

17. Biltagi, M.A., et al., *Omega-3 fatty acids, vitamin C and Zn supplementation in asthmatic children: a randomized self-controlled study.* Acta Paediatr, 2009. 98(4): p. 737-42.

18. Hinton, P.S. and L.M. Sinclair, *Iron supplementation maintains ventilatory threshold and improves energetic efficiency in iron-deficient nonanemic athletes.* Eur J Clin Nutr, 2007. 61(1): p. 30-9.

19. Khedr, E., et al., *Iron states and cognitive abilities in young adults: neuropsychological and neurophysiological assessment.* Eur Arch Psychiatry Clin Neurosci, 2008. 258(8): p. 489-96.

20. Lozoff, B., *Iron deficiency and child development.* Food Nutr Bull, 2007. 28(4 Suppl): p. S560-71.

21. Murray-Kolb, L.E. and J.L. Beard, *Iron treatment normalizes cognitive functioning in young women.* Am J Clin Nutr, 2007. 85(3): p. 778-87.

22. Otero, G.A., et al., *Working memory impairment and recovery in iron deficient children.* Clin Neurophysiol, 2008. 119(8): p. 1739-46.

23. Mousain-Bosc, M., et al., *Improvement of neurobehavioral disorders in children supplemented with magnesium-vitamin B6. II. Pervasive developmental disorder-autism.* Magnes Res, 2006. 19(1): p. 53-62.

24. Arnold, L.E. and R.A. DiSilvestro, *Zinc in attention-deficit/hyperactivity disorder.* J Child Adolesc Psychopharmacol, 2005. 15(4): p. 619-27.

25. Bilici, M., et al., *Double-blind, placebo-controlled study of zinc sulfate in the treatment of attention deficit hyperactivity disorder.* Prog Neuropsychopharmacol Biol Psychiatry, 2004. 28(1): p. 181-90.

26. D'Anci K, E., et al., *Voluntary dehydration and cognitive performance in trained college athletes.* Percept Mot Skills, 2009. 109(1): p. 251-69.

27. Edmonds, C.J. and B. Jeffes, *Does having a drink help you think? 6-7-Year-old children show improvements in cognitive performance from baseline to test after having a drink of water.* Appetite, 2009. 53(3): p. 469-72.

28. Kemp, A., *Food additives and hyperactivity.* BMJ, 2008. 336(7654): p. 1144.

29. Rowe, K.S., *Synthetic food colourings and 'hyperactivity': a double-blind crossover study.* Aust Paediatr J, 1988. 24(2): p. 143-7.

30. Boris, M. and F.S. Mandel, *Foods and additives are common causes of the attention deficit hyperactive disorder in children.* Ann Allergy, 1994. 72(5): p. 462-8.

31. Bateman, B., et al., *The effects of a double blind, placebo controlled, artificial food colourings and benzoate preservative challenge on hyperactivity in a general population sample of preschool children.* Arch Dis Child, 2004. 89(6): p. 506-11.

32. Waring, M.E. and K.L. Lapane, *Overweight in children and adolescents in relation to attention-deficit/hyperactivity disorder: results from a national sample.* Pediatrics, 2008. 122(1): p. e1-6.

33. Desch, S., et al., *Effect of cocoa products on blood pressure: systematic review and meta-analysis.* Am J Hypertens, 2010. 23(1): p. 97-103.

34. Bryant, C.A., et al., *Psychomotor performance: investigating the dose-response relationship for caffeine and theophylline in elderly volunteers.* Eur J Clin Pharmacol, 1998. 54(4): p. 309-13.

35. Heatherley, S.V., K.M. Hancock, and P.J. Rogers, *Psychostimulant and other effects of caffeine in 9- to 11-year-old children.* J Child Psychol Psychiatry, 2006. 47(2): p. 135-42.

36. Kaplan, G.B., et al., *Dose-dependent pharmacokinetics and psychomotor effects of caffeine in humans.* J Clin Pharmacol, 1997. 37(8): p. 693-703.

37. Rubin, J.T., et al., *Oral and intravenous caffeine for treatment of children with post-sedation paradoxical hyperactivity.* Pediatr Radiol, 2004. 34(12): p. 980-4.

38. Nobre, A.C., A. Rao, and G.N. Owen, *L-theanine, a natural constituent in tea, and its effect on mental state.* Asia Pac J Clin Nutr, 2008. 17 Suppl 1: p. 167-8.

39. Weber, C. S., Thayer, J. F., Rudat, M., Sharma, A. M., Perschel, F. H., Buchholz, K., Deter, H. C. *Salt-sensitive men show reduced heart rate variability, lower norepinephrine and enhanced cortisol during mental stress.* J Hum Hypertens. 2008; 22(6): p. 423-31

40. Pelsser, L.M., et al., *A randomised controlled trial into the effects of food on ADHD.* Eur Child Adolesc Psychiatry, 2009. 18(1): p. 12-9.

41. Tasiopoulou, S., et al., *Results of the monitoring program of pesticide residues in organic food of plant origin in Lombardy (Italy).* J Environ Sci Health B, 2007. 42(7): p. 835-41.

42. Lu, C., et al., *Dietary intake and its contribution to longitudinal organophosphorus pesticide exposure in urban/suburban children.* Environ Health Perspect, 2008. 116(4): p. 537-42.

43. Thomas, D., *A study on the mineral depletion of the foods available to us as a nation over the period 1940 to 1991.* Nutr Health, 2003. 17(2): p. 85-115.

44. Gyorene, K.V., A; Lugasi, A, *A comparison of chemical composition and nutritional value of organically and conventionally gorwn plant derived foods.* Orv Hetil, 2006. 29(147): p. 43.

45. Worthington, V., *Effect of agricultural methods on nutritional quality: a comparison of organic with conventional crops.* Altern Ther Health Med, 1998. 4(1): p. 58-69.

46. Hebeisen, D.F., et al., *Increased concentrations of omega-3 fatty acids in milk and platelet rich plasma of grass-fed cows.* Int J Vitam Nutr Res, 1993. 63(3): p. 229-33.

47. Leiber, F., et al., *A study on the causes for the elevated n-3 fatty acids in cows' milk of alpine origin.* Lipids, 2005. 40(2): p. 191-202.

Chapter 5

1. Taylor, A.F. and F.E. Kuo, *Children with attention deficits concentrate better after walk in the park.* J Atten Disord, 2009. 12(5): p. 402-9.

2.   Tsai, C.L., *The effectiveness of exercise intervention on inhibitory control in children with developmental coordination disorder: using a visuospatial attention paradigm as a model.* Res Dev Disabil, 2009. 30(6): p. 1268-80.

3.   Jensen, P.S. and D.T. Kenny, *The effects of yoga on the attention and behavior of boys with Attention-Deficit/ hyperactivity Disorder (ADHD).* J Atten Disord, 2004. 7(4): p. 205-16.

4.   Oka, Y., S. Suzuki, and Y. Inoue, *Bedtime activities, sleep environment, and sleep/wake patterns of Japanese elementary school children.* Behav Sleep Med, 2008. 6(4): p. 220-33.

5.   Dworak, M., et al., *Impact of singular excessive computer game and television exposure on sleep patterns and memory performance of school-aged children.* Pediatrics, 2007. 120(5): p. 978-85.

6.   Khilnani, S., et al., *Massage therapy improves mood and behavior of students with attention-deficit/hyperactivity disorder.* Adolescence, 2003. 38(152): p. 623-38.

7.   Field, T.M., et al., *Adolescents with attention deficit hyperactivity disorder benefit from massage therapy.* Adolescence, 1998. 33(129): p. 103-8.

Chapter 7

1.   Rubia, K., *The neurobiology of Meditation and its clinical effectiveness in psychiatric disorders.* Biol Psychol, 2009. 82(1): p. 1-11.

2.   Kjaer, T.W., et al., *Increased dopamine tone during meditation-induced change of consciousness.* Brain Res Cogn Brain Res, 2002. 13(2): p. 255-9.

3.   Chiesa, A. and A. Serretti, *A systematic review of neurobiological and clinical features of mindfulness meditations.* Psychol Med, 2009: p. 1-14.

4.   Holzel, B.K., et al., *Investigation of mindfulness meditation practitioners with voxel-based morphometry.* Soc Cogn Affect Neurosci, 2008. 3(1): p. 55-61.

5.   Lazar, S.W., et al., *Meditation experience is associated with increased cortical thickness.* Neuroreport, 2005. 16(17): p. 1893-7.

6.   Yamamoto, S., et al., *Medial profrontal cortex and anterior cingulate cortex in the generation of alpha activity induced by transcendental meditation: a magnetoencephalographic study.* Acta Med Okayama, 2006. 60(1): p. 51-8.

7.   Baron Short, E., et al., *Regional Brain Activation During Meditation Shows Time and Practice Effects: An Exploratory FMRI Study{dagger}.* Evid Based Complement Alternat Med, 2007.

8.   Chiesa, A., *Vipassana meditation: systematic review of current evidence.* J Altern Complement Med, 2010. 16(1): p. 37-46.

9.   Lee, J., et al., *Mindfulness-based cognitive therapy for children: Results of a pilot study.* Journal of Cognitive Psychotherapy, 2008. 22(1): p. 15.

10. Semple, R.J. and R.J. Semple, *Mindfulness-Based Cognitive Therapy for children: A randomized group psychotherapy trial developed to enhance attention and reduce anxiety.* Dissertation Abstracts International: Section B: The Sciences and Engineering, 2006. 66(9-B).

11. Napoli, M., et al., *Mindfulness Training for Elementary School Students: The Attention Academy.* Journal of Applied School Psychology, 2005. 21(1): p. 99.

12. Saltzman, A., A. Saltzman, and P. Goldin, *Mindfulness-based stress reduction for school-age children.* 2008: p. 139.

13. Broderick, P.M., S, *Learning to BREATHE: A pilot trial of a mindfulness curriculum for adolescents.* Advances in School Mental Health Promotion, 2009. 2: p. 35-46.

14. Flook, L., et al., *Effects of mindful awareness practices on executive functions in elementary school children.* Journal of Applied School Psychology, 2010. 26: p. 7-95.

15. Sibinga, E., et al. *Mindfulness-based stress reduction for urban youth.* in *Pediatric Academic Society Annual Meeting.* 2009. Baltimore, MD.

16. Barnes, V.A., L.B. Bauza, and F.A. Treiber, *Impact of stress reduction on negative school behavior in adolescents.* Health Qual Life Outcomes, 2003. 1: p. 10.

17. So, K.-T., K.-T. So, and D.W. Orme-Johnson, *Three randomized experiments on the longitudinal effects of the Transcendental Meditation technique on cognition.* Intelligence, 2001. 29(5): p. 419.

18. Rosaen, C. and R. Benn, *The experience of transcendental meditation in middle school students: a qualitative report.* Explore (NY), 2006. 2(5): p. 422-5.

19. Bogels, S., et al., *Mindfulness training for adolescents with externalizing disorders and their parents.* Behavioural and Cognitive Psychotherapy, 2008. 36(2): p. 193.

20. Birdee, G.S., et al., *Clinical applications of yoga for the pediatric population: a systematic review.* Acad Pediatr, 2009. 9(4): p. 212-220 e1-9.

21. Winbush, N.Y., C.R. Gross, and M.J. Kreitzer, *The effects of mindfulness-based stress reduction on sleep disturbance: a systematic review.* Explore (NY), 2007. 3(6): p. 585-91.

Chapter 8

1. Herrmann, M., K. King, and M. Weitzman, *Prenatal tobacco smoke and postnatal secondhand smoke exposure and child neurodevelopment.* Curr Opin Pediatr, 2008. 20(2): p. 184-90.
2. Froehlich, T.E., et al., *Association of tobacco and lead exposures with attention-deficit/hyperactivity disorder.* Pediatrics, 2009. 124(6): p. e1054-63.
3. Braun, J.M., et al., *Exposures to environmental toxicants and attention deficit hyperactivity disorder in U.S. children.* Environ Health Perspect, 2006. 114(12): p. 1904-9.
4. Rodriguez, V.M., M. Thiruchelvam, and D.A. Cory-Slechta, *Sustained exposure to the widely used herbicide atrazine: altered function and loss of neurons in brain monoamine systems.* Environ Health Perspect, 2005. 113(6): p. 708-15.
5. Christakis, D.A. and F.J. Zimmerman, *Violent television viewing during preschool is associated with antisocial behavior during school age.* Pediatrics, 2007. 120(5): p. 993-9.
6. Sharif, I. and J.D. Sargent, *Association between television, movie, and video game exposure and school performance.* Pediatrics, 2006. 118(4): p. e1061-70.
7. Zimmerman, F.J. and D.A. Christakis, *Associations between content types of early media exposure and subsequent attentional problems.* Pediatrics, 2007. 120(5): p. 986-92.
8. Johnson, J.G., et al., *Extensive television viewing and the development of attention and learning difficulties during adolescence.* Arch Pediatr Adolesc Med, 2007. 161(5): p. 480-6.
9. Landhuis, C.E., et al., *Does childhood television viewing lead to attention problems in adolescence? Results from a prospective longitudinal study.* Pediatrics, 2007. 120(3): p. 532-7.
10. Rushton, F.E., *Elementary school children with a television in their bedroom more likely to be diagnosed with attention deficit disorder.* J S C Med Assoc, 2005. 101(9): p. 315-7.

11. Kuo, F.E. and A.F. Taylor, *A potential natural treatment for attention-deficit/hyperactivity disorder: evidence from a national study.* Am J Public Health, 2004. 94(9): p. 1580-6.

Chapter 9

1. Ockene, I.S., et al., *Task force #4-adherence issues and behavior changes: achieving a long-term solution. 33rd Bethesda Conference.* J Am Coll Cardiol, 2002. 40(4): p. 630-40.

Chapter 12

1. Nikles, C.J., et al., *An n-of-1 trial service in clinical practice: testing the effectiveness of stimulants for attention-deficit/hyperactivity disorder.* Pediatrics, 2006. 117(6): p. 2040-6.
2. Nikles, C.J., et al., *Long-term changes in management following n-of-1 trials of stimulants in attention-deficit/hyperactivity disorder.* Eur J Clin Pharmacol, 2007. 63(11): p. 985-9.
3. Molina, B.S., et al., *The MTA at 8 years: prospective follow-up of children treated for combined-type ADHD in a multisite study.* J Am Acad Child Adolesc Psychiatry, 2009. 48(5): p. 484-500.
4. Jensen, P.S., et al., *3-year follow-up of the NIMH MTA study.* J Am Acad Child Adolesc Psychiatry, 2007. 46(8): p. 989-1002.
5. Koesters, M., et al., *Limits of meta-analysis: methylphenidate in the treatment of adult attention-deficit hyperactivity disorder.* J Psychopharmacol, 2009. 23(7): p. 733-44.
6. *Attention deficit hyperactivity disorder; Diagnosis and management of ADHD in children, young people and adults*, N.I.f.H.a.C. Excellence, Editor. 2008.
7. Brown, T.E., et al., *Effect of Atomoxetine on Executive Function Impairments in Adults With ADHD.* J Atten Disord, 2009.
8. Hammerness, P., et al., *Atomoxetine for the treatment of attention-deficit/hyperactivity disorder in children and adolescents: a review.* Neuropsychiatr Dis Treat, 2009. 5: p. 215-26.
9. Gould, M.S., et al., *Sudden death and use of stimulant medications in youths.* Am J Psychiatry, 2009. 166(9): p. 992-1001.

10. Mosholder, A.D., et al., *Hallucinations and other psychotic symptoms associated with the use of attention-deficit/hyperactivity disorder drugs in children.* Pediatrics, 2009. 123(2): p. 611-6.

11. Pappadopulos, E., et al., *Medication adherence in the MTA: saliva methylphenidate samples versus parent report and mediating effect of concomitant behavioral treatment.* J Am Acad Child Adolesc Psychiatry, 2009. 48(5): p. 501-10.

12. Adler, L.D. and A.A. Nierenberg, *Review of medication adherence in children and adults with ADHD.* Postgrad Med, 2010. 122(1): p. 184-91.

13. Setlik, J., G.R. Bond, and M. Ho, *Adolescent Prescription ADHD Medication Abuse Is Rising Along With Prescriptions for These Medications.* Pediatrics, 2009. 124(3):875-80

14. Coulter, M.K. and M.E. Dean, *Homeopathy for attention deficit/hyperactivity disorder or hyperkinetic disorder.* Cochrane Database Syst Rev, 2007(4): p. CD005648.

15. Sebastian, R.S., C. Wilkinson Enns, and J.D. Goldman, *U.S. adolescents and MyPyramid: associations between fast-food consumption and lower likelihood of meeting recommendations.* J Am Diet Assoc, 2009. 109(2): p. 226-35.

16. Guenther, P.M., et al., *Most Americans eat much less than recommended amounts of fruits and vegetables.* J Am Diet Assoc, 2006. 106(9): p. 1371-9.

17. Davis, D.R., M.D. Epp, and H.D. Riordan, *Changes in USDA food composition data for 43 garden crops, 1950 to 1999.* J Am Coll Nutr, 2004. 23(6): p. 669-82.

18. Murphy, K.R., PG; Jones, ST, *Relationship between yield and mineral nutrient concentrations in historical and modern spring wheat cultivars.* Euphytica, 2008. 163(3): p. 1573-5060.

19. Schoenthaler, S.J. and I.D. Bier, *The effect of vitamin-mineral supplementation on juvenile delinquency among American schoolchildren: a randomized, double-blind placebo-controlled trial.* J Altern Complement Med, 2000. 6(1): p. 7-17.

20. Kaplan, B.J., et al., *Improved mood and behavior during treatment with a mineral-vitamin supplement: an open-label case series of children.* J Child Adolesc Psychopharmacol, 2004. 14(1): p. 115-22.

21. Benton, D., R. Griffiths, and J. Haller, *Thiamine supplementation mood and cognitive functioning.* Psychopharmacology (Berl), 1997. 129(1): p. 66-71.

KATHI J. KEMPER, MD, MPH

22. Brenner, A., *The effects of megadoses of selected B complex vitamins on children with hyperkinesis: controlled studies with long-term follow-up.* J Learn Disabil, 1982. 15(5): p. 258-64.

23. Coleman, M., et al., *A preliminary study of the effect of pyridoxine administration in a subgroup of hyperkinetic children: a double-blind crossover comparison with methylphenidate.* Biol Psychiatry, 1979. 14(5): p. 741-51.

24. Malouf, R. and J. Grimley Evans, *The effect of vitamin B6 on cognition.* Cochrane Database Syst Rev, 2003(4): p. CD004393.

25. Williams, A.L., et al., *The role for vitamin B-6 as treatment for depression: a systematic review.* Fam Pract, 2005. 22(5): p. 532-7.

26. Konofal, E., et al., *Iron deficiency in children with attention-deficit/hyperactivity disorder.* Arch Pediatr Adolesc Med, 2004. 158(12): p. 1113-5.

27. Uckardes, Y., et al., *Effects of zinc supplementation on parent and teacher behaviour rating scores in low socioeconomic level Turkish primary school children.* Acta Paediatr, 2009. 98(4): p. 731-6.

28. Mousain-Bosc, M., et al., *Magnesium VitB6 intake reduces central nervous system hyperexcitability in children.* J Am Coll Nutr, 2004. 23(5): p. 545S-548S.

29. Lozoff, B., et al., *Poorer behavioral and developmental outcome more than 10 years after treatment for iron deficiency in infancy.* Pediatrics, 2000. 105(4): p. E51.

30. Otero, G.A., et al., *Iron supplementation brings up a lacking P300 in iron deficient children.* Clin Neurophysiol, 2004. 115(10): p. 2259-66.

31. Mousain-Bosc, M., et al., *Improvement of neurobehavioral disorders in children supplemented with magnesium-vitamin B6. I. Attention deficit hyperactivity disorders.* Magnes Res, 2006. 19(1): p. 46-52.

32. Starobrat-Hermelin, B. and T. Kozielec, *The effects of magnesium physiological supplementation on hyperactivity in children with attention deficit hyperactivity disorder (ADHD). Positive response to magnesium oral loading test.* Magnes Res, 1997. 10(2): p. 149-56.

33. Arnold, L.E., et al., *Serum zinc correlates with parent and teacher-rated inattention in children with attention-deficit/hyperactivity disorder.* J Child Adolesc Psychopharmacol, 2005. 15(4): p. 628-36.

34. Shekim, W.O., et al., *S-adenosyl-L-methionine (SAM) in adults with ADHD, RS: preliminary results from an open trial.* Psychopharmacol Bull, 1990. 26(2): p. 249-53.

35. Belanger, S.A., et al., *Omega-3 fatty acid treatment of children with attention-deficit hyperactivity disorder: A randomized, double-blind, placebo-controlled study.* Paediatr Child Health, 2009. 14(2): p. 89-98.

36. Vaisman, N., et al., *Correlation between changes in blood fatty acid composition and visual sustained attention performance in children with inattention: effect of dietary n-3 fatty acids containing phospholipids.* Am J Clin Nutr, 2008. 87(5): p. 1170-80.

37. Hamazaki, K., et al., *The effects of docosahexaenoic acid-rich fish oil on behavior, school attendance rate and malaria infection in school children—a double-blind, randomized, placebo-controlled trial in Lampung, Indonesia.* Asia Pac J Clin Nutr, 2008. 17(2): p. 258-63.

38. Owen, C., A.M. Rees, and G. Parker, *The role of fatty acids in the development and treatment of mood disorders.* Curr Opin Psychiatry, 2008. 21(1): p. 19-24.

39. Buydens-Branchey, L., M. Branchey, and J.R. Hibbeln, *Associations between increases in plasma n-3 polyunsaturated fatty acids following supplementation and decreases in anger and anxiety in substance abusers.* Prog Neuropsychopharmacol Biol Psychiatry, 2008. 32(2): p. 568-75.

40. Andersen, I.M., et al., *Melatonin for insomnia in children with autism spectrum disorders.* J Child Neurol, 2008. 23(5): p. 482-5.

41. Smits, M.G., et al., *Melatonin improves health status and sleep in children with idiopathic chronic sleep-onset insomnia: a randomized placebo-controlled trial.* J Am Acad Child Adolesc Psychiatry, 2003. 42(11): p. 1286-93.

42. Van der Heijden, K.B., et al., *Effect of melatonin on sleep, behavior, and cognition in ADHD and chronic sleep-onset insomnia.* J Am Acad Child Adolesc Psychiatry, 2007. 46(2): p. 233-41.

43. Weiss, M., et al., *Sleep Hygiene and Melatonin Treatment for Children and Adolescents With ADHD and Initial Insomnia.* J Am Acad Child Adolesc Psychiatry, 2006. 45(5):512-9.

44. Van Veen, M.M., et al., *Delayed Circadian Rhythm in Adults with Attention-Deficit/Hyperactivity Disorder and Chronic Sleep-Onset Insomnia.* Biol Psychiatry. 2010; 67(11):1091-6

45. Hoebert, M., et al., *Long-term follow-up of melatonin treatment in children with ADHD and chronic sleep onset insomnia.* J Pineal Res, 2009. 47(1): p. 1-7.

KATHI J. KEMPER, MD, MPH

46. Muller, S.F. and S. Klement, *A combination of valerian and lemon balm is effective in the treatment of restlessness and dyssomnia in children.* Phytomedicine, 2006. 13(6): p. 383-7.
47. Bryan, J., *Psychological effects of dietary components of tea: caffeine and L-theanine.* Nutr Rev, 2008. 66(2): p. 82-90.
48. Kuriyama, S., et al., *Green tea consumption and cognitive function: a cross-sectional study from the Tsurugaya Project 1.* Am J Clin Nutr, 2006. 83(2): p. 355-61.
49. Lillycrop, K.A., et al., *The octamer-binding protein Oct-2 represses HSV immediate-early genes in cell lines derived from latently infectable sensory neurons.* Neuron, 1991. 7(3): p. 381-90.
50. Rezai-Zadeh, K., et al., *Green tea epigallocatechin-3-gallate (EGCG) reduces beta-amyloid mediated cognitive impairment and modulates tau pathology in Alzheimer transgenic mice.* Brain Res, 2008. 1214: p. 177-87.
51. Niederhofer, H., *Ginkgo biloba treating patients with attention-deficit disorder.* Phytother Res, 2010 24(1):p. 26-7.
52. Lyon, M.R., et al., *Effect of the herbal extract combination Panax quinquefolium and Ginkgo biloba on attention-deficit hyperactivity disorder: a pilot study.* J Psychiatry Neurosci, 2001. 26(3): p. 221-8.
53. Trebaticka, J., et al., *Treatment of ADHD with French maritime pine bark extract, Pycnogenol.* Eur Child Adolesc Psychiatry, 2006. 15(6): p. 329-35.
54. Dvorakova, M., et al., *Urinary catecholamines in children with attention deficit hyperactivity disorder (ADHD): modulation by a polyphenolic extract from pine bark (Pycnogenol).* Nutr Neurosci, 2007. 10(3-4): p. 151-7.
55. Dvorakova, M., et al., *The effect of polyphenolic extract from pine bark, Pycnogenol on the level of glutathione in children suffering from attention deficit hyperactivity disorder (ADHD).* Redox Rep, 2006. 11(4): p. 163-72.

Chapter 13

1. Kaiser, N.M., B. Hoza, and E.A. Hurt, *Multimodal treatment for childhood attention-deficit/hyperactivity disorder.* Expert Rev Neurother, 2008. 8(10): p. 1573-83.
2. Langberg, J.M., et al., *Parent-reported homework problems in the MTA study: evidence for sustained improvement with behavioral treatment.* J Clin Child Adolesc Psychol. 39(2): p. 220-33.

3. Solanto, M.V., et al., *Efficacy of Meta-Cognitive Therapy for Adult ADHD.* Am J Psychiatry. 2010; 167(8): 958-68

4. Beauregard, M. and J. Levesque, *Functional magnetic resonance imaging investigation of the effects of neurofeedback training on the neural bases of selective attention and response inhibition in children with attention-deficit/hyperactivity disorder.* Appl Psychophysiol Biofeedback, 2006. 31(1): p. 3-20.

5. Becerra, J., et al., *Follow-up study of learning-disabled children treated with neurofeedback or placebo.* Clin EEG Neurosci, 2006. 37(3): p. 198-203.

6. Butnik, S.M., *Neurofeedback in adolescents and adults with attention deficit hyperactivity disorder.* J Clin Psychol, 2005. 61(5): p. 621-5.

7. Gruzelier, J., T. Egner, and D. Vernon, *Validating the efficacy of neurofeedback for optimising performance.* Prog Brain Res, 2006. 159: p. 421-31.

8. Heinrich, H., H. Gevensleben, and U. Strehl, *Annotation: neurofeedback—train your brain to train behaviour.* J Child Psychol Psychiatry, 2007. 48(1): p. 3-16.

9. Hirshberg, L.M., *Place of electroencephalograpic biofeedback for attention-deficit/hyperactivity disorder.* Expert Rev Neurother, 2007. 7(4): p. 315-9.

10. Leins, U., et al., *Neurofeedback for children with ADHD: a comparison of SCP and Theta/Beta protocols.* Appl Psychophysiol Biofeedback, 2007. 32(2): p. 73-88.

11. Levesque, J., M. Beauregard, and B. Mensour, *Effect of neurofeedback training on the neural substrates of selective attention in children with attention-deficit/hyperactivity disorder: a functional magnetic resonance imaging study.* Neurosci Lett, 2006. 394(3): p. 216-21.

12. Monastra, V.J., et al., *Electroencephalographic biofeedback in the treatment of attention-deficit/hyperactivity disorder.* Appl Psychophysiol Biofeedback, 2005. 30(2): p. 95-114.

13. Pop-Jordanova, N., S. Markovska-Simoska, and T. Zorcec, *Neurofeedback treatment of children with attention deficit hyperactivity disorder.* Prilozi, 2005. 26(1): p. 71-80.

14. Strehl, U., et al., *Self-regulation of slow cortical potentials: a new treatment for children with attention-deficit/hyperactivity disorder.* Pediatrics, 2006. 118(5): p. e1530-40.

15. Weiskopf, N., et al., *Physiological self-regulation of regional brain activity using real-time functional magnetic resonance imaging (fMRI): methodology and exemplary data.* Neuroimage, 2003. 19(3): p. 577-86.

16. Xiong, Z., S. Shi, and H. Xu, *A controlled study of the effectiveness of EEG biofeedback training on-children with attention deficit hyperactivity disorder.* J Huazhong Univ Sci Technolog Med Sci, 2005. 25(3): p. 368-70.

17. Doehnert, M., et al., *Slow cortical potential neurofeedback in attention deficit hyperactivity disorder: is there neurophysiological evidence for specific effects?* J Neural Transm, 2008. 115(10): p. 1445-56.

18. Drechsler, R., et al., *Controlled evaluation of a neurofeedback training of slow cortical potentials in children with Attention Deficit/Hyperactivity Disorder (ADHD).* Behav Brain Funct, 2007. 3: p. 35.

19. Gevensleben, H., et al., *Distinct EEG effects related to neurofeedback training in children with ADHD: a randomized controlled trial.* Int J Psychophysiol, 2009. 74(2): p. 149-57.

20. Surmeli, T. and A. Ertem, *Post WISC-R and TOVA improvement with QEEG guided neurofeedback training in mentally retarded: a clinical case series of behavioral problems.* Clin EEG Neurosci, 2010. 41(1): p. 32-41.

21. Thompson, L., M. Thompson, and A. Reid, *Neurofeedback outcomes in clients with Asperger's syndrome.* Appl Psychophysiol Biofeedback, 2010. 35(1): p. 63-81.

22. Tryon, W.W., et al., *Reducing hyperactivity with a feedback actigraph: initial findings.* Clin Child Psychol Psychiatry, 2006. 11(4): p. 607-17.

23. Miller, L.G. and I.A. Kraft, *Application of actigraphy in the clinical setting: use in children with attention-deficit hyperactivity disorder.* Pharmacotherapy, 1994. 14(2): p. 219-23.

24. Colman, R.S., et al., *The effects of fluorescent and incandescent illumination upon repetitive behaviors in autistic children.* 1976. 6(2): p.157-62.

Chapter 14

1. Beider, S. and C.A. Moyer, *Randomized controlled trials of pediatric massage: a review.* Evid Based Complement Alternat Med, 2007. 4(1): p. 23-34.

2. Buckle, J., et al., *Measurement of regional cerebral blood flow associated with the M technique-light massage therapy: a case series and longitudinal study using SPECT.* J Altern Complement Med, 2008. 14(8): p. 903-10.

3. Takeda, H., et al., *Differences between the physiologic and psychologic effects of aromatherapy body treatment.* J Altern Complement Med, 2008. 14(6): p. 655-61.

4. Hernandez-Reif, M., M. Diego, and T. Field, *Preterm infants show reduced stress behaviors and activity after 5 days of massage therapy.* Infant Behav Dev, 2007. 30(4): p. 557-61.

5. Pelaez-Nogueras, M., et al., *Depressed mothers' touching increases infants' positive affect and attention in still-face interactions.* Child Dev, 1996. 67(4): p. 1780-92.

6. Field, T., et al., *Massage reduces anxiety in child and adolescent psychiatric patients.* J Am Acad Child Adolesc Psychiatry, 1992. 31(1): p. 125-31.

7. Billhult, A. and S. Maatta, *Light pressure massage for patients with severe anxiety.* Complement Ther Clin Pract, 2009. 15(2): p. 96-101.

8. Maddigan, B., et al., *The effects of massage therapy & exercise therapy on children/adolescents with attention deficit hyperactivity disorder.* Can Child Adolesc Psychiatr Rev, 2003. 12(2): p. 40-3.

9. Field, T., et al., *Massage therapy reduces anxiety and enhances EEG pattern of alertness and math computations.* Int J Neurosci, 1996. 86(3-4): p. 197-205.

10. Feijo, L., et al., *Mothers' depressed mood and anxiety levels are reduced after massaging their preterm infants.* Infant Behav Dev, 2006. 29(3): p. 476-80.

11. Field, T., et al., *Massage therapy reduces pain in pregnant women, alleviates prenatal depression in both parents and improves their relationships.* J Bodyw Mov Ther, 2008. 12(2): p. 146-50.

12. Pilkington, K., et al., *Acupuncture for anxiety and anxiety disorders—a systematic literature review.* Acupunct Med, 2007. 25(1-2): p. 1-10.

13. Duan, Y.E., *Treatment of child extensive anxiety disorder with catgut implantation of point plus western medicine.* Zhongguo Zhen Jiu, 2007. 27(5): p. 341-3.

14. Gibson, D., et al., *Effects of acupuncture as a treatment for hyperventilation syndrome: a pilot, randomized crossover trial.* J Altern Complement Med, 2007. 13(1): p. 39-46.

15. Lang, T., et al., *Prehospital analgesia with acupressure at the Baihui and Hegu points in patients with radial fractures: a prospective, randomized, double-blind trial.* Am J Emerg Med, 2007. 25(8): p. 887-93.

KATHI J. KEMPER, MD, MPH

16. Luo, W.Z., H.J. Liu, and S.Y. Mei, *Clinical study on "Jin's three-needling" in treatment of generalized anxiety disorder.* Zhongguo Zhong Xi Yi Jie He Za Zhi, 2007. 27(3): p. 201-3.

17. Mora, B., et al., *Auricular acupressure as a treatment for anxiety before extracorporeal shock wave lithotripsy in the elderly.* J Urol, 2007. 178(1): p. 160-4; discussion 164.

18. Wang H, Qi H, Wang BS, Cui YY, Zhu L, Rong ZX, Chen HZ. *Is acupuncture beneficial in depression: a meta-analysis of 8 randomized controlled trials?* J Affect Disord. 2008; 111(2-3): p. 125-34.

19. Yuan, Q., et al., *Effect of Jin-3-needling therapy on plasma corticosteroid, adrenocorticotrophic hormone and platelet 5-HT levels in patients with generalized anxiety disorder.* Chin J Integr Med, 2007. 13(4): p. 264-8.

20. Leo, R.J. and J.S. Ligot, Jr., *A systematic review of randomized controlled trials of acupuncture in the treatment of depression.* J Affect Disord, 2007. 97(1-3): p. 13-22.

21. Wang, S.M., et al., *Extra-1 acupressure for children undergoing anesthesia.* Anesth Analg, 2008. 107(3): p. 811-6.

22. Wang, L., et al., *Systematic evaluation of therapeutic effect and safety of acupuncture for treatment of depression.* Zhongguo Zhen Jiu, 2008. 28(5): p. 381-6.

23. Chen, H.Y., et al., *Auricular acupuncture treatment for insomnia: a systematic review.* J Altern Complement Med, 2007. 13(6): p. 669-76.

24. Lee MS, Shin BC, Suen LK, Park TY, Ernst E. *Auricular acupuncture for insomnia: a systematic review.* Int J Clin Pract. 2008; 62(11): p. 1744-52.

25. Cheuk, D.K., et al., *Acupuncture for insomnia.* Cochrane Database Syst Rev, 2007(3): p. CD005472.

26. MacPherson, H., et al., *A prospective survey of adverse events and treatment reactions following 34,000 consultations with professional acupuncturists.* Acupunct Med, 2001. 19(2): p. 93-102.

27. White, A., et al., *Survey of adverse events following acupuncture (SAFA): a prospective study of 32,000 consultations.* Acupunct Med, 2001. 19(2): p. 84-92.

28. Giesen, J.M., D.B. Center, and R.A. Leach, *An evaluation of chiropractic manipulation as a treatment of hyperactivity in children.* J Manipulative Physiol Ther, 1989. 12(5): p. 353-63.

29. Gillespie, B.R., *Case study in attention-deficit/hyperactivity disorder: the corrective aspect of craniosacral fascial therapy.* Explore (NY), 2009. 5(5): p. 296-8.

30. Cuthbert, S.C. and M. Barras, *Developmental delay syndromes: psychometric testing before and after chiropractic treatment of 157 children.* J Manipulative Physiol Ther, 2009. 32(8): p. 660-9.

31. Karpouzis, F., H. Pollard, and R. Bonello, *A randomised controlled trial of the Neuro Emotional Technique (NET) for childhood Attention Deficit Hyperactivity Disorder (ADHD): a protocol.* Trials, 2009. 10: p. 6.

KATHI J. KEMPER, MD, MPH

INDEX

D

E

F

KATHI J. KEMPER, MD, MPH

Louv, Richard
Last Child in the Woods, 93

M

magnesium, 27, 29, 120, 139, 163
Mandel, Howie, 10
massage, 44, 134-35, 168
mastery, 21, 46, 48, 54, 56, 74, 81,
  97, 138, 140
Mazlish, Elaine
  How to Talk so Kids Will Listen &
  Listen so Kids will Talk, 74
medications, v, 2, 4, 45, 112, 114-15,
  162
  nonstimulant, 115, 117
  problems with, 117-18
  side effects of, 7
  stimulant, i-ii, 7, 32, 34, 45, 114-
    16, 118-19, 123, 126, 161
meditation, 44, 78-81, 149
melatonin, 45, 122, 164
Mental Health America, 132-33
metacognitive therapy, 127, 166
Metadate, 116
Methylin, 116
methylphenidate, ii, 114, 116, 161-63
minerals, 4, 25-26, 29, 37, 113, 119-
  20, 140, 146
minimal brain dysfunction (MDB).
  See attention deficit disorder
  (ADD)
mint, 44
mistakes, management of, 69-70, 139
Monastra, Vincent
  Parenting Children with ADHD, 49
moodiness, 2, 4, 8, 11
moods, 11, 30, 32, 35, 79, 120, 162,
  164, 168

mood swings, 9
movement, 4, 45, 75, 79, 128, 139
music, 91-92, 129, 131, 139-40

N

National Federation of Families of
  Children's Mental Health, 132-
  33
National Institute for Health and
  Clinical Excellence (NICE), 15,
  116
National Mental Health Association.
  See Mental Health America
nature, 5, 40, 44, 91, 93, 139
neurofeedback. *See*
  electroencephalographic (EEG)
  biofeedback
N-of-1 trial, 114-15, 125, 161
nutrition, 101, 112, 117, 139

O

organic food, 36-37, 39
organization, 4, 6, 20, 98, 127, 136,
  143-44

P

Parenting Children with ADHD
  (Monastra), 49
passionflower, 44, 123
patience, vi, 54, 75, 98, 138
pesticides, i, 93, 113, 138, 145
  atrazine, 90, 140, 160
  dieldrin, 90, 140
  toxic, 36-37
Phelps, Michael, 3, 12
pine bark extract, 124, 140, 165

Poe, Edgar Allan, 10
Pollan, Michael
  Food Rules, 138
polybrominated biphenyls (PBB), 89, 140
polybrominated diphenyl ethers (PBDE), 89, 140
polychlorinated biphenyls (PCB), 89, 122, 140
Pycnogenol, 124, 165

Q

qigong, 79, 86, 146
quantitative electroencephalogram (qEEG), 3-4, 167

R

Raising an Emotionally Intelligent Child (Gottman), 56
religion, 1
Remen, Rachel Naomi, 73
Ritalin, ii, 34, 116, 161-63
Rosemond, John
  Well-Behaved Child, The, 56
rules, 47, 51, 54-55, 59

S

s-adenosylmethionine (SAM or SAM-E), 121, 163
Saint-John's-wort, 114
salt, 34-35
school, 11, 13, 30, 39, 42, 127-31, 133, 144
Scouts, 140
Seinfeld, Jessica
  Deceptively Delicious, 39

selenium, 120
self-discipline, vi-1, 53-55, 75, 93, 139
self-esteem, 1, 11, 41, 48
Sher, Barbara
  Attention Games, 74
side effects, 15, 76, 117, 120
single photon emission computerized tomography (SPECT) scan, 4, 167
sleep, 42, 44, 112, 117, 122-23, 134, 139, 164
  deprivation of, 42
  improvement of, 43
SMART (specific, measurable, achievable, relevant, timely) plan, 49, 94, 101, 104-5, 140
smoking, 62, 88, 109
snacks, 25
Sneaky Chef, The (Lapine), 39
spirituality, 1
sports, 11, 20, 58, 131
Strattera, ii, 117-18, 161
stress, 56, 62, 75-79, 81, 139
supplements, 29, 31, 112-13, 120-21, 125, 144, 146

T

tae kwon do, 42
tai chi, 41-43, 79, 86, 139, 146
tea, 34, 44, 113, 123, 125, 165
  black, 34
  green, 34, 45, 123, 139, 165
  iced, 34, 124
  oolong, 34
theanine, 34, 45, 123, 165
thyroid, 6-7, 89
time, 49, 65-66, 68, 139, 166

Tourette's syndrome, 11
tracking, 98-99, 105-7, 109-10

V

valerian, 45, 123, 165
vegetables, 26-29, 35-37, 39, 138, 162
Vitamin B, 27, 29, 120, 139
  B6, 120
Vitamin C, 120
Vitamin E, 120
Vitamin K, 120
Vyvanse, 116

W

water, 30, 89, 93, 138
Well-Behaved Child, The (Rosemond),
  56

Y

yoga, 41-43, 79, 86, 139, 141, 146

Z

zinc, 27, 29, 120, 139

What people are saying
about *Addressing ADD, Naturally:*

"A primer for parents who want to positively change their child's life. I cannot wait to give this book to my patients' parents."

—Chris Magryta, MD Pediatrician,
Salisbury Pediatric Associates, NC

"This book is fantastic! It is written by a founding member of the field who is able to combine a wealth of knowledge with practical experience to offer effective guidance for a challenging condition. Dr. Kemper helps guide the reader to use a process of treatment that enhances confidence for the child so they can become resilient towards overcoming the labels that our culture is so ready to attach. A must read for any clinician or parent."

—David Rakel, MD Editor of *Integrative Medicine,*
Family Physician, University of Wisconsin

"This short, sweet, practical book is comprehensive, evidence-based, and gives step by step directions for successful change. It is helpful for the individual and entire family. I love the big picture aspect as well as the individual."

—Paula Gardiner, MD, MPH Family Medicine,
Boston Medical Center

"Comprehensive, easy-to-read – a must have for parents, teachers, and health care providers who want to help children focus. Written by one of the most respected experts in pediatric integrative medicine. If you can't take your child to be seen by Dr. Kemper, at least you can benefit from her sound advice and guidance."

—Sunita Vohra, MD, Director CARE
Program for Integrative Health and Healing,
University of Alberta, Canada